CHRISTIANITY ON TRIAL

The Bishop Henry McNeal Turner/Sojourner Truth Series
in Black Religion

Editor: Dwight N. Hopkins
  The University of Chicago, The Divinity School

Associate Editors:
  James H. Cone, Union Theological Seminary, New York
  Katie G. Cannon, Temple University
  Cain Hope Felder, Howard University, School of Divinity
  Jacquelyn Grant, The Interdenominational Theological Center
  Delores S. Williams, Union Theological Seminary, New York

The purpose of this series is to encourage the development of biblical, historical, theological, ethical, and pastoral works that analyze the role of the churches and other religious movements in the liberation struggles of black women and men in the United States, particularly the poor, and their relationship to struggles in the Third World.

Named after Bishop Henry McNeal Turner (1843-1915) and Sojourner Truth (1797?-1883), the series reflects the spirit of these two visionaries and witnesses for the black struggle for liberation. Bishop Turner was a churchman, a political figure, a missionary, and a pan-Africanist. Sojourner Truth was an illiterate former slave who championed black emancipation, women's rights, and the liberating spirit of the gospel.

Previously published in the Turner Series:

1. *For My People* by James H. Cone
2. *Black and African Theologies* by Josiah U. Young
3. *Troubling Biblical Waters* by Cain Hope Felder
4. *Black Theology USA and South Africa* by Dwight N. Hopkins
5. *Empower the People* by Theodore Walker, Jr.
6. *A Common Journey* by George C.L. Cummings
7. *Dark Symbols, Obscure Signs* by Riggins R. Earl, Jr.
8. *A Troubling in My Soul* by Emilie Townes
9. *The Black Christ* by Kelly Brown Douglas

In the Turner/Truth Series:

10. *Christianity on Trial* by Mark L. Chapman

The Bishop Henry McNeal Turner/Sojourner Truth Series
in Black Religion, Volume X

CHRISTIANITY ON TRIAL

African-American Religious Thought Before and After Black Power

Mark L. Chapman

ORBIS BOOKS

Maryknoll, New York 10545

The Catholic Foreign Mission Society of America (Maryknoll) recruits and trains people for overseas missionary service. Through Orbis Books, Maryknoll aims to foster the international dialogue that is essential to mission. The books published, however, reflect the opinions of their authors and are not meant to represent the official position of the society.

Library of Congress Cataloging in Publication Data

Chapman, Mark L.
    Christianity on trial : African-American religious thought before
and after Black power / Mark L. Chapman.
        p.   cm. — (The Bishop Henry McNeal Turner/Sojourner Truth series
in Black Religion; v. 10)
    Includes bibliographical references and index.
    ISBN 1-57075-044-0 (alk. paper)
    1. Afro-American—Religion.   2. Theology, Doctrinal—United
States—History—20th century.   3. Black Muslims.   4. Black Power—
United States.   5. Black theology.   6. Womanist theology.
7. United States—Religion—20th century.   I. Title.   II. Series.
BR563.N4C45   1996
277.3'082'08996073—dc20   95-43642
                                                                CIP

In loving memory of my grandmother
Mary Madeline Chapman

In honor of my parents
the Rev. Dr. William L. and Joyce E. Chapman

and

To my wife
Teri
and
daughter
Quincey

Contents

Acknowledgments

God has richly blessed me with a loving family and supportive friends! It is no cliché when I acknowledge that without their love and constant encouragement, I would not have completed this project. Numerous professors, friends, relatives, and church members have supported me throughout my studies. While it is not possible to name every individual who encouraged me along the way, I wish to acknowledge those persons who supported me throughout the writing of this book.

There would be no way for me adequately to express in words my deep gratitude to my mentor, Dr. James H. Cone. When I was a first-year seminarian, Dr. Cone inspired me and challenged me to become a theologian. His passionate commitment to serve God's people as a scholar, teacher, and writer reminded me that Christian ministry extends beyond the local parish and that there are a "variety of gifts" the same Spirit gives to each of us for the work of ministry (1 Corinthians 12: 4-11). Later, as a graduate student, I had the privilege of serving as Dr. Cone's research assistant, where I began to learn firsthand what it means to be a scholar and theologian. Without his encouragement, patience, advice, and friendship, I would not have written this book.

I am also grateful to other professors at Union Seminary who helped me in my studies, especially Christopher Morse, Kosuke Koyama, Beverly Harrison, Tom Driver, and James Washington. I also thank Harold Dean Trulear of New York Theological Seminary for offering his encouragement and response to my work. A fellow Morehouse alumnus, Dr. Trulear's commitment to scholarship and pastoral ministry challenged me to bridge the gap between academic theology and the black church.

From the time I first met Gayraud S. Wilmore as a first-year seminarian, he has been a source of inspiration and encouragement. Dr. Wilmore instilled in me a love for African-American religious thought and history in his classes at New York Theological Seminary and later invited me to serve as his teaching assistant. Early in the writing of this book he let me know I was on the right track and offered helpful insights. His warm spirit and his genuine love for the church and the academy ministered to me as I wrestled with my own vocational calling. For his advice and support I am eternally grateful.

I also wish to thank those who granted me interviews and shared their ideas, including Charles Shelby Rooks, Delores Williams, and Metz

Rollins. I am grateful to J. Oscar McCloud and the Fund for Theological Education for financial assistance and moral support. Thanks also to several excellent librarians, including Betty Bolden and Seth Katsen of Union and Irene Owens of Howard Divinity School, for helpful research assistance.

There are many other people who helped me. My doctoral colleagues at Union challenged and encouraged me. My friends Howard Wiley, Choon Seo Koo, Annie Ruth Powell, Sally MacNichol, JoAnne Terell, and Augustine Musopole were a source of tremendous support. Dennis Wiley, Dwight Hopkins, Kelly Brown Douglas, and Alonzo Johnson also helped me in my studies. My dear friends Revs. Willie C. Martin, Anthony Bennett, Allen Pinckney, Horace James, Ed Turner, and Derrick Harkins prayed with me, as did several others, when I felt like giving up.

Three faith communities provided spiritual guidance and supported me with their prayers: Grace Congregational Church of Harlem where my father, the Rev. Dr. William L. Chapman, pastored for twenty-five years; the Mariners' Temple Baptist Church, pastored by the Rev. Dr. Suzan D. Johnson-Cook; and the Neighborhood Prayer Room in Corona, Queens, led by the late Deacon Jessie McAllister (who went on to glory on Christmas day 1994) and Rev. Willie C. Martin, my friend and father-in-law. My spirituality and understanding of ministry have been shaped by these communities, and I thank God for them. I extend a special thanks to Revs. Henrietta Carter, Carolyn Holloway, and Ministers Sheila Grimes, Valerie Eley, Letha Johnson, and Gladys Lawrence of Mariners' Temple Baptist Church for their love and support during the completion of this book. While Dr. Johnson-Cook was serving as a White House Fellow in Washington, D.C., for the year 1993-94, we served as assistant co-ministers and had a wonderful experience of ministry together.

I must also thank my former colleagues at Rollins College (Winter Park, Florida) where I served as Visiting Instructor of Religious Studies for 1991-92. Drs. Yudit Greenberg, Arnold Wettstein, Tom Cook, Hoyt Edge, Rev. John Langfitt, and Mrs. Doris Lynn all helped to make my first teaching experience a rewarding one. I am also very appreciative of the tremendous support I receive from my colleagues in the African-American Studies Department at Fordham University. My friends and mentors Drs. Claude Mangum and Mark Naison have been extremely helpful, as have Francesca Thompson, Irma Watkins-Owens, and Fawzia Mustafa. I am also grateful to Dr. Jerome Contee, Assistant Vice President for Academic Affairs, and Dean Joseph McShane for their support of my work. Thanks also to Robert Ellsberg of Orbis Books for his patience and assistance in bringing this work to completion.

Most important, my family supported me when I was unproductive and discouraged. My wife, Teri, deserves an award for putting up with me throughout this entire process. Words cannot express the debt of gratitude I owe her. Teri gave birth to our daughter, Quincey, during the early drafts of this project and allowed me to complete it by fulfilling some of my parental responsibilities. Now, two years later, as I rewrite sections of the manuscript for publication, Quincey's constant question upon still seeing me in front of a computer screen is, "Daddy still workin'?" Thank God for that question and the inspiration it gave me to finish.

I have also been blessed with a loving mother and father, who went out of their way to make sure that my brothers and I had a solid education and a supportive home environment; I could not have asked for more loving parents, and I thank God for them daily. My brothers Mike and Bill and their families have been extremely supportive, and many cousins, uncles, and aunts have expressed their support. My in-laws Delle, Willie, Michelle, Bridgette, and Christopher have all been wonderful throughout this process.

Finally, I honor my beloved Grandma, Mary Madeline Chapman, who died before seeing this finished book. Although she is not physically present with us, her spirit still guides and comforts me along the way.

Introduction

Christianity: Source of Black Liberation or Oppression?

The Christian religion as it has functioned in America has been both the friend and the foe of the Negro. Despite the paradoxes and the feebleness with which it is practiced in the American Social Order, it is potentially, and at times actually, the most powerful weapon a minority group has to press its claim for equal opportunities for survival.
                                                        —Benjamin E. Mays, 1939

This is the question which individuals and groups who live in our land always under the threat of profound social and psychological displacement face: Why is it that Christianity seems impotent to deal radically, and therefore effectively, with the issues of discrimination and injustice on the basis of race, religion and national origin? Is this impotency due to a betrayal of the genius of the religion, or is it due to a basic weakness in the religion itself? The question is searching, for the dramatic demonstration of the impotency of Christianity in dealing with the issue is underscored by its apparent inability to cope with it within its own fellowship.
                                                        —Howard Thurman, 1949

What does the Christian gospel have to say to powerless black men whose existence is threatened daily by the insidious tentacles of white power? Is there a message from Christ to the countless number of blacks whose lives are smothered under white society? . . . Is it possible to strip the gospel as it has been interpreted of its "whiteness," so that its real message will become a live option for radical advocates of black consciousness? Is there any relationship between the work of God and the activity of the ghetto? Must black people be forced to deny their identity in order to embrace the Christian faith? . . . These are hard questions. To answer these questions, however, we need to discuss, first, the gospel of Jesus as it relates to black people.
                                                        —James H. Cone, 1969

Christianity and the Struggle to Believe

More than any other issue in the history of African-American religious thought, the meaning of Christianity and its relation to black

1

oppression has generated ongoing controversy and debate. Indeed, the above quotations by Benjamin Mays, Howard Thurman, and James Cone, three of the most respected interpreters of African-American Christianity in the twentieth century, all reflect the serious theological issues that have been, and still are, debated in black communities across the nation. In fact, no interpretation of black life in America can ignore the manner in which the debate concerning Christianity has affected the social, political, and religious dimensions of the African-American freedom struggle, especially in the civil rights and Black Power movements of the 1950s and 1960s.

Needless to say, black people have never forgotten that they were introduced to Christianity by their enslavers. This historical reality produced in African-Americans a feeling of deep ambivalence and skepticism about the value of Christianity as a source of black liberation. Writing at the height of the Black Power movement, Vincent Harding, Professor of Religion and Social Transformation at Iliff School of Theology in Denver, Colorado, poignantly captured the source of this dilemma in his seminal essay, "Black Power and the American Christ" (1967):

> This ambivalence is not new. It was ours from the beginning. For we first met the American Christ on slave ships. We heard his name sung in hymns of praise while we died in our thousands, chained in stinking holds beneath the decks, locked in with terror and disease and sad memories of our families and homes. When we leaped from the decks to be seized by sharks we saw his name carved on the ship's solid sides. When our women were raped in the cabins they must have noticed the great and holy books on the shelves. Our introduction to this Christ was not propitious. And the horrors continued on America's soil. So all through the nation's history many black men have rejected this Christ—indeed the miracle is that so many accepted him.[1]

Certainly, it was not easy for black people to embrace a faith that was given to them by their enslavers. Indeed, as Harding suggests, the widespread acceptance of Christianity among African-Americans points to the miracle-working power of a God who resurrected the crucified Jesus and made him alive in the hearts and minds of black slaves and their descendants. Nevertheless, from the time white missionaries told Africans that Christianity compels slaves to "obey your earthly masters with fear and trembling" (Eph 6:5) through the present, the struggle to believe that "God could make a way (freedom) out of no way (slavery)" was often a severe test of faith. To be sure, some slaves rejected Christianity and religion altogether, while others clung to Islam or new adaptations of traditional African religions. But those who accepted Christianity—despite their oppression at the hands of white "Christian" slave masters—created a distinct expression of the faith that enabled them to maintain their dignity in the midst of a brutal, dehumanizing institution. As Gayraud Wilmore demonstrated in his classic text *Black Religion and Black Radicalism,* a stream of radicalism has flowed through black Christianity inspiring slave revolts, emigration movements, and other forms of resistance.[2] But whether they have embraced the faith or rejected it, I believe an analysis of African-American religious thought will show that black people have always put Christianity on trial. The basic theological dilemma they have continually addressed is whether Christianity is a source of black liberation or oppression.

Therefore, this book poses the very question black people have asked throughout history: Is Christianity a liberating reality in African-American life or is it an oppressive ideology that hinders black freedom? This is the question African-American religious thinkers have pondered with intensity, especially in the years after World War II. It is no accident that this query about the efficacy of Christianity intensified during the civil rights and Black Power movements of the 1950s and 1960s. As black people's hope regarding integration soared in the postwar years, so did their belief that Christianity was the force that would help them to realize the beloved community articulated by Martin Luther King, Jr. But the optimism of the 1950s and early 1960s turned to hopelessness and despair as African-Americans in the urban North discovered that the passage of civil rights legislation had no bearing on their economic plight. Still crowded in ghettos with little or no employment opportunities, the militant voices of the discontented began to drown out the hopeful proclamations of Christian integrationists.

As the gap between the promise of democracy and the reality of poverty widened, so did the perception that Christianity could help solve the race problem in America. Increasingly alienated from the institutional structures of white power, young blacks began to feel that violence was the only way to make their voices heard. Significantly, this mounting disillusionment regarding integration was accompanied by harsh critiques of Christianity leveled by the Nation of Islam, Black Power militants, and radical black clergy leaders sensitive to the cries of the masses.

Similarly, black women's increasing frustration and disappointment over the oppressive sexism of black men and the racism of white feminists were followed by a prophetic womanist theological critique of Christianity. Indeed, male and female indictments of racist and sexist manifestations of Christianity before and after Black Power constitute an important African-American theological tradition that is often overlooked.

Pre- and Post-Black Power Critiques of Christianity

Throughout this study, I refer to "Negro" and "pre–Black Power" theologians interchangeably, as I do with "black" and "post–Black Power" theologians. Because African-Americans before the rise of Black Power most commonly referred to themselves as Negroes (including Benjamin Mays, Howard Thurman, George Kelsey, and Martin Luther King, Jr.) I have used it when describing their views. However, it must be emphasized that my use of the word *Negro* is not intended in a pejorative sense—as Elijah Muhammad, Malcolm X, and Black Power radicals used it to demean leaders they considered "Uncle Toms"—but is rather employed to help illustrate points of discontinuity between pre– and post–Black Power theologians. Similarly, after the emergence of Black Power, African-Americans increasingly referred to themselves as black people. Here, it is important to underscore the point that the term "black theologian" is not primarily a description of the theologian's ethnic background using language that reflected the community's new racial consciousness (though it is that); more important, it is a description of a theological perspective, much like "liberal," "neo-orthodox," or "feminist" theologian. With this in mind, this book examines the various indictments of Christianity articulated by African-American religious thinkers before and after the Black Power movement. The critiques and interpretations of Christianity found in these two historical periods were greatly influenced by the political ideologies of integration and nationalism. Perhaps the most important religious thinkers in the pre–Black Power period were Benjamin Mays, Howard Thurman, George Kelsey, and Martin L. King, Jr. As educators, preachers, and theologians, their thought epitomizes the best of the integrationist tradition that challenged church and society to "practice what it preached" in the area of race. While these thinkers were proud of their racial heritage, it is important to note that they did not (and indeed could not) think of themselves as *black* theologians. Their approach to religious experience and commitment to the ideology of integration led them to think of ethnic and cultural background as *incidental* to the doing of theology. They believed that all life is interrelated, and so they put forward an interpretation of Christianity that was consistent with integrationist philosophy. Their personal experiences of being *excluded* made them acutely aware of the need to develop inclusive theologies that would transcend the categories of race.

However, alongside the dominant integrationist tradition stood a rich legacy of black nationalism that interpreted Christianity in an entirely different light. Christian black nationalists from Henry McNeal Turner to Albert Cleage emphasized racial particularity and the importance of Africa, while non-Christian black nationalists such as Elijah Muhammad and Malcolm X rejected Christianity altogether as "the white man's religion."[3] These two ideological forces—integration and black nationalism—collided in 1966 when the cry of "Black Power" was heard above the "Freedom Now" slogan of the mainline civil rights movement. This shift in political ideology also caused a shift in religious thought. As young civil rights activists began to embrace the spirit of black nationalism, a new way of interpreting the gospel emerged among progressive ministers and theologians who now sought to interpret Christianity in light of the black community's search for cultural as well as political liberation. Religious thinkers after Black Power made bold theological claims that integrationist scholars would not have made: God and Jesus Christ are black and are present in the spirit of Black Power!

Clearly, there are significant points of tension between the perspectives of Negro and black theologians. Whereas pre–Black Power religious leaders attempted to make Christianity relevant for a generation of young people fighting racial segregation in the South, post–Black Power ministers and theologians in the 1960s and 1970s faced the challenge of making the gospel speak to the frustrations of black youth fighting institutional racism, joblessness, and police brutality in the urban North. In this latter period, African-Americans were more conscious of the fact that racism was supported by deep structural and economic roots; consequently, the younger generation changed its focus from integration and civil rights to a new emphasis on black nationalism and self-determination. If the black church and its theologians could not answer Elijah Muhammad's claim that "Christianity is the white man's religion," then they wanted no part of it.

Although there are sharp differences in the critique and interpretation of Christianity articulated by pre– and post–Black Power religious thinkers, there is also a strong line of continuity. Interpreters in both periods attacked the racism of the white church and insisted that authentic Christianity had to address the social, political, and economic realities of the African-American community. Moreover, pre– and post–Black Power Christian thinkers issued a prophetic internal critique of the black church when it failed to relate its ministry to the poor and the disinherited. There is, therefore, an important stream of continuity between pre– and post–Black Power Christian thought that demands more scholarly attention. In fact, it can be said that the black theologians of the late 1960s and 1970s "stood on the shoulders" of the Negro theologians of the 1930s, '40s and '50s.[4]

As a student of history and theology, this integral relationship between pre– and post–Black Power religious thinkers intrigued me greatly. During my undergraduate years at Morehouse College in the early 1980s, I read the autobiographies of Benjamin Mays and Howard Thurman (while living in dormitories named in their honor) and attended worship services in the chapel named after the school's most distinguished alumnus, Martin Luther King, Jr. I was proud to know that many of the leading figures in twentieth century African-American religious thought (Benjamin E. Mays, Howard Thurman, George Kelsey, and Martin Luther King, Jr.) had been students, administrators, and professors at my alma mater; indeed, the several occasions I met and talked with Dr. Mays before his death in 1984 are among my most cherished memories.

Yet, I was also drawn to the more militant writings of James Cone, especially his *Black Theology and Black Power*. Cone's work addressed another part of me that pre–Black Power thinkers did not emphasize: radical black consciousness and skepticism about nonviolence as the *only* Christian means of struggle. My subsequent graduate studies at Union Seminary, therefore, highlighted a subconscious inner tension regarding my appreciation for the work of both pre– and post–Black Power theologians. On the one hand, I had tremendous respect for the accomplishments of Mays, Thurman, and King; I admired their moral and intellectual courage and respected their profound commitment to Jesus' nonviolent ethic. Yet, I also knew I had serious doubts about my ability to participate in civil rights demonstrations without retaliation and hatred. Did this mean that I was not an authentic Christian, inasmuch as Jesus himself taught forgiveness, repudiated violence, and told his disciples to love their enemies?

In this respect, I sympathized with Cone's rage and passionate critique of integration and nonviolence as the *sole* Christian response to white racism. I knew from personal experience (a gang of whites once chased me through the streets of Greenwich Village, New York, with the intention of doing me serious bodily harm) how difficult it is to love the enemy and desire reconciliation with people who seek to destroy you. While I still valued the contributions of Mays, Thurman, and King, I realized that no interpreter of the history of black people in the United States could fail to appreciate the dramatic impact the Black Power movement had on African-American religious thought.

The radical black theology that emerged in the late 1960s and 1970s marked the most exciting outpouring of African-American religious thought in the twentieth century. After the 1969 appearance of Cone's *Black Theology and Black Power*, a steady stream of books and articles sought to reinterpret Christianity in light of the new mood of black consciousness. Drawing on the insights of radical nineteenth-century male figures such as Nat Turner, David Walker, and Henry McNeal Turner, and the more recent leadership of Martin Luther King, Jr., and Malcolm X, male post–Black Power thinkers emphasized the theological significance of blackness and the need for social, political, and economic liberation from the oppressive structures of white racism. Unfortunately, black male theologians adopted the patriarchal views of secular black nationalists and therefore ignored the problem of sexism in the black church and community. Consequently, the post–Black Power era also saw the emergence of black female religious scholars who rediscovered the theology and feminist political activism of their radical nineteenth-century foremothers. With the rise of womanist theology in the mid 1980s, Christianity as interpreted by progressive black male preachers and theologians was itself put on trial. With prophetic zeal and compassion, womanist theologians asked how black theology can be a theology of liberation when it ignores and participates in the oppression of black women? Certainly, womanist theology is a prophetic critique of the limitations of both pre– and post–Black Power male theologians.

Bridging the Generation Gap

Given the sharp differences between pre– and post–Black Power theologians, I was initially unable to resolve my inner conflict regarding seemingly opposite traditions that shaped my thinking. Indeed, the outpouring of religious thought after Black Power caused many scholars to neglect the work of Negro theologians and their influence on black theology. Recently, however, there has been a renewed interest in the work of pre–Black Power theologians, especially Howard Thurman.[5] For example, an important 1989 conference celebrating the fortieth anniversary of Howard Thurman's *Jesus and the Disinherited* and the twentieth anniversary of James Cone's *Black Theology and Black Power* was held at the Benjamin E. Mays Hall of the Howard University School of Divinity in Washington, D.C. (November 8-9, 1989). The theme of the conference was "Black Theology in Retrospect and Prospect: Discontent, Revolt, and New Ferment," and scholars including Luther Smith, Gayraud Wilmore, Delores Williams, and J. Deotis Roberts began to address some of the continuities between pre– and post–Black Power theology.[6] However, to the best of my knowledge, a comprehensive study has not been done comparing and contrasting African-American religious thought before and after Black Power. The present work seeks to fill that void by examining key figures in both periods who responded to the black community's ongoing debate concerning the value of Christianity as a source of liberation.

In *Christianity on Trial* I argue that despite the important differences between pre– and post–Black Power religious thought, there is a common thread that ties these two generations together. In both periods African-American Christian and non-Christian thinkers exposed the racism of the white church and sought to make black faith a powerful resource in the struggle against oppression. Moreover, the history of both periods shows that the African-American Christian community subjected its faith to serious internal critique. Prophetic theologians and pastors challenged the black church to be true to the liberating gospel of Jesus, even as they were confronted with the presence of sexism and other weaknesses in their own perspectives. Indeed, the research presented in this study confirms my strong belief that the African-American community *must* continue to critique manifestations of Christianity from inside and outside the church walls if the black institutional church is to be an effective witness to the liberating gospel of Jesus Christ.

Apart from the sharp cultural focus of black theology in the late 1960s and beyond, the difference between it and pre–Black Power religious thought is largely one of emphasis. For pre–Black Power thinkers, the emphasis on the *universality* of the Christian faith was derived from their primary concern about integration and improved race relations; for post–Black Power theologians, the emphasis on the *particularity* of the gospel stemmed from a growing nationalist consciousness that glorified blackness and stressed racial unity. Yet, it is important to note that pre–Black Power theologians' emphasis on the universality of the faith did not mean that they denied the importance of their African heritage, nor did black theologians' emphasis on the theological significance of blackness mean that they rejected the universality of the Christian gospel.

An African-American Tradition of Theological Critique

All five chapters of *Christianity on Trial* seek to illustrate my central thesis that the relevancy of Christianity to the reality of black oppression was intensely scrutinized by the African-American community in the years following World War II. Each chapter highlights a principal thinker whose ideas are representative of a major trend in African-American religious thought: Benjamin Mays, Elijah Muhammad, Albert Cleage, James Cone, and Delores Williams. More than any of their contemporaries, I believe, these theologians epitomize their respective schools of thought and serve to focus our attention on the major theological issues raised at the time. In each chapter I address the historical context that shaped the theological discussion and provide a brief biographical sketch of the featured theologian. Equally important, *Christianity on Trial* seeks to highlight the chorus of other important voices that contributed to the dialogue and helped reinforce the perspective of the major thinker under examination.

Chapter 1 analyzes the Negro theology of race relations that emerged in the years before and after World War II. As Negroes during this period intensified their political struggle for civil rights, religious scholars sharpened their critique of white Christianity and developed a theology of race relations based on the community's desire for integration. The major architect of this theological trend was Benjamin E. Mays, the renowned scholar, ecumenical church leader, and educator. Mays was an instructor at Morehouse during Howard Thurman's student days in the early 1920s, and was president when Martin Luther King, Jr., matriculated there in the mid 1940s. Mays had a profound impact on Thurman, King, and other students who went on to make significant contributions to the civil rights movement. In fact, I selected Mays as the principal thinker in this chapter because I agree with historian Orville Vernon Burton, who wrote, "King's fame overshadows Mays's, but I believe there could not have been a Martin Luther King, Jr., if there had been no Benjamin Elijah Mays. From their days together at Morehouse, through the years of the civil rights struggle, and until King's death, the pair shared the same philosophy and goals."[7]

Chapter 2 examines Elijah Muhammad's nationalist critique of Christianity as "the white man's religion." Muhammad's biting critique of Negro Christian preachers and theologians is representative of non-Christian voices in the pre–Black Power era who understood Christianity to be a chief source of black oppression. The mentor-student relationship of Mays and King is similar to that of Elijah Muhammad and Malcolm X. Although Malcolm's fame exceeds Elijah Muhammad's, the latter laid the theological foundation that Malcolm and others built upon. What truth, if any, is found in the Nation of Islam's critique, and what can the black church learn from the theological challenge Elijah Muhammed and Malcolm X present? I argue that the Nation of Islam's critique of Christianity prompted the articulation of black liberation theology as much, if not more, than the emergence of Black Power in the summer of 1966.

In chapter 3 I examine the emergence of Black Power and its impact on the rise of black theology. How did the black church respond to the new call for Black Power? I analyze the important role the National Committee of Negro Churchmen (later the National Conference of Black Churchmen, and finally the National Conference of Black Christians) played in bridging the gap between pre– and post–Black Power religious thought. These progressive ministers from black and white denominations knew that the credibility of Christianity and the black church depended on how they responded to Black Power. Gilbert H. Caldwell, the first black district superintendent in the history of New England Methodism, expressed this concern in a way that demonstrates his awareness that Christianity was on trial in the African-American community:

> Is it or is it not possible to be black and true to the aspirations of the black community and still be a part of white Christianity? The jury is still out on that one, and it will not be coming in with the verdict for some time to come.[8]

The development of black theology within the NCBC and the black caucuses of the white denominations answered Caldwell's question with an emphatic "Yes!" In fact, the new theology that emerged was so decisive that Gil Caldwell was moved to testify in a manner similar to ministers in the Nation of Islam:

> All praises be to the National Committee of Black Churchmen, to the black caucus movement as it has developed in all the white denominations . . . I have the feeling that if these structures had not emerged a lot of us would have received "calls" to preach in places other than the church.[9]

The major figure highlighted in the second half of the chapter is Albert Cleage, a United Church of Christ minister and the first pastor to develop a black nationalist theology in the wake of Black Power. Indeed, Cleage and others like him developed a black theology that sought to respond to Elijah Muhammad's claim that "Christianity is the white man's religion."

Chapter 4 examines the pivotal role James Cone played in the academic formulation of black theology. After addressing the misgivings of pre–Black Power thinkers regarding the rise of black theology, I analyze Cone's work as a response to Black Power, white and Negro theologians, and Elijah Muhammad's Nation of Islam. A close reading of Cone's perspective will show that although he radically departed from Negro theologians in key areas, he also learned from them and incorporated some of their insights into his theology. Lastly, Cone's critique of white and black churches is examined; more than any other black male theologian, his relentless critique of the American churches makes an enduring contribution to the African-American theological tradition.

Chapter 5 analyzes the prophetic challenge womanist theology presents to the ministry and theology of the black church. I examine the problem of sexism in the black church, the civil rights and Black Power movements, and the work of black male theologians. The emergence of womanist theology is then discussed as a response to the limitations of white feminist and black male theologians. Here, the pioneering work of Delores Williams is highlighted. More than any other womanist theologian, Williams has researched the history, literature, and religious experience of African-American women as sources for a constructive womanist perspective. Her pioneering study of the biblical woman Hagar's experience and its relation to the social, political, and economic plight of black women established her as a major voice in American theology in general and African-American theology in particular. Lastly, Williams's critique of the denominational black churches is discussed in relation to the work of male pre– and post–Black Power theologians.

The concluding chapter highlights the continuities and discontinuities between African-American religious thought before and after Black Power. What similarities and differences exist between pre– and post–Black Power theologies? The critiques of Christianity examined in each chapter are briefly summarized to show how an African-American theological tradition was created that fostered prophetic internal critique. I believe the contemporary black church can learn from this tradition as it seeks to make Christianity relevant to the urgent needs of the black community. Thus, an appeal for more self-criticism and constructive dialogue in black churches is made in the hope that the African-American Christian community will be a more effective and prophetic witness to the liberating message of Jesus Christ.

Self-critique is a biblical mandate and an important part of the African-American theological tradition. Dialogue in the churches must be seen as an act of worship, just like preaching, singing, and praying. Moreover, as *Christianity on Trial* seeks to show, dialogue with those outside the "household of believers" can be a source of renewal pushing the church to reinterpret its message for a new generation of African-Americans who have serious questions about the relevancy of Christianity and the black church. Let the dialogue continue.

PART ONE

1945-1965

CHAPTER 1

"The Christian Way in Race Relations"

Benjamin E. Mays and the Theology of Race Relations

We are what we do and not what we say. We are as democratic as we live and we are as Christian as we act. If we talk brotherhood and segregate human beings, we do not believe in brotherhood. If we talk democracy and deny it to certain groups, we do not believe in democracy. If we preach justice and exploit the weak, we do not believe in justice. If we preach truth and tell lies, we do not believe in truth. We are what we do.
—Benjamin E. Mays, 1945

It is not enough for us to call upon members of different races to be decent toward one another for the sake of humanity, science, or democracy. The basis for good relations is found in the Christian religion, in the proper understanding of the Christian doctrine of man, Christ, and God, and in the application of Christian insights and convictions in everyday living.
—Benjamin E. Mays, 1957

No issue placed a greater strain on the faith of African-American Christians than the problem of racial segregation and the support it received from white churches. How could white Christians bar black people from their churches and yet claim to read the same Bible and worship the same Jesus as African-American Christians? For some blacks, the contradiction between basic Christian faith claims and the racist practices of white churches was too powerful to overcome; consequently, these persons renounced Christianity as an impotent religion incapable of solving the nation's race problem.

Pre–Black Power religious intellectuals in the 1930s and 1940s were also painfully aware of the wide gulf between genuine Christianity and white American Christianity. For example, when they travelled overseas and encountered Muslims and Hindus, they were frequently put in the awkward position of having to explain their allegiance to a religion that discriminated against them. Benjamin Mays was confronted by Muslims in Egypt who told him that Islam, unlike Christianity, had no racial barriers, while Hindus in India accused Howard Thurman of being a "tool of the Europeans."[1] Indeed, the sharp criticism Thurman received from one Hindu educator poignantly captures the dilemma of Negro Christian leaders who visited parts of Africa and Asia: "I think that an intelligent young Negro such as yourself, here in our country on behalf of a Christian enterprise, is a traitor to all darker peoples of the earth. How can you account for yourself being in this unfortunate and humiliating position?"[2]

Despite such interrogation, Negro Christian thinkers before and after World War II insisted that the genuine application of Christian principles to the problem of race relations offered the most promising solution to America's moral dilemma.[3] Accordingly, they continuously urged the nation and its churches to live up to their democratic and Christian ideals by practicing what they preached in the area of race.

No pre–Black Power religious thinker had a greater impact on discussions of Christianity and race in the 1940s and 1950s than Benjamin Elijah Mays. Throughout his long and distinguished career,[4] Mays summoned the national and international Christian community to implement the demands of the gospel by eradicating racism in its own fellowship and leading the fight against it in the world at large. In fact, the theology and educational philosophy of Benjamin Mays shaped the direction of student activism that eventually inspired Martin L. King, Jr., and other civil rights leaders.[5] As scholar Keith D. Miller notes in his recent landmark study of King's language and its sources, "What Mays had been to liberal black (and to a lesser degree white) religious and academic circles King–with the benefit of a huge political movement and television–would be to America."[6] Therefore, because of his far-reaching impact, an understanding of the life and thought of Mays is essential for our discussion of African-American religious thought before and after Black Power. What did he have to say about the Christian gospel and its relationship to American racism and imperialism?

CHRISTIANITY, AMERICA, AND THE WORLD

The life and thought of Benjamin Mays epitomized black people's enduring faith in Christianity and America. Despite the painful awareness that their religion (as interpreted by many whites) and country considered them inferior, Negro Christians continued to believe in the noble principles of Christianity and democracy. In fact, they maintained that the actual implementation of Christian and democratic principles offered the only viable solution to America's race problem. Accordingly, Benjamin Mays and other integrationist thinkers articulated a theology of race relations which they believed would lead to the redemption of the church and nation they so deeply loved. A brief examination of Mays's life and career will reveal the abiding faith pre–Black Power religious scholars placed in Christianity as an instrument of social change in America and around the world.

Biographical Sketch

Benjamin Mays was born in Greenwood County, South Carolina, on August 1, 1894. The youngest of eight children born to Hezekiah and Louvenia Mays, Benjamin was raised in a proud black southern community that did its best to shelter him from the brutal realities of racial violence and legal segregation. But the world into which Mays was born was becoming increasingly hostile toward African-Americans. In 1895 legislators from South Carolina overturned the political gains made possible by Federal Reconstruction by disfranchising blacks throughout the state. The following year the Supreme Court of the United States ruled in *Plessy v. Ferguson* that segregation was the accepted law of the land. This climate of political repression was accompanied by an increase in white terrorist violence against African-Americans. Before young Benjamin reached his fifth birthday, he experienced the paralyzing fear that haunted the lives of all southern blacks in the late nineteenth and early twentieth centuries. Indeed, the white lynch mob that rode through Greenwood County and taunted his father while Benjamin stood by and cried was a poignant symbol of the racial violence that characterized black life in the deep South. Reflecting on the impact of this traumatic experience, Mays wrote in his autobiography:

> Since my earliest memory was of a murderous mob, I lived in constant fear that someday I might be lynched . . . The flimsiest excuse manufactured by a white mob would suffice to insure a Negro's being brutally beaten or lynched. So whenever I saw a crowd of whites together I was ill at ease and, if possible, I avoided contact with them.[7]

Despite the pervasive atmosphere of white racism, the institutions of family, church, and school sought to combat the myth of black inferiority by reinforcing the self-esteem of Negro children. Like other black children of his generation, Mays spent his early years working on the farm with his siblings (his father was a sharecropper), attending a one-room schoolhouse from November through February, and participating in the life of the local church. Indeed, these three things—hard work, education, and religion—stood at the center of Mays's life and thought throughout his career.[8]

Although young Benjamin enjoyed work on the farm (which began at sunup and ended at sundown), he especially looked forward to the four months of uninterrupted formal education at the Greenwood County School for Negroes. Even at an early age the pursuit of learning was the driving force in his life. Having been taught the basics of reading and writing by his older sister, Benjamin was well ahead of the other students when he began his academic journey at the county's one-room schoolhouse. Therefore, when the nine-year-old Mays recited from memory the entire fifth chapter of the Gospel According to St. Matthew, the members of the Mount Zion Baptist Church hailed him as the next Booker T. Washington or Frederick Douglass. Mays described their response like this:

> After my recitation, the house went wild: old women waved their handkerchiefs, old men stamped their feet, and the people generally applauded long and loud. It was a terrific ovation, let alone a tremendous experience, for a nine-year-old boy. There were predictions that I would "go places" in life. The minister said I would preach; and from that moment on the Reverend Marshall manifested a special interest in me.[9]

Although the members of Mount Zion never contributed "one dime" toward his educational expenses, Mays believed they gave him "something far more valuable" in the form of praise, encouragement, and confidence. Indeed, the enthusiastic support Benjamin received from his schoolteacher, pastor, and church deepened his commitment to further his education, despite the objections of his father.[10] Not surprisingly, Mays's early prayer life, which was cultivated by his mother, revolved around his unquenchable thirst for an education:

> I sought a way out through prayer. I prayed frequently as I worked in the field and many nights alone in the moonlight. I often plowed to the end of the row, hitched the mule to a tree, and went down into the woods to pray. On moonlight nights, I would leave the house and go into the field and pray. My prayers were all variations of the same theme: a petition to God to enable me to get away to school. My desire for an education was not only a dream but a goal that drove and prodded me, day and night. I left the farm not to escape it but to find *my* world, to become myself.[11]

Clearly, from the beginning, education and religion went hand in hand for Benjamin Mays. Essentially, they were two sides of the same coin enabling him to make sense out of a world intent on stifling his God-given potential. Therefore, when the seventeen-year-old Mays entered the high school program at South Carolina State College in

Orangeburg, he resolved to take advantage of every educational opportunity available to him.

Mays graduated from high school in 1916 at the age of twenty-two,[12] determined to matriculate at a prestigious New England college. He desperately wanted to prove to himself and the world that Negroes could compete on the same intellectual level as whites. Mays was particularly disturbed about the "myth of Negro inferiority," and the manner in which blacks "accepted their denigration." As he saw it, their lackluster response "tended to make each new generation believe that they were indeed inferior." Therefore, in September 1917, after spending his freshman year at Virginia Union University, Mays set out for Bates College in Lewiston, Maine in order to "prove my worth, my ability." It is significant to note that while Mays rejected the myth of Negro inferiority, he wanted to compete academically against Northern whites, whom he considered at the time the measuring rod of intellectual ability, so that he might have "*prima facie* evidence that Negroes were not inferior."[13]

The three years Mays spent at Bates College had a decisive impact on his thinking. For the first time in his life he met white people who treated him as a human being. No doubt, this positive experience with Northern whites helped to shape his conviction that there was, in fact, a "Christian way in race relations" capable of producing justice and harmony between blacks and whites. Mays described his encounters with white students and faculty at Bates in this fashion:

> We met and mingled as peers, not as "superior" and "inferior." This was a new experience for me. I was getting another view of the white man—a radically different view. They were not all my enemies. For the first time, whether on campus or in the town of Lewiston, whether alone or in a group, I felt at home in the universe.[14]

Consequently, Mays produced an impressive record at Bates and graduated as the fifth ranking student in the senior class of 1920.[15] Having successfully proven that "superiority and inferiority in academic achievement had nothing to do with skin color," Mays decided to continue his education at the Divinity School of the University of Chicago. Interestingly enough, his decision to pursue graduate study in religion was not an easy one. Although he had been licensed to preach in 1919, he entered his senior year at Bates undecided about the ministry as a full-time profession; he had also considered doing graduate work in mathematics or philosophy. Not being one who appreciated sensationalized accounts of ministerial callings, Mays succinctly described his vocational decision without drama or fanfare: "Religion finally won out over both philosophy and mathematics."[16] Mays was ordained in 1921.

However, Mays's goal of obtaining the Ph.D. in religion took many turns and detours before he finally completed the degree in March 1935. After spending only three quarters at the University of Chicago, Dr. John Hope, President of Morehouse College, lured Mays away from his studies in 1921 to teach mathematics and psychology at the Atlanta-based school. In addition to his teaching responsibilities, Mays served as acting dean; coached the debating team (of which Howard Thurman was a member)[17]; and pastored his first and only church, Shiloh Baptist Church in Atlanta. After three enjoyable years at Morehouse, Mays returned to the University of Chicago to complete his master's degree in 1925.[18]

After receiving his M.A. in religion, Mays took several other positions before resuming work on his doctorate in 1932. He served as an English instructor at South Carolina State College (1925-26); Executive Secretary of the National Urban League in Tampa, Florida (1926-28); student secretary for the National YMCA (1928-30); and research fellow (along with Joseph W. Nicholson, a C.M.E. minister and Ph.D. from Northwestern University) commissioned by the Institute of Social and Religious Research to conduct a nation-wide study of the black church in the United States (1930-32).

Indeed, Mays considered the latter invitation a "heaven-sent" opportunity to cultivate his life-long interest in scholarship, religion, and the black church. The Mays-Nicholson study, which appeared in 1933 under the title *The Negro's Church*, along with the publication of his doctoral thesis, *The Negro's God* (1938), quickly became *the* classic texts on the black church and its theology, and established Mays as a preeminent interpreter of the African-American religious experience. In these and other writings Mays emphasized the importance of constructive criticism of the black church and its ministers, and the need for a socially relevant theology that addressed the plight of the Negro community.[19]

Having completed all his course requirements by the summer of 1934, Mays accepted the deanship of the School of Religion at Howard University in Washington, D.C. Thereafter, his reputation as an educator and churchman spread rapidly throughout the nation and the world. In 1936 Mays was one of thirteen Americans selected to attend the 1937 YMCA World Conference in Mysore, India, where he was also elected to the organization's World Committee.[20] By the end of 1939 he had attended three more ecumenical meetings in England, Stockholm, and Amsterdam. In *Born to Rebel* Mays described the significant impact these international gatherings had on his thinking:

> These conferences enabled me to learn from experience, from observation, and from wide contact with people across the world that the black-white problem was a major problem . . . and that

our Christian people, Negro and white, have their work cut out for them if Christianity is to play the decisive role in solving the problem of race, war, and poverty and thus avoid world catastrophe.[21]

Indeed, these trips abroad while dean of Howard University's School of Religion, strengthened Mays's resolve to relate the gospel to the pressing social and political realities facing America and the world.

After a successful six-year term at Howard University,[22] Mays accepted his greatest challenge to date: the presidency of Morehouse College, where he had begun his teaching career nineteen years earlier. In addition to strengthening the college financially and academically, Mays also found time to continue his participation in national and international ecumenical organizations. In 1944 he became the first African-American to be elected vice president of the Federal Council of Churches of Christ in America, which was organized in 1912 (now the National Council of Churches). Four years later he attended the organizing meeting of the World Council of Churches in Amsterdam, Holland, and was chosen to represent the National Baptist Convention, Inc., on the Council's Central Committee (the official voice of the organization between Assemblies). Between 1948 and the Second World Assembly in 1954, Mays, one of two Negroes on the ninety person committee, attended meetings in Switzerland, England, Canada, and India.[23]

In many respects Mays's participation in the ecumenical movement epitomized the dilemma of Negro Christians in the post–World War II years. On the one hand, he experienced moments of spiritual exultation and renewal upon witnessing the embodiment of Christian universalism in the World Council of Churches. Noting the lack of segregation at international meetings, Mays argued that "one would have to be in an Assembly of the World Church to really know what Christian fellowship is." Even more significant was his description of a communion service at the 1948 Amsterdam meeting, where he "noted a Methodist sitting next to a Baptist, an Anglican sitting next to a Presbyterian, a Chinese communing beside a Japanese, an American white man seated with an American Negro, and an African communing with a Dutchman."[24]

But despite feelings of optimism produced by the achievement of integration and ecumenicity at world meetings, Mays knew that the realities of segregation and discrimination awaited him when he returned to the United States—as with African-American soldiers who experienced social equality in Europe during World War II. Yet another important reality that tempered Mays's idealism was his recognition that even "in world gatherings, as elsewhere, the Negro is likely to be the forgotten man." Mays was referring to his belief that if it were not for the persistence of African-American delegates, the World Council's pronouncements on race would be weak and blacks would be overlooked for positions of influence and leadership.[25] Mays also knew that church resolutions and pronouncements at international conferences (no matter how strong) would not, in and of themselves, solve the race problem in America. Indeed, the reality of racism at home and abroad kept Mays from an exclusive commitment to theological liberalism.

Having worked and prayed his way through high school, college, and graduate school; received significant appointments in the Federal and World Council of Churches; and succeeded in the academy far beyond many of his white peers, Mays had demonstrated that education, religion, and positive race relations were effective means by which the poorest Negro child could transcend the limitations of his or her environment.[26] In his capacity as president of Morehouse College from 1940 to 1967, and a frequent public speaker at church conferences, colleges, and universities across the country, Mays repeated this message to thousands of students, preachers, and educators. In similar fashion, he told the American community at large that its credibility as a world leader depended on it being a nation where all people—regardless of race, sex, or creed—could rise above their limitations to achieve their goals and dreams.

America and World Leadership

More than any other African-American religious scholar in the postwar years, Benjamin E. Mays consistently emphasized the global implications of the American race problem. As we have seen, Mays was an internationally respected church leader who travelled extensively. He knew from personal experience that "the eyes of the world are upon America." Whether he was in Asia, Africa, or Europe, Mays was constantly asked about the status of race relations in the United States. He used these opportunities to put the racist, un-Christian, and un-democratic practices of America and its churches before the scrutiny of world opinion. Like other pre–Black Power thinkers, Mays reminded the American public that the news of segregation and discrimination was known throughout the world:

> For good or for ill, we can no longer live in isolation. Whether we like it or not, what happens in one corner of the earth resounds around the world. In attitudes and ideas, we may be thousands of miles apart; but in time and space we are very near. The press, the radio, the airplane, and sheer economic necessity now make isolation impossible.[27]

America could no longer hide. Advances in technology meant that the nation's race problem was now a global issue, discussed in the most remote corners of the earth. Ironically, America had invited this close international scrutiny because it presented itself as the leader of the democratic world. Therefore, Mays reminded the nation:

Today the eyes of the world are upon America to see how she treats today and will treat tomorrow the minorities within her borders such as Jews, Mexicans, American Indians, Negroes, and Japanese who are loyal American citizens. Our moral leadership in the post-war world will be greatly advanced or retarded on this point.[28]

Like other Negro leaders, Mays argued that America's international influence depended on its treatment of the poor and oppressed in its own backyard. Clearly, if America was to claim moral leadership on the international level, it would first have to practice democracy at the domestic level. Pre–Black Power religious thinkers made this point unmistakably clear as they reminded the nation of its moral obligation to practice the democracy it so eloquently preached.

Yet it was precisely America's wartime propaganda that fueled black people's historic quest for freedom. Having fought in World War I to "make the world safe for democracy," African-American soldiers returned to the states expecting to share in the fruits of democracy; certainly, their disappointment was still fresh in their minds when they fought again in World War II. Convinced that World War II pronouncements "helped India, made the Africans restless, and stimulated Negroes in the United States," Mays described the impact of these experiences on the black freedom struggle:

Each time, we fought for a way of life for all peoples . . . As a result of what we claimed we were fighting for, the race crisis has become global in character. We intensified the aspiration for equality of treatment and equality of opportunity on the part of American Negroes and the colored races throughout the world. The race problem can no longer be localized. It is now global.[29]

Just as W.E.B. Du Bois prophesied in 1903 that "the problem of the twentieth century is the problem of the color line,"[30] Benjamin E. Mays predicted in 1946 that the postwar years would be full of global racial tension. Mays stated his position forthrightly: "Either the colored races will obtain more than they have now, or there will be increasing tension in the years ahead."[31]

Having travelled to Africa and Asia as early as 1937, Mays knew firsthand that "the colored races of the earth do not share in world control." But even worse, Mays observed that "they do not have the decisive word even in their own native lands." European imperialism meant that "the 992 million colored peoples in Asia are not free to shape and mould their own lives," and "the 142 million Africans neither own nor control Africa." Furthermore, Mays noted, "the 13 million Negroes in the United States live only on the periphery of American democracy."[32]

However depressing the plight of colored peoples around the world, Mays argued that there was reason for hope. As he saw it, this hope was to be found in the people's determination to be free, which is why "the pressure from below will increase rather than diminish in the postwar years":

> The colored races of the world will never be less submissive than they are now; they will never want less than they want now; they will never be less vocal in their assertion of their desire for equal opportunity than they are today. Increasingly and more vigorously they will oppose exploitation, segregation, and discrimination based on color and race.[33]

But Mays also knew that in their struggle for justice, the oppressed would encounter unyielding white resistance. Predicting that "the way of the colored races in the postwar world is going to be exceedingly difficult," Mays paraphrased the oft-repeated maxim of Frederick Douglass that "power concedes nothing without a demand." Mays put it like this:

> Those who occupy vantage points are seldom willing to share their privileges with the less privileged. Persons in control usually do all they can to keep persons not in control from rising to their level. They may help them a bit but rarely to the point of equality.[34]

As Mays viewed it, colored peoples around the world shared the same fate; they will experience agony and frustration as the white nations continually "close the doors of opportunity" in their faces. But Mays urged the world's struggling peoples not to lose heart. His firm belief in Christianity led him to the conviction that "in the final analysis, the forces of evil and reaction cannot win." Like other pre–Black Power religious thinkers, he argued that there was a "moral order in the universe" that leaned in the direction of justice. Consequently, he urged the American churches to muster "the Christian courage to solve the color problem within its own borders" by becoming "Christian in their daily lives, private and public," and demanding that the government treat the oppressed in light of the Christian principles of love, justice, and equality. Mays firmly believed that American Christians had all "the tools with which to work" (the teachings of Christ, the Declaration of Independence, and the U.S. Constitution); all they needed now was the *will* to "practice what the church has been teaching for 1900 years."[35]

Ultimately, Mays was hopeful because he believed that the world climate in the postwar years meant that "the number of people who believe in justice and equality for all races will never be fewer than they are today." Therefore, he concluded that the struggle for racial justice around the world must be waged with courage and determination:

> The battle will not be easy but those who believe in Jesus, in God, in justice, and in equality cannot and will not retreat. Upon complete victory in this area, hangs the welfare of all mankind.[36]

All Life Is Interrelated

In addition to calling on America to fulfill its claim to moral world leadership, pre–Black Power religious thinkers waged a theological battle against white racist interpretations of Christianity that undergirded segregation. These racist distortions of the faith were based on the false notion that black humanity is defective and therefore not worthy of fellowship with whites. As George Kelsey (a Morehouse graduate, professor, and Director of Morehouse School of Religion from 1945 to 1948) noted in his classic text *Racism and the Christian Understanding of Man*, segregation developed as a plan of political action to separate "inferior," "defective" black being (the out-race) from "superior," "godlike" white being (the in-race).[37] In light of this gross distortion of the Christian doctrine of humanity, pre–Black Power theologians articulated a theological anthropology that emphasized "the oneness of humanity," and the "interrelatedness of all life."

Perhaps the most important element that shaped Negro theologians' views on Christianity, America, and the world was their firm conviction that God is the creator of all human life, and thus all men and women, regardless of race or nationality, are brothers and sisters. Benjamin Mays, George Kelsey, Howard Thurman, and others pointed to the Genesis creation story to demonstrate their claim that "the human family began in unity." In a speech delivered at the Eighth Congress of the Baptist World Alliance in Cleveland, Ohio, Mays underscored this view by clarifying the Christian doctrine of creation. As Mays saw it, Christianity does not speak of

> one origin for the French and another for the German; not one for the English and another for the Irish; not one for the Chinese

and another for the Japanese; not one for the Bantus and another
for the Dutch of South Africa; and not one for the Russian and
another for the American.[38]

No, for Mays and other pre–Black Power religious thinkers, Christianity declares that "the various races and nations of the earth have a common ancestry and that ancestry is God, for God 'has made of one blood all nations of men to dwell on all the face of the earth.'"[39]

Second, Mays contended that modern scientific research supported the Christian claim that "all life is interrelated." In his sermons and addresses across the country, he frequently referred to the work of anthropologists Ruth Benedict and Margaret Mead to reinforce his belief in the oneness of humanity. Furthermore, Mays argued, "we could quote scientist after scientist on the question as to whether there is or is not an inherent superiority which one race possesses over another."[40]

On the contrary, Mays proclaimed that "the structure of the body proves kinship." Here again, he emphasized the obvious in his attempt to demonstrate the absurdity of racist conceptions of humanity:

> In all normal human beings, we find the same number of toes, fingers, teeth, muscles, and bones. There are tall people and short people in all parts of the world. There are long heads and round heads among all races. There are brilliant people and stupid people in every race of mankind.[41]

In addition, Mays contended that science repudiates the notion that there is such a thing as "Negro blood" or "white blood"; in reality, there are four blood types (A, B, O, and AB) that are found in all peoples throughout the world. Therefore, Mays, citing John Donne's poem "No Man Is an Island," concluded that "whether we like it or not," all nationalities "must inhabit the globe together."[42] Indeed, Martin Luther King, Jr., also frequently quoted John Donne to emphasize "the interrelated structure of reality" that makes all people "links in the great chain of humanity."[43] Howard Thurman used similar language to express his belief in the interrelated structure of human life. In his essay "God and the Race Question," Thurman stressed that

> The human lungs, heart, liver, and so forth, are all the same. The blood types are the same. The air we breathe and the food we eat serve the same purpose in every human body. Physical death and birth are the same for all mankind. For better or for worse we must live together on this planet.[44]

Finally, pre–Black Power religious thinkers argued that the unity of the human family compelled Christians to be concerned about the welfare of *every* human being. Since "we are tied together with an inescapable destiny," Mays told the 1945 graduating class of Howard University, "what affects one, affects all. What affects the sharecropper in Mississippi, affects the millionaire on Park Avenue. What hurts the poor Negro hurts the poor whites."[45] Indeed, Mays's famous protégé, Martin Luther King, Jr., used similar metaphors in the early 1960s to articulate his vision of the American dream and its role in the creation of the beloved community.[46]

It is important to emphasize, however, that before King's rise to international prominence in the wake of the 1955 Montgomery bus boycott, Benjamin Mays was the most assertive public spokesman for the theology of race relations; his active participation in ecumenical conferences throughout the world made him one of the most visible Negro churchmen of his time. As noted earlier, Howard Thurman was also profoundly committed to the development of a Christian perspective on integration and race relations; indeed, his theology also influenced Martin Luther King, Jr., and other students who went on to make important contributions to the civil rights movement.[47] Therefore, a discussion of Thurman's ministry is essential for a more complete understanding of pre–Black Power theologians' interpretation of "the Christian way in race relations."

The Ministry of Howard Thurman

Like Benjamin Mays, Howard Thurman shaped his ministry out of the firm conviction that "all life is interrelated." But unlike Mays, he was not primarily interested in exposing America's racial sins before the world community; nor did he spend a lot of time making impassioned appeals to the moral conscience of the nation, seeking to remind the church and the government of their Christian and democratic principles. Instead, Thurman sought to demonstrate the interrelatedness of human life through the practice of religious experience. In his pastoral work in Ohio and San Francisco, and his teaching and campus ministries at Howard and Boston Universities, Thurman experimented with creative worship styles that would appeal to congregants from different cultural, religious, social, and ethnic backgrounds. Essentially, he believed that authentic religious experience transcends "all superficial categories that separate and divide" people and allows them to sense their relatedness to all humanity.[48]

Like Mays, Thurman believed that nations, ethnic groups, and religious communities inhibit the realization of human community when they emphasize the differences that separate people instead of the common ties that bind them together. Indeed, for pre–Black Power thinkers, the ideology of integration was simply the political expression of

Christian teaching on the interrelatedness of human life. Thurman eloquently captured the essence of this perspective:

> To experience oneself as a human being is to feel life moving
> through one and claiming one as a part of it . . . It is not the
> experience of oneself as male or female, as black or white, as
> American or European. It is rather the experience of oneself as
> being. It is at such a time that one can hear the sound of the
> genuine in other human beings.[49]

The opportunity to explore further his convictions about the unify-
ing nature of the religious experience came in 1944 when Thurman
was invited to join Dr. Alfred G. Fisk (a white Presbyterian minister
and college professor) as the co-pastor of a new interracial church in
San Francisco. After prayerful consideration, Thurman left his tenured
professorship and position as Dean of Rankin Chapel at Howard University and ventured westward excited about the challenges of an interracial ministry:

> Here at last I could put to the test once more the major concern
> of my life: Is the worship of God the central and most significant
> act of the human spirit? Is it really true that in the presence of
> God there is neither male nor female, child nor adult, rich nor
> poor, nor any classification by which mankind defines itself in
> categories, however meaningful?[50]

The racial makeup of San Francisco in 1944 made it the ideal loca-
tion for the testing of Thurman's fundamental theological concern.
Whites, Asian-Americans, Mexican-Americans, Native Americans, and
African-Americans lived side by side during a time of deep ethnic tension. Specifically, the steady arrival of black migrants in search of jobs
in the war industries; the white backlash to increased racial diversity;
and the relocation of Japanese-Americans to concentration camps, created a social climate that was a potential racial powderkeg.[51] In this
environment Thurman wanted to prove that through authentic religious experience, people could transcend racial barriers and appreciate the interrelatedness of all humanity.

The Church for the Fellowship of All Peoples (officially organized
in October 1944) developed a program and liturgy especially designed
to foster unity in the midst of cultural and religious diversity. Both
children and adults were regularly exposed to the contributions of different ethnic groups through worship experiences, forum discussions,
lectures, games, recitals, art exhibits, and international dinners. As a
result, "slowly there began to emerge a climate in which the fruits of

culture could be appreciated, assimilated, and shared without patronage and condescension."[52]

In addition, Fellowship Church cultivated an openness to religious truth beyond the confines of Hebrew-Christian thought. The members expressed their ecumenical attitude in the spirit of Galatians 3:28:

> It is our faith that in the presence of God—with His dream of order—there is neither male nor female; white nor black, Gentile nor Jew; Protestant nor Catholic; Hindu nor Buddhist nor Moslem—but a human spirit, stripped to the literal substance of IT-SELF.[53]

This declaration of faith was the lifeblood of Fellowship Church. After nine years of ministry there (which included nationwide preaching tours and writing about the San Francisco experience), Thurman was satisfied that his vision of ministry had made an impact on American religion. Therefore, in 1953, he accepted an invitation to become Dean of Marsh Chapel and Professor of Spiritual Disciplines and Resources at Boston University.

Through the practice of ministry, Thurman demonstrated that there was "a Christian way in race relations" capable of tearing down the walls of hostility. Interestingly enough, Albert Cleage, who served as interim co-pastor with Alfred Fisk until Thurman arrived from Washington, D.C., had a very different assessment of the viability of interracial congregations like Fellowship Church.[54] Nevertheless, Thurman's ministry embodied pre–Black Power theologians' belief that a strong emphasis on the interrelatedness of human life was a necessary precondition for any Christian theology of race relations.

CHRISTIANITY AND RACE RELATIONS

Pre–Black Power Critique of American Christianity

Pre–Black Power religious thinkers exposed the sins of American Christianity just as they revealed America's hypocritical claim to be the moral leader of the democratic world. They attacked American Christianity for failing to take a bold stand against racism and segregation, proclaiming that the church functioned as "a taillight instead of a headlight." As they saw it, the overwhelming majority of white churches refused to "rock the boat"; shunned their responsibility to "the least of these"; and made "a mockery of the gospel" by condoning racism in the church and society. Accordingly, Negro theologians in the 1940s and 1950s constantly reminded the American churches that they must use their spiritual and material resources to help solve the race problem in the nation. Indeed, they insisted that the institutional church could "break the back of segregation" and racial discrimination if it only applied its efforts toward that end. Refusing to let the church off the hook, pre–Black Power religious intellectuals understood their role as that of prophets sent by God to pluck the conscience of American Christianity. Their message was essentially this: Struggle with the oppressed to eliminate racial segregation and discrimination, or renounce your claims to Christianity and democracy.

Negro theologians consistently challenged the church to live out the demands of the gospel in the area of race relations. Indeed, Benjamin Mays took full advantage of every opportunity to urge white Christians to apply the basic principles of their faith to the problematic area of race relations. Likewise, William Stuart Nelson, who succeeded Benjamin Mays as dean of Howard University's School of Religion, warned the white church that "the increasing tension between White and Negro Americans is of the deepest and most immediate concerns to the religious community, for it poses a serious threat to America's internal peace and conceivably to our social and religious structure."[55] Like Mays and other Negro theologians, Nelson challenged the American churches to re-order their priorities by making the race problem more important than fundraising, passing resolutions, holding theological debates, and building new structures.[56]

The important issue pre–Black Power theologians wanted to underscore was that the institutional church failed to take the problem of racism and segregation seriously. As veteran churchmen, they knew from experience that even when denominations and other national church bodies passed resolutions condemning racism, local white ministers and their parishioners continued to shun their moral responsibility, and refused to challenge segregation in their churches and communities. However, the realism of Negro theologians did not lead them to conclude that Christianity was impotent in the fight against racism. On the contrary, they reminded Americans that "the religious impulse" fueled the anti-slavery movement and was responsible for efforts to provide an education for blacks after emancipation.[57] Evaluating the contemporary church in light of these historical moments, Nelson captured the essence of pre–Black Power theologians' critique of American Christianity:

> Except for philanthropy, the period since the Civil War has proved almost completely barren of any determined effort initiated and sustained by the religious community to solve the problem of Negro-White relations in America.[58]

Segregation: *"The Greatest Scandal within the Church"*

For Benjamin Mays, the failure of the American religious community effectively to challenge racial segregation in the church and society was a source of deep anguish. As noted earlier, his wide range of experience as a preacher, teacher, college president, and ecumenical leader showed him that racism was pervasive in every facet of American life. And while Mays encountered less discrimination abroad, he nevertheless lamented, "Nowhere can a black man escape. On sea and on land, at home and abroad, the same stupid and cruel discrimination spreads its tentacles."[59] Mays understood segregation to be "the greatest curse that can be imposed upon any one" because it denies individuals respect as full human beings, restricts their opportunities, and leads to a climate of violence against the segregated group. But more important, Mays interpreted racial segregation as a sin against God. In a 1952 address at Yale Divinity School, he made this point crystal clear:

Segregation on the basis of color or race is a wicked thing because it penalizes a person for being what God has made him and for conditions over which he has no control. If one were segregated because of ignorance, he could learn and change the situation. If one were segregated because of poverty, he could work and improve his economic status. If he were segregated because of uncleanliness, he could bathe and become acceptable. But if one is segregated and stigmatized because of his race, he is penalized for something which he cannot change. And to do this is tantamount to saying to God you made a mistake in making a man like this. *Of all the sins, this is the greatest.*[60]

Clearly, Mays hated racial segregation with every fiber of his being, and he dedicated his life to eradicating it. But he especially despised segregation in the church, calling it "a great strain on my religion."[61] Unlike secular organizations, which made no pronouncements about the sacredness of human life and the meaning of reconciliation, the church is blatantly hypocritical. In fact, Mays argued that "hypocrisy" is the mildest term one can apply to a church that "maintains a segregated house, and simultaneously preaches the fatherhood of God and the brotherhood of man."[62] Mays lamented the fact that the local churches lag far behind secular bodies such as professional boxing, major league baseball, theaters, universities, and the public schools in advocating social change in the area of race. Accordingly, in an address before the Second Assembly of the World Council of Churches in 1954, he cautioned, "It will be a sad commentary on our life and time if future historians can write that the last bulwark of segregation based on race and color in the United States and South Africa was God's church."[63]

Although Mays criticized the white church for its failure to eliminate racial segregation, he was careful to add, "I certainly do not want to give the impression that the blame is all on the side of white churches." As he saw it, "the exclusively racial church" (black or white) is an inadequate expression of Christian community; therefore, Negro congregations that opposed the *full* integration of the churches, for whatever reasons, "may be just as un-Christian at this point as the white church."[64] Indeed, Mays and other pre–Black Power theologians reminded the Negro church and community that it had a pivotal role to play in the creation of better race relations in America. Yet, like black theologians in the late 1960s and 1970s, Negro theologians insisted that self-love is a prerequisite for better race relations.

"The Moral Obligations of Negro Christians"

Having lived in the South for the majority of his life, Benjamin Mays knew firsthand the devastating effect segregation had on the Negro community. On countless occasions he suffered the indignities of discrimination, and several times even feared for his life. As an educator, Mays also knew the impact that segregation had on the minds of black youth; therefore, he dedicated his career to instilling character and pride in young people as he encouraged them to fight segregation and oppression. The first thing Mays sought to do was to combat the inferiority complex that accompanied legalized segregation. The simple message he proclaimed to thousands of young Negroes year after year was, "You are as good as anybody. And you have the right to aim at the stars and make your mark in the world." Mays knew that legalized segregation, along with the prejudice and violence that accompanied it, placed a "badge of inferiority" on every black child. The system of segregation meant that blacks had inferior schools, jobs, and accommodations. As a result, Mays observed that many Negroes grew up believing that they were inferior to whites, and that their subordinate role was ordained by God. Segregation meant that for many youth, "the nerve of aspiration was cut, ambitions dulled, hopes shattered, and dreams killed." Mays elaborated:

> The segregated system with its inevitable consequences of inequality has warped the minds and spirits of thousands of Negro youths. They either grow to manhood accepting the system, in which case they aspire to limited racial standards; or they grow up with bitterness in their minds. It is the rare Negro child who comes through perfectly normal and poised under the segregated system.[65]

However, Mays consistently preached that Negroes could throw off the "badge of inferiority," even as they fought to end racial segregation and discrimination. He noted the impact of the two world wars on the black freedom struggle, claiming that they helped to intensify agitation for justice on the homefront. Suggesting that "morale is caught more than taught," Mays argued that as children associated "with parents, teachers and adults who were cringing and kow-towing, less and less," they too would gain self-esteem and pride.[66]

In his effort to combat the effect of segregation on the black community, Mays consistently referred to the achievements of famous Negroes who succeeded under the most adverse circumstances. Recalling the impact Booker T. Washington, Frederick Douglass, and Paul Lawrence Dunbar had on his life, Mays noted that "every Negro who achieves significantly is a builder of morale for the Negro child." Indeed, Mays frequently cited the accomplishments of figures such as Jackie Robinson, Joe Louis, Marian Anderson, Paul Robeson, Richard Wright, Charles Drew, and Ralph Bunche, to let young people know that they too could achieve if they put their minds to it. As Mays understood it, parents, teachers, and ministers must continually tell children the same things that were told to him as a child growing up on a farm in South Carolina: "Character and ability are the important things. You are as good as anybody."[67]

While Mays emphasized the importance of building pride and self-esteem, as a minister of the gospel he also knew the dangers of self-righteousness and hatred. He cautioned Negroes not to think that they were more virtuous than whites simply because they were oppressed. Accordingly, Mays told Negroes that, "no one race has a monopoly on virtue and no one race has a monopoly on things that are evil. We are potentially no worse and potentially no better than other races."[68] As he viewed it, Negroes must not only criticize the un-Christian behavior of whites, they must also be critical of un-Christian conduct in their own community, where all too often "Negroes are just as brutal and cruel to each other as the members of the dominant group are to Negroes." Indeed, Mays claimed that if Negro Christians were to avoid the sin of hypocrisy and self-righteousness, they should "earn the right to criticize" whites by practicing democracy and justice in those areas where they have complete control. When this is done, Negroes can criticize white Christians "with cleaner hands," and participate more effectively in improving race relations.[69] Emphasizing the value of self-criticism for interracial fellowship, Mays concluded:

> Criticisms are likely to be more effective and better received when those who give them accept the fact that they themselves are not perfect, and that they are part and parcel of the evil they condemn.[70]

In addition, Mays believed that Negroes participate in the evil of seg-regation when they are dishonest and evasive when discussing the race problem with whites. He understood that the violence inflicted upon blacks during slavery and Reconstruction made them develop techniques of survival when dealing with the white community. To be sure, these were times when it was safer to tell whites what they wanted to hear if blacks were to survive in a hostile environment. Mays knew that even in 1945 it required a degree of courage to express one's true feelings about racism to whites. Nevertheless, he noted that now "a critical Negro public is demanding that Negro Christian leadership be straightfor-ward and honest" in its interactions with white leaders. Like other pre—Black Power thinkers, Mays believed that a commitment to honesty and integrity was the only way to achieve genuine progress in race relations.[71]

Not surprisingly, Mays was disturbed by Negro leaders who, out of selfish motivation, were hypocritical and evasive in order to promote themselves to a position of prestige in the eyes of the white community. In fact, in his weekly column for the *Pittsburgh Courier,* he described this type of leader (who had the respect of neither Negroes nor whites) in a style that anticipated the scathing critique of Black Power advocates:

> "Uncle Thomas" has two outstanding traits. He is afraid and he is extremely selfish. He seeks in his every mode to please the white folk. He is physically afraid. He is also afraid he will not hold his position nor stand well in the eyes of the ruling majority if he says or does something which the white people do not like. He usually finds out their wishes before he puts forth his program. Mingled with fear and awe of and respect for the white man, he idolizes that which is white. He just cannot stand on his feet and strongly express a point of view at variance with white people.[72]

Finally, Mays urged Negro Christians to reject the spirit of hatred and revenge, because they too will be under God's judgment if they seek to oppress others. Mays insisted that Negroes must continue to open their church doors to all people and be free of prejudice against other minority groups such as Native Americans, Mexican-Americans, Asian-Americans, Jews, West Indians, and "other minority peoples."[73] But it is important to emphasize that despite the ethical weaknesses of white and black churches, Benjamin Mays deeply believed that the Christian religion, when practiced with boldness and integrity, could help solve the problem of race relations in America.

"Democratizing and Christianizing America"

Mays combined the social justice theme of the Old Testament proph-ets with the liberative element of black religion as he reminded America and the church of its obligation to practice democracy and equality. Whether he was speaking to a black or white audience, he emphasized the importance of themes such as justice for the oppressed, individual honesty and integrity, self-help, and Christian service. At colleges, universities, and ecumenical conferences throughout the nation, Benjamin Mays persistently challenged Christians to apply the power of the gospel to the problem of racism in America.

In a 1945 commencement address at Howard University, Mays spoke about these issues in a manner that was characteristic of pre–Black Power religious intellectuals. Mays challenged the graduating class to be "prophets of a new day" by working to democratize and Christianize America in their generation. Reminding his audience that "it does not take a hundred years to perfect social change," Mays reasoned that

> if Germany through brutal means can build a kingdom of evil in one decade and if Russia, through brutal processes, can construct a new order in two decades, we can democratize and Christianize America in one generation.[74]

Of course, when Mays spoke of democratizing and Christianizing America, he knew that there was already some level of democracy and Christianity practiced in the United States. However, he emphasized that America never intended for its democracy to function effectively "as Hitler planned his kingdom of evil to function effectively"; nor has America been committed to Christianity in the way Russian leaders were committed to building a new political and economic structure.

Mays noted that in the area of race, America's ability to practice democracy and Christianity is put under the severest strain; accordingly, he reasoned that "it is probably easier to be Christian in any other area of life than in the area of race."[75] Nevertheless, Mays clung to the belief that the federal government and the Christian churches of America would ultimately be forced to practice what they preached:

> The United States is *obligated* by virtue of its Federal Constitution and by virtue of its Christian pronouncements to become Christianized and democratized. If America is to maintain integrity of soul, and if our Government is to escape the label of hypocrisy and deception, it has no choice but to plan deliberately to bring to full fruition the four freedoms—for which we claim we fought on the battlefields of Europe and Africa; and for which we claim we are fighting in the Pacific.[76]

Clearly, Mays had faith that America would live up to its obligations to treat all of its citizens with justice and equality. Like other pre–Black Power religious thinkers, he appealed to the moral conscience of America in an effort to improve the plight of oppressed blacks. Mays referred to the noble ideas contained in the Declaration of Independence and the Bill of Rights to assure Howard University students that America had no choice but to extend the rights of full citizenship to Negroes. Moreover, he sought to remind the graduates that it was their responsibility to put pressure on the federal government to take a more active role in solving the basic problems that confront the Negro community. For example, Mays contended that the government could end unemployment "within less than a decade" if it were truly committed to democracy. Concomitantly, he believed that once the problem of unemployment was solved, many other obstacles would also be overcome: friction between the races would be minimized; healthcare could be provided for every citizen (those who could pay and those who could not); delinquency would decrease; slums could be eliminated and decent housing provided for all; and educational facilities (especially in the South) would be enhanced. Speaking in the heart of the nation's capital, Mays reminded the graduates and the politicians that it was "the responsibility of the federal government to see that these things are done." Anticipating criticism, he added:

> Let those who oppose these measures on the ground of cost, bear in mind that we spend more in one year to prosecute this war than we would spend in twenty-five years in constructive measures such as these.[77]

Most important, Mays argued that the government must abolish segregation in all areas where federal money is spent. Accordingly, Mays urged the government to end discrimination in federal agencies in Washington, the Armed Forces, employment, education, housing, hospitalization, and wherever else "the people's money is spent." Indeed, Mays spoke as a prophet of social justice as he urged the church to be Christian and the government to be democratic; he reminded both institutions that "we are what we do and not what we say. We are as democratic as we live and we are as Christian as we act."[78]

Mays concluded his commencement address by emphasizing themes that were hallmarks of his educational pedagogy and oratorical style. He told the graduates to develop strong moral character by practicing honesty and integrity in their personal and professional lives. Whether they became doctors, lawyers, ministers, teachers, or politicians, they should stand for principles and not for that which is expedient:

> Let it be known in your community and in your profession that you are not for sale . . . that you are not putty to be molded and twisted in the pattern of injustice and incorruption. Develop strong, rock-ribbed, steel girded characters so that whoever bumps up

against you, will bounce back because they came up against a man or a woman who is not for sale.[79]

Anticipating the liberation theology of the post–Black Power era, Mays told students that if they were to democratize and Christianize America in their generation, they had to stand with the oppressed in their struggle for freedom. He urged the graduates to be in solidarity with disfranchised blacks in the South, poor whites, the untouchables of India, persecuted Jews, and "the millions in Africa who are groping for freedom." By speaking out against injustice wherever they find it, they "will be symbols of the new day," and "express the hopes and aspirations of the suppressed peoples everywhere." As they struggle against injustice in America and around the world, they must never lose hope, because God is on the side of the oppressed:

> You can not lose. The future is on your side. The moral order of the universe will support your views. The planets, the sun, the moon, and the stars in their courses will fight on your side. Even God will fight on your side. History proves that all injustice defeats its own end.[80]

CHRISTIANITY, THE BIBLE, AND NONVIOLENCE

No examination of the theology of race relations espoused by Benjamin Mays and others would be complete without a brief analysis of their understanding of the Bible and its impact on their interpretation of Christianity and nonviolence. Essentially, Mays sought to expose the fallacy of racist interpretations of scripture and provide a biblical hermeneutic that would reinforce the Negro community's quest for integration.

"Of One Blood": Biblical Support for Integration

Perhaps the most important aspect of Mays's biblical interpretation is his assertion that *nothing* in the Hebrew and Christian scriptures supports racial segregation. On the contrary, Mays underscored the biblical affirmation that faith and not race is the standard by which God judges human beings. In fact, Mays noted, "the nations that surrounded Israel belonged to the same racial stock as Israel," and converts from other nations and races were always welcomed. Indeed, for Mays, a careful study of the Hebrew scriptures will show that no support for racial segregation can be found there; when Israelite religion proscribed intermarriage with surrounding cultures, it was done solely on the basis of preserving their distinctive religious tradition, not to maintain racial purity.[81]

Likewise, Mays emphasized that the Christian scriptures advocate universalism and repudiate segregation based on race. First, Mays referred to the teachings of Jesus to support his claim that "to deny the universalism in the teachings of Christ is to deny the very genius of Christianity." Jesus' parable of the Good Samaritan (Lk 10:25-37); his declaration about finding more faith in a Roman centurion than in all Israel (Lk 7:1-10); and his teaching in Nazareth about God's concern for the non-Israelite (Lk 4:23-30) all show that "from the beginning of his career, Jesus proclaimed a religion that was supraracial, supranational, supracultural, and supraclass."[82]

Additionally, Mays noted that the early church opened its fellowship to all persons regardless of ethnic background, class, or gender. As he saw it, the descent of the Holy Spirit at Pentecost (Acts 2:1-11); Peter's realization that "God is no respecter of persons" (Acts 10:34-35); Paul's declaration that in Christ Jesus there are no distinctions that divide humanity (Gal 3:28) and his sermon in Athens proclaiming God as the Creator of all human beings (Acts 17:24-28), all demonstrate that the early Christian church was an integrated community that renounced all forms of segregation and discrimination. Finally, and most important, Mays argued that the "universalism in the gospel is climaxed and attested to by the fact that Christ died for all mankind." Therefore, he concluded that those who seek biblical support for racism and segregation will search in vain; instead of supporting racial segregation, it is a manual for integration and universalism.[83]

The Ministry of Jesus: Love for God and Humanity

Like other pre–Black Power religious scholars, Mays believed that genuine Christianity was based on Jesus' teaching that "all the law and the prophets" are based on fervent love for God and humanity (Mt 22:35-40). For Mays, it was Jesus' profound love for God *and* human beings that brought him into conflict with the religious establishment:

> If Jesus had gone throughout the Palestinian or Greco-Roman world merely talking about God and doing nothing to help man, he would hardly have run into trouble because almost everyone in the world of his day believed in God or in gods. Jesus got into trouble because he believed in man, a belief interlaced and interwoven with his concept of God.[84]

Referring to Jesus' many confrontations with the Pharisees (see Mk 3; Mt 23), Mays emphasized Jesus as a defender of the poor. Again, he contended that it was Jesus' "belief in man, which went with his belief in God, that sent Jesus to the cross."[85] Based on Jesus' example and teaching, Mays concluded that genuine Christianity combines an equal love for God, self, and neighbor; in fact, "the religion of Jesus might be thought of as a triangular religion, and an equilateral triangle at that."[86]

Mays also examined the parables to highlight the social aspects of Jesus' ministry and to underscore the responsibilities of contemporary Christians. For example, in an address at Bucknell University in 1954, he interpreted the parable of the Rich Man and Lazarus as a Christian call to social responsibility. Mays argued that Jesus did not condemn the rich man because he was a bad, immoral person who exploited the poor; nor, for that matter, does Jesus praise Lazarus as a man of virtue. For Mays, the rich man went to hell because he had no social conscience, which was indicated by his inability to see the suffering of Lazarus.[87]

Mays also frequently referred to Jesus' teaching on the judgment (Mt 25:31-46) to emphasize his belief that God is concerned about how we treat "the least of these." For Mays, the test of true Christianity is "not how I treat the educated, but how I treat the man who can't write his name":

> The test of good religion is not how we treat our peers and those above us, but how we treat those beneath us; not how we treat the man highest up, but how we treat the man farthest down.[88]

As Mays saw it, the Christian scriptures are clear in their emphasis on the love of God *and* humanity. "And yet how strange it is," he lamented, "that this aspect of the life and teachings of Jesus has become such a neglected area in our daily practices."[89]

Love, Reconciliation, and Nonviolence

Negro theologians understood nonviolence to be the only Christian means of struggle validated in scripture. Indeed, for Mays, Thurman, and others in their generation, the praxis of Jesus was the authoritative source for Christian living in the area of race, and therefore, they rejected hatred, bitterness, and violence as acceptable Christian behavior. For them, nonviolence was the *only* way Negro Christians could be true to the love ethic of Jesus. Mays expressed this view in his sermons and speeches, but it is also found in the writings of Howard Thurman, George Kelsey, and of course Martin Luther King, Jr.

Underlying Negro theologians' thinking on love, reconciliation, and nonviolence is a firm belief in the power of Christianity to transform lives. In fact, Mays referred to the apostle Paul's Damascus road experience and the conversion of St. Augustine to illustrate his claim that "as pessimistic as any Christian may be about man, he can never deny the power of the Christian religion to make men better."[90] Therefore, Mays interpreted Jesus' teaching on forgiveness, reconciliation, and love for the enemy quite literally, stating that "there is no limit to what the religious man must do to perfect reconciliation or right relationship with his fellowman." Accordingly, Mays argued that *Christian* nonviolence—not all who participated in nonviolent demonstrations embraced it as a philosophy based on religious conviction—is rooted in a profound love that seeks to redeem oppressors, not to humiliate or destroy them.[91]

In addition to the teachings of the Christian scriptures, Mays noted that nonviolence was rooted in the history of the black experience of protest and resistance. He contended that the spirituals are not songs of hate, revenge, or conquest, but rather songs of the soul that helped slaves survive and protest without bitterness and violence. Mays also cited the leadership of Frederick Douglass, Harriet Tubman, Booker T. Washington, W.E.B. Du Bois, and the NAACP to show that a tradition of nonviolence has shaped black people's drive for full citizenship.[92]

Finally, Mays's December 1936 conversation with Gandhi helped to shape his understanding of the philosophy of nonviolence as "an active force" that requires spiritual and moral courage.[93] Indeed, as Sudarshan Kapur has demonstrated in his landmark book *Raising Up a Prophet* (1992), Negro intellectuals' encounter with Gandhi in the 1930s and 1940s (including Benjamin Mays, Howard Thurman, and William Stuart Nelson) laid the theological foundation that Martin Luther King, Jr., later built upon in the 1950s and 1960s.[94]

By the early 1960s Benjamin Mays had seen great progress in race relations in America. He was encouraged by the early successes of the civil rights movement, and interpreted the National Conference on Religion and Race held in Chicago from January 14-17, 1963 as a historic moment for the American religious community.[95] Chaired by Mays, this interfaith meeting (conceived as a religious commemoration of the one hundredth anniversary of the Emancipation Proclamation) brought together for the first time leaders from the Jewish, Roman Catholic, Orthodox, and Protestant faiths to "speak to the nation with a united voice" about the problem of racism in American society. In his opening address to the delegates, Mays expressed an optimism that was characteristic of pre–Black Power Christian integrationists:

> We come this week to think together, to work together, to pray together and to dedicate ourselves to the task of completing the job which Lincoln began 100 years ago . . . We believe that this conference will create in us a new sense of urgency to do in the next ten years what we failed to do in the past 100 years—abolish from among us racial discrimination and prejudice.[96]

Seven months later, the American religious community gathered again to reaffirm its commitment to the ideal of racial equality. The celebrated March on Washington, which culminated in Martin Luther King, Jr.'s eloquent "I Have a Dream" speech on the steps of the Lincoln Memorial, gave Mays and his contemporaries a profound hope that under the leadership of their young, dynamic colleague "the Christian way in race relations" was beginning to change the nation. But not all pre–Black Power religious leaders shared their views about the power of Christianity to transform America. We turn now to the nationalist critique of Elijah Muhammad, who repudiated Christianity as an impotent, white religion specifically designed to enslave and oppress black people.

CHAPTER 2

"Christianity Is the White Man's Religion"

Elijah Muhammad's Nationalist Critique of Christianity

Christianity is a religion organized and backed by the devils for the purpose of making slaves of black mankind . . . Our first step is to give back to the white man his religion, Christianity.
—Elijah Muhammad, 1957

Christianity is a religion that teaches you to love your enemies and hate your friends, and seek reward after death. It has produced more division and hate than all the other religions combined.
—Elijah Muhammad, 1957

Christianity is one of the most perfect black-slave-making religions on our planet. It has completely killed the so-called Negroes mentally.
—Elijah Muhammad, 1965

Unlike Benjamin E. Mays and the other integrationist thinkers, Elijah Muhammad and his followers in the Nation of Islam did not think the Christian religion, no matter how it was interpreted, was a viable resource for improving race relations in America. To the contrary, they proclaimed that Christianity was a hindrance to the African-American community's quest for freedom, justice, and equality. Instead of being an instrument of black liberation, it is actually a "chain of slavery" that will keep black people in bondage as long as they continue to believe in it. Therefore, Muhammad urged African-Americans to renounce "the white man's Christianity" and accept Islam, the true religion of all dark-skinned peoples throughout the world. "Regardless of your prayers to the Father and the Son," Muhammad told African-American Christians, black people will never get justice from the hands of their former Christian slavemasters. The teachings and doctrines of Elijah Muhammad's Nation of Islam, therefore, were specifically developed as a critique of Christianity and its disastrous effect upon "the so-called Negroes in the wilderness of North America."

In this chapter I will examine Elijah Muhammad's critique of Christianity, using the major categories applied in chapter 1: Christianity, America, and the world; Christianity and race relations; and Christianity, the Bible, and self-defense (nonviolence).

CHRISTIANITY, AMERICA, AND THE WORLD

Biographical Sketch

Like Benjamin E. Mays, Elijah Poole was born in the deep South at the close of the nineteeth century. Born in Sandersville, Georgia, in 1897, one of thirteen children of Wali and Marie Poole, Elijah knew the harsh realities of southern racism just as Mays did. But unlike Mays, who left the South in pursuit of a New England college education, Poole dropped out of school after the fourth grade, and in 1923 moved to Detroit with his wife and two children in search of economic security.[1]

Although he had been a Baptist preacher in Georgia (as was his father), Poole became a disciple of Wallace D. Fard, a mysterious man who sold silks and satins from door to door while advising blacks to stop eating pork and to renounce Christianity. Fard had appeared in Detroit in 1930 claiming to be a prophet of Allah from the Holy City of Mecca. His stated mission was to teach blacks in America about their true religion (Islam) and to give them a proper knowledge of themselves and their enemies (the white race).[2]

Impoverished blacks in the overcrowded ghettoes of Detroit responded to the teachings of Wallace D. Fard in such large numbers that it was no longer possible to hold meetings in the homes of his followers. Hence, the group rented an auditorium and the Nation of Islam was born. Poole, one of Fard's most devoted disciples, was duly rewarded with the title Muhammad, a name meaning "one worthy of praise." Thereafter known as Elijah Muhammad, Poole was designated as chief minister of the movement, a position he used to spread the teachings of the new organization.[3]

Muhammad's background as a Baptist preacher gave him the necessary administrative skills to establish new temples—the first being Temple Number Two, which he organized in Chicago in 1932. Moreover, his thorough knowledge of the Bible enabled him to make the message of Islam understandable to poor blacks who had become disillusioned with Christianity and the black church. In light of such skills, Elijah Muhammad was the likely successor to Fard, who mysteriously vanished from Detroit in June 1934.[4] But Muhammad's leadership of the movement did not go unchallenged by some of the leaders in Detroit, and he ultimately was forced to move the headquarters of the Nation of Islam to Chicago. Subsequently, Elijah deified his teacher, proclaiming that "God came to us in the person of Wallace D. Fard," and then presented himself as the sole Messenger of Allah. Indeed, Muhammad solidified his authority by emphasizing his divine calling and unique relationship with Allah:

> I am not a man who has grabbed a suitcase with a bible in it upon my own impulses. No! I stand before you as a man who has been chosen for you by God Himself. I did not choose myself. This must be made clear . . . I was in the presence of God for over three years, and I received what I am teaching you directly from His Mouth . . . I did not receive this gospel from a paper, nor a book, nor from a vision, nor from an angel, but directly from the Mouth of Almighty God Himself.[5]

America and World Leadership

Whereas Benjamin Mays and other Christian thinkers of the post-war period emphasized the need for global unity, Elijah Muhammad preached a doctrine of racial separation that drew sharp lines between whites from Europe and America on the one hand, and the dark-skinned peoples of Africa and Asia on the other. To be sure, both Mays and Muhammad applauded the revolutionary movements in the Third World, interpreting them as God's liberating activity in history. But whereas Mays's religious faith linked him to the white *Christian* nations responsible for the oppression of third-world nations, Muhammad's religious faith connected him to "725 million more brothers and sisters in the World of Islam," who were fighting to throw off the chains of European imperialism. Despite these differences, both men sought validation by their respective international communities: Mays through his active participation in numerous ecumenical conferences overseas, and Muhammad by his pilgrimage (hajj) to the Holy City of Mecca.[6]

As the sole Messenger of Allah, Muhammad used his authority to proclaim the divine solution to the problems of the so-called Negroes in America. Essentially, he taught that Allah would destroy America for its treatment of black people, who had been made deaf, dumb, and blind by the slavery teachings of the white man's Christianity. Just as God punished Egypt for enslaving the Israelites, America would pay for its treatment of its poor black slaves—"the only difference is that Egypt still exists while America will not."[7] Accordingly, Muhammad proclaimed that the divine solution to the problems of the African-American community was the complete separation from white Christian America and the full acceptance of Allah's religion of Islam.

In addition, Muhammad proclaimed that Negroes who believed in integration and Christianity would suffer the same fate as white America. Like an overzealous Christian preacher who admonishes his hearers about the hellfire and damnation that await unbelievers, Muhammad warned that Negroes who reject his message and refuse to join the Nation of Islam will suffer a punishment so terrible "you will wish that you were dead."[8] Those so-called Negroes who are "seduced" into accepting the false friendship of their enemies will meet certain death; but those who believe in Allah and join the Nation "will be put on the road to success overnight . . . on the road toward complete independence in a home of your own, where you will never any more have to beg anyone for freedom, justice, or equality."[9]

Central to Muhammad's critique of Christianity is his claim that America, a so-called Christian nation, has denied freedom, justice, and equality to its black Christian brothers and sisters. Indeed, Muhammad noted that the express purpose of Allah's appearance in the person of Wallace D. Fard was to make manifest the sins of America and to proclaim its destruction. America, Muhammad taught, was Allah's "number one enemy on His list for destruction." Although it presented itself as "a friend and defendant to all peace-loving and freedom-loving people," the history of America proves that it, along with Germany, is one of the "worst, vicious, evil, destructive, trouble-makers of the entire nation of (the) earth."[10] For Muhammad, America's wholesale murder of the Indians and its enslavement of the so-called Negroes are just the beginning of the list of the country's many sins. Like all the white Christian nations of the West, Muhammad described America as the enemy of dark humankind, forever seeking opportunities to oppress the peaceful people of Africa and Asia. Not only will the country pay for its treatment of the so-called Negroes, it will also be punished for its participation in white imperialism:

> This evil people (the white race) have worked all their lives making trouble, causing bloodshed among the peaceful people of the earth and themselves. Their greed in ruling the black people of the earth is unequaled . . . Let the world ponder—what does history show that the white man can call his own outside Europe? However, they spread out and into the homes of black mankind of the earth, taking by armed force the black people's home and making slaves of them for many centuries.[11]

To be sure, both Benjamin Mays and Elijah Muhammad exposed the hypocrisy of America's claim to be the leader of the free world. But whereas Mays appealed to the moral conscience of the nation, emphasizing its democratic and Christian principles in his effort to gain justice for African-Americans, Muhammad preached that America's time was up and its doom was impending. As he saw it, there was no use in attempting to embarrass America before the international community for its racial sins, because its destruction (along with the other Christian nations of the West) had already been determined by Allah:

> Today America's doom is set like a die. She cannot escape; it is impossible. For her to escape would classify the prophets of God and God Himself as predicting lies. When God appeared to me in the person of Master Fard Muhammad, to whom Praises are due forever, in 1931 in Detroit, Michigan, He said that America was His number one enemy on His list for destruction.[12]

It is also important to note that while Mays and other Christian thinkers, though critical of America's treatment of people of color, supported the United States' involvement in World War II, Elijah Muhammad taught African-Americans that since all non-whites were blacks, their interests were best served by a Japanese victory. Consequently, in 1942 he was arrested by the FBI on charges that he conspired to promote the success of the enemy by encouraging blacks to resist the draft. While incarcerated at the federal prison at Milan, Michigan, Muhammad maintained his firm leadership of the Nation of Islam. Upon his release in 1946, he continued to teach that it was foolish for African-Americans to fight against the Japanese, since they too were the victims of white racism. Instead of fighting their own black brothers and sisters in Asia, Muhammad urged African-Americans to prepare themselves for "the Battle of Armageddon," the final showdown between the black and white races.[13] As he saw it, the judgment of Allah upon the white Christian nations of the West was at hand:

> Shall not the God of Peace and Justice deal with such trouble-making people as He did with those before you of old? I warn everyone of you, my people, fly to Allah with me! As I warned you, the judgement of this world has arrived! Get out of the church and get into the Mosques and join onto your own kind, the Nation of Islam! The house you are in shall surely fall and never rise again.[14]

Muhammad's call for blacks to "get out of the church and into the Mosques" was based on more than his utter disdain for the Christian religion; it was also based on an elaborate religious mythology that undergirded the theology of the Nation of Islam. Therefore, in order fully to understand Muhammad's critique of Christianity, it is necessary to grasp the mythology that shaped the worldview of his followers.[15]

White Devils and Black Gods

Whereas Mays, Thurman, and King proclaimed the unity of the human family, emphasizing their conviction that "all life is interrelated," Elijah Muhammad advocated the division of humanity along racial lines and developed a counter-racist doctrine of black superiority and white inferiority.[16] First, Muhammad (along with his most articulate disciple, Malcolm X) took great delight in reminding his followers that Africa was the birthplace of civilization. He often noted that this "dark continent" was a great educational center for the study of architecture, mathematics, and science at a time when Europeans were still "living in caves," "climbing trees," and "crawling on all fours." More important, Elijah Muhammad explained this vast difference in the level of achievement between Africans and Europeans by proclaiming the biological and moral superiority of the black race. But the question Muhammad had to address was this: If blacks are superior to whites, then why have they been oppressed and subjugated by an inferior people for so long?

To be sure, every religious system has its own unique explanation for the existence of human sin and evil. The mythology espoused by Elijah Muhammad's Nation of Islam was commonly referred to as "Yakub's History." This complex myth begins with the belief that black people constitute the "original man," and have therefore existed ever since the earth was created six trillion years ago.[17] As the original people, they were created in the image of Almighty God, who is also black. Contrary to the Christian claim that God is a Spirit, Muhammad taught that Allah was the Divine Black Man, the Supreme Being among a nation of divine black people:

> God is not a mystery today. He is not something invisible. He is not a spirit. He is not something other than flesh and blood; He is in the flesh and in the blood. God is a human being! God would have no joy or pleasure in humans (us) if He Himself were something other than a human being. God would have no joy or pleasure in the material universe if He Himself were other than material.[18]

According to Black Muslim mythology, God appointed twenty-four scientists to be responsible for predicting the future and recording the history of the black nation. These scientists foresaw that one day, when 30 percent of the people were dissatisfied with the present state of affairs, a man named Yakub would be born from that number who would create a race of people destined to rule the black nation for six thousand years. Yakub was born 6,600 years ago in fulfillment of the prophecy, and at a very young age began scientific experiments that would eventually contribute to his creation of the white race. According to the myth, at the age of six, Yakub was playing with two pieces of steel and discovered that the magnetic power of one was able to attract the other; whereupon he said to his uncle, "Uncle, when I get to be an old man, I am going to make a race of people who shall rule you." Elijah Muhammad explained the significance of this initial experiment, as it would influence his interpretation of Christianity as "a trick and a lie" used by the white man to enslave the black race:

> And it was at that moment, the boy Yakub, first came into the knowledge of just who he was—born to make trouble, break peace, kill and destroy his own people with a made enemy to the black nation. He learned his future from playing with steel . . . The one attracting and drawing the other under its power. In this, he saw an unlike human being, made to attract others, who could, with the *knowledge of tricks and lies*, rule the original black man—until that nation could produce one greater and capable of overcoming and making manifest his race of tricks and lies, with a nation of truth.[19]

Later, at the age of eighteen, Yakub discovered that the black man had two germs in him, one black and the other brown. The weaker brown germ, Yakub learned, could be grafted to progressively lighter stages until a white race was created. Armed with this knowledge he began recruiting converts in Mecca for the purpose of grafting this new race of people. Yakub gathered 59,999 followers, posing such a serious threat to the authorities that he and his converts were exiled to the island of Pelan (Patmos in the Bible).[20] He coerced his recruits to follow his evil plan,[21] and after six hundred years of grafting the white race was created. Subsequently, the new white race carried out Yakub's instructions: they returned to the black nation, creating havoc and disunity for six months until they were banished to the hills of West Asia (now Europe), as far from the Holy East as possible. In fact, the proclivity of the white race to sow discord among black people is the reason they are often referred to as Caucasians—meaning, "One whose evil effect is not confined to one's self alone, but affects others."[22]

Elijah Muhammad used the Yakub myth to support his claim that the white race is inherently evil. He reasoned that whites were, by nature, incapable of pursuing truth and righteousness, because they were created for the expressed purpose of spreading lies, evil, and murder. Following this logic, Muhammad even argued that whites were not to blame for their own wickedness:

You can't blame one for the way he or she was born, for they had nothing to do with that. Can we say to them why don't you do righteousness when Nature did not give righteousness to them? Or can we say to them why are you such a wicked devil? Who is responsible—the made or the maker?[23]

It is also important to note that Elijah Muhammad's assertion regarding the devilish nature of the white race was not simply an ontological statement about white being. For him, it was also a claim based on the actual events of recorded history. Muhammad frequently referred to the gas chambers of Germany, the bombing of Hiroshima, the genocide of Native Americans, the institution of American slavery, the rape of black women, and the lynching of black men, as concrete historical proof that white people behaved like real devils. Malcolm X supported his teacher, asserting that black people "speak with the authority of history" when they refer to whites as a race of devils. Indeed, because of their collective historical record of murder and oppression, Muhammad concluded that

the human beast—the serpent, the dragon, the devil, and Satan—all mean one and the same: the people or race known as the white or Caucasian race, sometimes called the European race.[24]

In sharp contrast to "the evil white race," Muhammad declared that "black people have a heart of gold, love and mercy."[25] As we have already noted, he taught that blacks were the "original people," and therefore morally and physically superior to whites. But the disastrous error made by the so-called Negroes was to accept "the white man's Christianity" and believe that integration was the solution to their problems. Accordingly, Muhammad argued that Christianity and integration inhibit African-Americans from recognizing whites for who they really are: the created enemies of black humankind. Therefore, Elijah Muhammad proclaimed that his divine mission was to awaken the "so-called Negroes in the wilderness of North America" to the proper knowledge of themselves (the original people), their enemies (the white race and Christianity), and their natural religion (Islam).[26]

CHRISTIANITY AND RACE RELATIONS

Like Benjamin E. Mays and other Christian thinkers, Elijah Muhammad presented a harsh critique of American Christianity. Both Mays and Muhammad exposed the hypocrisy of the white church for preaching Christian love on the one hand, and practicing segregation on the other. But whereas Mays believed the Christian religion, when genuinely practiced, offered a viable solution to America's race dilemma, Muhammad understood Christianity to be the very source of black people's problems. As he viewed it, Christianity is a religion concocted by the white race for the purpose of enslaving the African-American community. Moreover, Muhammad argued that Christianity has sown disunity among blacks and made them more concerned about loving their enemies than they are about loving one another. Elijah Muhammad was committed, therefore, to revealing the disastrous effect that Christianity had on the so-called Negroes in "the wilderness of North America."

Slavery and Christianity

For Muhammad, the fact that blacks became slaves and Christians at the same time was enough to discredit Christianity. He urged the African-American community to examine the history of slavery and see for themselves that Christianity is nothing but a "slave-making religion," designed to kill black people mentally and spiritually. In fact, Muhammad argued that the prevailing problems facing the African-American community can be traced directly back to the evil relationship between slavery and Christianity. He reminded his followers that

> it was white Christians who brought our forefathers into slavery, and it is their false religion that is keeping you a subject people today. They rape and murder your families and bomb your homes and churches if you demand equal rights with them and justice.[27]

As Elijah Muhammad saw it, the matter was quite simple: If there were "any saving power in the white race's churches of Christianity," Negroes would not be begging for civil rights that are supposedly guaranteed in the Constitution of the United States.[28] Again, he reasoned that Christianity has no "saving power" to help African-Americans because it was intentionally created to enslave, not to liberate. Central to Muhammad's critique of Christianity, therefore, is his claim that it is a religion "organized by the white race for the purpose of making slaves of black mankind." After creating this "slave-making religion," whites "placed the name of Jesus on it being the founder and author to deceive black people into accepting it."[29] Muhammad repudiated the notion that Christianity was a liberating religion that enabled African slaves to endure the psychological, spiritual, and physical assault on their humanity. On the contrary, he argued that the slaves' uncritical acceptance of the white man's religion compounded their oppression even more. Although some black Christian historians and theologians might object to this view,[30] in the minds of his ardent followers

Muhammad's interpretation of Christianity's negative effect on the slave community and subsequent generations of African-Americans was the unadulterated, gospel truth.

As Elijah Muhammad viewed it, the institution of slavery and its aftermath completely robbed African-Americans of their name, language, religion, and culture. This history of oppression began in the year 1555,[31] when John Hawkins, a Christian slave trader from England, "brought our forefathers here (from Africa) on a ship named 'Jesus.'" For Muhammad, mental and spiritual bondage compounded physical oppression when later generations of slaves forgot that the Negro spiritual "Give me Jesus" referred to the ship, and not the man from Nazareth:

> Our foreparents stared at the old slave ship as it departed and begged to be carried back, but to no avail, and they said that "you can have this new Western world but give us the ship Jesus back to our people and country."[32]

Elijah Muhammad's central argument is that the enslavement of the dark world was aided by the "tricks and lies" of the white man's Christianity. For him, the two most harmful "tricks and lies" of Christianity's "slavery teachings" concerned instructions about heaven and hell and loving the enemy. First and foremost, Muhammad urged African-Americans "to bring their minds out of the sky" and "stop being spooky." Like Benjamin Mays, Muhammad was critical of the otherworldly, compensatory element in slave religion.[33] As long as the so-called Negroes look for their reward "beyond the grave," he argued, they will never enjoy freedom, justice, and equality alive on this earth. Therefore, Muhammad taught his followers that

> there is no such thing as a heaven up in the sky or a hell down in the ground. All that is fantasy, false stories made up by your slave master to further enslave you . . . *Heaven and hell are two conditions*, and both are experienced in this life right here on this earth. You have already suffered the worse kind of hell in the hands of the only real devil.[34]

Muhammad believed that the Christian idea of heaven made blacks "deaf, dumb, and blind" to the social, political, and economic realities that oppressed them. Elaborating on the negative effect this concept has had on the African-American community, Malcolm X noted that "white people have taught us to shout and sing and pray until we die." While black people are looking "for some dreamy heaven-in-the-hereafter," Malcolm argued, "this white man has his milk and honey in the streets paved with golden dollars right here on this earth."[35] Therefore, instead of waiting until death for a heaven up in the sky, Elijah Muhammad and his ministers urged African-Americans to seek heaven right here on earth: "Freedom, Justice, Equality; money, good homes and friendship in all walks of life."[36] Just as Jesus proclaimed the Kingdom of God already present in the midst of the faithful, Muhammad promised that all who accept Allah and join the Nation of Islam "will begin enjoying the above life here and now." For Muhammad, black Christians talked too much about "spooks coming up out of graves to meet God," and too little about the actual transformation and rehabilitation of lives in the present. That is why he invited African-Americans across the country to

> accept Allah and His religion and follow me and I will lead you to Him and to a heaven right here on this earth. Come and follow me, and you will not have to wait until you die to enjoy a heaven somewhere up in the sky.[37]

The second harmful slavery teaching of the white man's Christianity is the religious mandate to love one's enemies. For Muhammad, the problems facing black people in the area of race relations were exacerbated when slaves were brainwashed into believing that it was their religious duty to love their masters. Muhammad considered the words attributed to Jesus in Luke 6:27-29 "another poison addition of the slavery teaching of the Bible"; and wondered how African-Americans could accept a religion that not only told them to obey their white slavemasters, but also to love and forgive them—even as they were brutally beaten, raped, and killed. These false teachings demonstrated the mastery of the white race when it comes to deceiving and enslaving black people. Indeed, their effect on the African-American community caused Muhammad to conclude that, "The slavemasters couldn't have found a better teaching for their protection against the slaves' possible dissatisfaction of their masters' brutal treatment."[38]

Elijah Muhammad told blacks to exercise basic common sense and reject the Christian notion that God demands the oppressed to love their oppressors. Contrary to the claim of Christian thinkers like Benjamin Mays, Howard Thurman, and Martin Luther King, Jr., Muhammad proclaimed that "it is against the very nature of God, and man, and all life, to love their enemies":

> Would God ask us to do that which He Himself cannot do? He hates His enemies so much that He tells us that He is going to destroy them in hellfire, along with those of us who follow His enemies.[39]

Instead of seeking to love and forgive their open enemies (the white race), Muhammad urged blacks to gain an understanding of them based in reality. As he viewed it, Christianity fails to give African-Americans a proper knowledge of their enemies, because it does not view whites as the created rivals of black humankind. Accordingly, Muhammad believed that African-American Christian thinkers who emphasized the interrelatedness of life do more harm than good. Contrary to those who wasted energy trying to find "the Christian way in race relations," Muhammad proclaimed that, "My followers and I can and are getting along with them (whites) in a more understandable way than ever, because we know them." That is why he taught that "a true knowledge of the white race removes once and for all the mistakes that would be made in dealing with them."[40] For Muhammad, blacks should love themselves and not their enemies; they should forgive one another, but "it is not left to the slave to forgive his master." Muhammad concluded, therefore, that these "lying and slavery teachings of the white man's Christianity," which have "crucified our people all over the earth, must be given up!"[41]

Love Your Own Kind

Whereas pre–Black Power Christian thinkers primarily focused their attention on the problem of *interracial* fellowship, Elijah Muhammad and his disciples in the Nation of Islam urged the African-American community to concentrate on the need for *intraracial* love and harmony. For Muhammad, the lack of love for self and one another is "one of the gravest handicaps among the so-called Negroes"; in fact, it is "the root cause of hate (dislike), disunity, disagreement, quarreling, betraying, stool pigeons and fighting and killing one another."[42] Muhammad attributed this lack of unity in the African-American community directly to the negative influence of Christianity. As he saw it, the slavery teachings of the "white man's Christianity has robbed us of the knowledge of self and kind and destroyed our love for one another."[43] Drawing on the Yakub myth, Muhammad insisted that Christianity is, by nature, incapable of giving African-Americans a proper love and knowledge of self, because it was created by whites for the purpose of enslaving blacks physically, mentally, and spiritually. Therefore, as long as African-Americans cling to Christianity, they will "remain asleep to the knowledge of themselves," and depend on whites for what they can and should do for themselves.

Muhammad believed that "a proper knowledge of self and kind" was a prerequisite for the achievement of black unity. Once blacks learned to love themselves as individuals, they would be able to show the proper love and respect for one another. Like the slavery teaching regarding love for the enemy, the lack of self-love in the African-American community has had a devastating effect on black unity. Noting that blacks are often "afraid to act too friendly towards each other," Muhammad instructed his followers to "seek FIRST the friendship of your own people and then the friendship of others (if there is any friendship in others)."[44] He lamented the fact that "every race of people want unity with their own kind first, except my people, the so-called Negro in America."[45] That is why he detested African-Americans who appeared to show more love for whites than for their own kind:

> Curse be to the black man or woman who loves this open enemy, the devil, and hates his own black skin and kind! May the chastisement of Allah choke you until you submit that: There is no God but Allah and that Muhammad in the wilderness of North America is His Messenger![46]

Muhammad was especially critical of black preachers. He characterized them as "ministers of the white man's Christianity," who did nothing but "preach the gospel of being an American citizen," and criticize his efforts to achieve black unity. He considered these "so-called spiritual leaders" to be "more of an enemy to his people than the real white devils." Muhammad described the behavior of black preachers in this way:

> They want to please the enemy at the expense and destruction of their own people. They are more upset (the clergy) over the preaching of justice for our people and a home on this earth that we can call our own than the white man himself.[47]

Some of Elijah Muhammad's most biting statements about black preachers were directed at Martin Luther King, Jr., who began to indirectly challenge the "black supremacy" teachings of the Nation of Islam in the early 1960s. In a 1961 commencement address at Lincoln University, King, in opposition to Muhammad, remarked that "black supremacy is as dangerous as white supremacy, and God is not interested merely in the freedom of black men and brown men and yellow men." Not surprisingly, King's commitment to integration and Christian universalism led him further to declare that "God is interested in the freedom of the whole human race and the creation of a society where all men can live together as brothers."[48] Two years later in his famous "Letter from Birmingham City Jail," King was more explicit when he expressed concern about the "bitterness and hatred" of "various black nationalist groups that are springing up over the nation, the largest and best known being Elijah Muhammad's Muslim movement."[49]

King's presentation of himself and the civil rights movement as the moderate, intelligent alternative to the bitter and violent teachings of black nationalist groups eventually drew the scorn of Elijah Muhammad, who was considerably more tame than the fiery Malcolm X.

Muhammad was especially critical of what he regarded as King's inordinate universalism. As a black nationalist, Muhammad believed that it was totally absurd for an African-American leader to preach that "God is not interested merely in the freedom of black men and brown men and yellow men," as if whites were somehow wrongfully excluded. For Muhammad, people of color were the *only* oppressed groups that deserved God's loving attention; while whites, the ones responsible for the oppression, deserved God's wrath and punishment. Therefore, when King, after receiving the 1964 Nobel Peace Prize, was quoted as telling blacks that, "We must not seek to rise from a position of disadvantage to one of advantage substituting injustice of one type for that of another," Muhammad responded harshly:

> I have never heard such talk coming from a leader's mouth in all my life. If a man is NOT going to rise from a position of disadvantage why is he preaching for the passage of the Civil Rights Bill for his people? . . . He is ignorant, preaching for brotherhood of white people and destruction of his own people . . . This kind of talk coming from a theological college graduate is almost unbelievable.[50]

For Muhammad, King's theology was a perfect example of the negative effect "the slavery teachings of the white man's Christianity" had on African-Americans. He believed King's concern about black supremacy being "just as dangerous as white supremacy" was designed to placate whites, and thus "all blacks should disregard anything that a man like this says."[51] Indeed, just as King presented himself to whites as the reasonable alternative to Muhammad, Muhammad presented himself to blacks as the only sensible alternative to King:

> Rev. King is of no good among black people. What are you going to do? Are you going to follow such teachings, or will you turn around and join your own kind?[52]

In sum, Elijah Muhammad not only rejected the teachings of Martin Luther King, Jr., but he believed that Christianity in general was completely incapable of producing "love of self and kind" among blacks. Therefore, he proclaimed Islam as the only divine solution to the spiritual, social, political, and economic problems of the African-American community.

Islam to the Rescue

Elijah Muhammad was unrelenting in his critique of Christianity. He almost always articulated the benefits of Islam against the backdrop of Christianity's failure to rehabilitate and liberate the African-American community. Consequently, Louis Lomax, one of the first interpreters of the Nation of Islam, observed that "broadsides at Christianity" seemed to illicit the greatest reactions from the Muslim audiences.[53]

First and foremost, Muslim ministers pointed to the reality of racial segregation as the basis for their indictment of Christianity. Why would African-Americans want to follow a religion that practices segregation and denigrates blackness, they asked? Whereas white Christians segregate and humiliate their fellow black Christians, Elijah Muhammad proclaimed that "a Muslim is *truly* the brother of another Believer, regardless of how black the skin or kinked the hair."[54]

In addition to emphasizing the legacy of white racism in the Christian tradition, Muslim ministers criticized black Christians for failing to practice the Christian morality they professed. Newspaper accounts of clergymen having affairs with female members; fights and arguments among church leaders leading to lawsuits; and general reports of the churches' tolerance of drunkenness and fornication among members, provided the ammunition for the Nation's attack on Christianity. Louis Lomax aptly described this process:

> The Black Muslims take the Christian ethic as a measuring stick; they then arouse the guilt complex of the wayward Christians in the audience and then go on to blame Christianity for the individual's moral failure. This, to be sure, is a contorted argument. But it works. Christians sit in the temple audience and confess their Christian failing, then they repent themselves right out of the Christian church.[55]

Indeed, the fact that former Christians constituted the majority of the group's membership is clear proof that Elijah Muhammad and his ministers were successful prosecuting attorneys in the trial of Christianity before the court of African-American opinion.[56] Furthermore, most interpreters would agree with Lomax that the Nation attracted "three times as many fellow travelers as ... members." Of course, Muslim ministers were even more optimistic, claiming that for every one member, there were ten blacks in the ghetto who shared the same views.[57]

In proclaiming Islam as the religious solution to the problems of the African-American community, Muhammad first emphasized that unlike Christianity (which was a "European-organized white man's religion"), Islam developed in the East, and was the natural religion of all the non-white peoples of Africa and Asia. As a non-white religion, he believed that Islam automatically gave black people a sense of racial dignity that Christianity was incapable of producing. Therefore,

Muhammad preached that Islam was "the master key" to the spiritual, political, social, and economic salvation of the African-American community. Yet, it is important to note that Elijah Muhammad was not primarily concerned about the distinctive theological claims of orthodox Islam; he was concerned about repudiating Christianity and developing a *black* religion that could speak directly to the social and psychological needs of poor blacks in the urban ghettos of America.[58]

Now let us examine two of Muhammad's central claims about the failure of Christianity and the success of Islam in meeting the social needs of the African-American community. First, Muhammad and his ministers emphasized their success in rehabilitating the lives of ex-convicts, drug addicts, alcoholics, criminals, and prostitutes, while pointing out the failure of the black Christian church to do the same. Indeed, ever since Elijah Muhammad himself was incarcerated in 1942, the Nation of Islam has targeted prison inmates, ex-convicts, and addicts in its recruitment efforts. Significantly, Muhammad's greatest convert, Malcolm X, was introduced to the Nation of Islam while serving time in a Massachusetts prison. Whereas mainline Christian churches had little or no outreach to the prison population, Elijah Muhammad's organization aggressively sought membership there. As a result, ex-convicts swelled the ranks of the Nation. In his widely circulated newspaper column, Muhammad explained the process:

> I receive many letters from inmates of jails and correctional institutions across the country. They are from the so-called Negroes who want to accept Islam . . . as soon as they are free, they should report to the nearest Temple of Islam in person and formally join on to their own Holy Nation of Islam.[59]

Ex-convicts, addicts, and prostitutes were welcomed by the Nation with open arms. At the same time, however, they were held to a strict code of morality and discipline designed to transform radically their former behavior. First and foremost, all new converts were required to work, either in Muslim-owned businesses or other secular jobs. Equally important, they were expected to pray five times a day—paying special attention to the proper ablutions—and attend the temple twice a week. In addition to these ritual requirements, the use of alcohol, tobacco, and drugs was strictly forbidden, as was fornication and sexual immorality. Through this strict program of rehabilitation, former criminals and addicts made a complete break from their old lifestyles and became disciplined Muslims and law-abiding citizens.[60]

Needless to say, the Nation of Islam took great pride in its ability to transform lives. Muslim ministers praised the Honorable Elijah Muhammad as the messianic leader who did more to improve the morals of the African-American community than all the Christian churches combined. Indeed, Malcolm X, Muhammad's most ardent admirer, was living proof of the Messenger's ability to convert criminals and drug addicts into shining examples of morality. Malcolm carried the "soul-stirring, life-giving Message of the Honorable Elijah Muhammad" to cities across the country, testifying that Muhammad had accomplished in "such a short time" what Christian leaders "have failed to do for one hundred years."[61] In proclaiming the moral superiority of the Nation of Islam, Malcolm pointed to the members whose lives were transformed by the teachings of Elijah Muhammad:

> His Message of Truth has cured us of Drunkenness and dope addiction and other vices that were destroying our morals . . . Among those of us who follow him adultery and fornication has completely disappeared. Lying and stealing has been stamped out.[62]

To be sure, the Nation of Islam's moral requirement kept many sympathizers from actually joining the organization. Quite humorously, the story of Malcolm's attempt to convert a black Baptist was spread throughout the movement. When the Baptist asked about the rules of the Nation, Malcolm responded, "My brother, you have to stop drinking, stop swearing, stop gambling, stop using dope, and stop cheating on your wife." Having heard enough and desiring to end the discussion, the potential convert replied, "Hell, I think I had better remain a Christian."[63] Although many other blacks also chose not to join the Nation, the organization was widely respected in the African-American community for its successful rehabilitation programs and genuine efforts at outreach and recruitment among the urban underclass. Dan Burley, a journalist for one of Chicago's black newspapers, expressed the views of a growing segment of African-Americans who criticized the black church and its preachers for failing to reach out to the black underclass as Elijah Muhammad and the Nation of Islam did. Burley put it like this:

> The Negro preachers and comfortable and self-righteous "Amen corner" regulars chide me for patting Muhammad on the back and telling him in print, to "Go, Man Go!" But I don't see the reverends getting out of their Cadillacs to go among the thugs, thieves, harlots and hustlers to pass out invitations to come to the House of God.[64]

C. Eric Lincoln made a similar observation about the failure of African-American Christians to match the missionary zeal of the Black Muslims. Lincoln urged the black church to respond to the Nation of

Islam and other black nationalist organizations that were quickly making new converts out of potential Christians:

> It used to be a Christian tradition to go into the hedges and byways in search of souls for Christ. Once it was not uncommon for Christian denominations even to compete with each other. All this is passe. The man (sic) in need of salvation today must make it to the church on his own—and even then he may not get in. But the Muslims have taken over this rich reserve abandoned by the churches. In the pool halls, the barbershops, the chicken shacks, the jails and the prisons they have reaped an impressive harvest— not for Christ, but for Muhammad.[65]

Whereas many black churches adopted a judgmental attitude toward non-Christians engaged in immoral behavior, the Nation of Islam told these individuals that they did not become thieves and drunkards until they were stolen from their homeland and brainwashed into the evil practices of whites. It is important to note that while Elijah Muhammad was critical of the low moral standards in the African-American community, he blamed the problem on white Christians who implemented a deliberate plot to keep blacks from accepting the divine truth of Islam. According to Muhammad, this plot involved pornography, alcohol, vulgar music, and other social vices designed to encourage blacks "in indulgence of the baser instincts."[66] Consequently, Muhammad concluded that "whatever my people (the so-called Negroes) are today, the devils (the white Christian race) made them that."[67]

In addition to the overwhelming success of his rehabilitation program (compared to the relative failure of Christian leaders), Elijah Muhammad argued that Islam creates unity among blacks, while Christianity sows division. As noted earlier, Muhammad characterized Christianity as a religion of "tricks and lies" created by whites for the purpose of enslaving and dividing the African-American community. Thus, while Christianity may have succeeded in making blacks love their white enemies, it was completely incapable of making them love one another. Accordingly, Muhammad told African-Americans that "regardless to how long and how hard you try to be a good Christian, you will never have a sincere, true love for your own black brother and sister as you should." Therefore, Muhammad and his ministers presented Islam as the only religion that could awaken African-Americans from their mentally and spiritually dead condition and create the unity they so desperately needed.[68]

None of Muhammad's ministers presented this argument more effectively than Malcolm X. For Malcolm, Christianity divided the black community into many different denominations that kept African-

Americans forever competing against each other; Islam, on the other hand, united blacks and taught them to love their brothers and sisters in America and around the world. Moreover, unlike Christianity, which produced power-hungry leaders who "set up factions of their own," Islam "is bringing us together today, and uniting us into a vast Brotherhood under ONE GOD ALLAH overnight." Malcolm celebrated the spirit of unity found among members of Elijah Muhammad's Nation of Islam, declaring that:

> We now have ONE GOD, ONE RELIGION, ONE LEADER and TEACHER, this ONENESS gives us a UNITY never before attained by any other people (in such a short period of time) in history.[69]

However, Muhammad's own words provide the best summary of his claims about the success of Islam and the failure of Christianity regarding efforts to unite and liberate the African-American community. Essentially, Muhammad argued that Islam rescued blacks from the ineffectiveness of Christianity, producing results the black church has failed to match:

> I am doing that for thousands (of my people) which Christianity failed to do—that is, uniting the so-called Negroes and making them to leave off evil habits that the preachers of Christianity haven't been able to do for a hundred years. We are that in Islam what Christianity offers beyond the grave.[70]

CHRISTIANITY, THE BIBLE, AND SELF-DEFENSE

No interpretation of Elijah Muhammad's critique of Christianity would be complete without an analysis of his understanding of the Bible and its relationship to the plight of the African-American community. Ironically, Muhammad relied on the Bible more heavily than the Qur'an in his presentation of Islam as the spiritual solution to social and political problems of the "so-called Negroes." He referred to the Bible more frequently because he knew that his audience was primarily ex-Christian and would understand biblical stories better than passages from the Holy Qur'an. Common sense told Muhammad that his attempt to wean African-Americans away from Christianity would fail if he did not make wide use of the scriptures his potential converts already knew and respected.[71] Therefore, he used the thorough knowledge of the Bible he acquired as a former Baptist preacher to make his version of Islam understandable to African-Americans who had become disillusioned with Christianity, America, and the black church.

Although Elijah Muhammad held two contradictory views of the Bible—on the one hand it was a "poison book" that constituted "the graveyard of my people," and on the other, it was a book of prophecy and parables that revealed the truth about the condition of the black community—he used it effectively in his efforts to persuade African-Americans that Islam and not Christianity was the only intelligent religious option open to them.

The "Poison Book"

The basic foundation of Muhammad's biblical interpretation is his claim that whites "tampered with the truth of the Divine Scripture" when they translated it into the English language by the authority of King James in 1611. According to Muhammad, both the original Torah and the gospel God gave to Moses and Jesus respectively were "holy" until white Jewish and Christian scholars "started tampering." These scholars made the Bible a "commercialized book," enabling many persons "to rewrite or revise it."[72] Therefore, although the Bible contains truth—despite it being tampered with by whites—Muhammad argued that it is not a "holy" book in the truest sense of the word, because "holy means something that is perfectly pure, and we just can't say that of the Poison Bible."[73]

For Muhammad, not only was the Bible corrupted by white scholars who distorted its true meaning, but it was grossly misinterpreted by African-American Christian preachers who lacked the wisdom to understand it properly. Consequently, Muhammad lamented that the Bible "is like a rattlesnake in the hands of my people," because they have accepted the poisonous teachings passed on to them by their misinformed preachers. If black Christian preachers have failed to grasp the true meaning of scripture, what then, according to Elijah Muhammad, is the correct interpretation of the Bible that will reveal the true Word of God for the African-American community?

Essentially, Muhammad viewed the Bible as a book of symbols, prophecies, and parables about the condition of black people in America. He taught African-Americans that everything currently happening to them in America was foretold in the Bible thousands of years earlier. For example, the enslavement of the Hebrews and God's selection of Moses as their liberator corresponded to black people's mental, spiritual, and political enslavement to white America and the appearance of Elijah Muhammad as the modern-day Moses sent to deliver them.[74] Moreover, just as God called for the separation (exodus) of the enslaved Israelites from their Egyptian oppressors, so Muhammad proclaimed the separation of blacks from whites as the divine solution to the nation's race problem:

Separation of the so-called Negroes from their slavemasters' children is a MUST. It is the only SOLUTION to our problem. It was the only solution, according to the Bible, for Israel and the Egyptians, and it will prove to be the only solution for America and her slaves.[75]

Additionally, Muhammad emphasized the Old Testament theme of judgment to proclaim God's impending destruction of America. As he saw it, the fall of ancient Babylon was a foreshadowing of what God would do to America. Muhammad put it like this:

I compare the fall of America with the fall of ancient Babylon. America's wickedness (sins) is the same as the history shows of ancient Babylon. Only America is modern and much worse . . . and as God (Allah) dealt with ancient peoples, so will He deal with modern Babylon (America).[76]

Likewise, Muhammad referred to the flood (Gn 7:11-24) and the destruction of Sodom and Gomorrah (Gn 19:24-28) to reinforce his interpretation of God as the Righteous Judge who punishes wicked, evil people. Again, he reasoned that since America will be destroyed, separation was the only intelligent religious and political option available to African-Americans. Why would anyone want to integrate with a sinful nation on the verge of destruction, Muhammad asked? Therefore, the Islamic leader emphasized the Old Testament themes of separation and judgment to support his critique of Christianity (integration) and advance his presentation of Islam (black separatism) as the most viable religio-political philosophy for the African-American community.[77]

In like manner, Elijah Muhammad understood the New Testament as a book of prophecy and parables that African-American Christians have completely misinterpreted. For example, he taught that the parables of Jesus in Luke 15 refer not to the Jews but to the lost condition of black people in America. Just as the dutiful shepherd forsook everything to search for the one lost sheep, Elijah Muhammad presented himself as the Messenger of Allah sent to reclaim the mentally and spiritually lost black people "in the wilderness of North America." Likewise, Muhammad interpreted the parable of the Prodigal Son as the perfect description of a spiritually lost African-American community, which preferred the immoral practices of whites over the dignity and respect of its own people.[78]

Muhammad especially liked the parable of the Rich Man and Lazarus in Luke 16. Whereas Benjamin Mays highlighted the condemnation of the rich man for his lack of compassion and social concern, Muhammad criticized Lazarus for his dependence on charity and lack of ambition. As he saw it, African-Americans have made the same mistake of the beggar Lazarus, "who was so charmed over the wealth and food of the rich man that he couldn't leave his gate to seek the same for himself."[79] Accordingly, Muhammad urged African-Americans to "stop relying on the white man to care for us," and to "become an independent people." He compared black activists who accepted insult and injury from white segregationists to the pitiful Lazarus, who continued to beg "regardless of the disgraceful condition in which the rich man puts him, even to sending his dogs to attack him."[80] Therefore, Muhammad's biblical interpretation reinforced his claim that Islam "produces an industrious people who are self-independent," while Christianity "makes the so-called Negroes lazy, careless and dependent people."[81]

Confusing Doctrines

Muhammad also critiqued Christianity on the basis of its orthodox faith claims about the person of Jesus. He repeatedly told African-American Christians that Jesus was only a prophet "who did his work and is dead like others of his time." Moreover, for Muhammad, Jesus was a Muslim who "knew nothing about Christianity in those days"; rather, Jesus taught his followers Islam, just as did Abraham, Noah, and Moses.[82] Since Jesus was only a prophet, Muhammad argued that he was incapable of hearing or answering prayers "any more than Moses or any other dead prophet." Therefore, instead of looking to Jesus as a divine savior, Muhammad told Negro Christians to join the Nation of Islam and worship Allah, the only one who "can hear your prayers and answer them."[83]

Muhammad's doctrinal critique also called into question orthodox Christian claims about the trinity, virgin birth, and the resurrection. For Muhammad, the doctrine of the trinity totally confused Negro Christians into believing in three gods; even more confusing was the Christian claim that Jesus the son was equal to God the father. Muhammad cited Jesus' words from the cross, "My God, my God, why hast Thou forsaken me?" (Mt 27:46) to prove his claim that Jesus "did not consider himself to be God or a Son of God or equal to him," but rather "only a man and prophet of Allah (God)." Therefore, he urged his followers to use their common sense and reject the Christian doctrine of the trinity.[84]

Muhammad also considered the Christian doctrine of the virgin birth an absurd teaching. As he saw it, the concept made God guilty of breaking one of God's own commandments—"Thou shalt not commit adultery."[85] Therefore, Muhammad challenged Negro Christians to think deeply about the faith claims they accepted so uncritically:

My beloved brothers and sisters, how could you accept a religion that teaches you to believe the God of Righteousness was responsible for making a virgin girl in Palestine pregnant with a child 2,000 years ago, called this child his "son," and let this "son" die for the sins of the wicked world?[86]

Likewise, Muhammad explained that Negro Christians had misinterpreted the Bible's teaching on the resurrection. The resurrection is not a literal, historical event where Jesus rises from the grave, he said, but rather the spiritual resurrection of the mentally dead so-called Negroes who have awakened from the grave of ignorance and are no longer deaf, dumb, and blind.[87]

Finally, it is important to underscore the point that Muhammad's rejection of Christianity was based on more than the ethical failure of white and Negro Christians; it was also based on a theological critique of orthodox Christianity that evidently appealed to a significant number of dissatisfied Negro Christians who had legitimate questions about the veracity of orthodox Christian faith claims. Attempts to understand the widespread appeal of the Nation of Islam, therefore, must also consider the theological position of Elijah Muhammad concerning classical Christianity. Indeed, black theologians would do well to consider the theological objections some blacks have to doctrinal Christianity; this might lead to a constructive reinterpretation of Christian theology that addresses the theological concerns of the African-American community.

The Right of Self-Defense

Muhammad also used the Bible to critique the nonviolent ideology of Martin Luther King, Jr. As noted earlier, he viewed the "love your enemy" teaching of Jesus to be a "poisonous" addition made by whites who tampered with the scriptures. Instead, Muhammad invoked the *lex talionis* of the Hebrew scriptures: "eye for an eye, and tooth for a tooth." He taught that the right of self-defense was a religious right bestowed by God. Although the Qur'an teaches Muslims never to be the aggressors, Muhammad argued that "it is a Divine Law for us to defend ourselves if attacked." Suggesting that Jesus might have been "more successful" if he had let Peter and the other disciples use the sword, Muhammad urged civil rights demonstrators to defend themselves from brutal attacks by dogs and policemen.[88] Contrary to the white media's portrayal of the Nation of Islam as a violent organization, Muhammad declared that "by nature the black people are for peace," and by nature "the white people are for war and bloodshed." Interestingly, however, Muhammad enforced a strict "no arms policy" to ensure that Muslims remained peaceful and were never the initiators of violence.[89]

African-American pastors in the late 1960s were increasingly forced to respond theologically to the nationalist indictment of Christianity as "the white man's religion." In fact, when the theology of Elijah Muhammad joined forces with the cry of Black Power, the trial of Christianity in the African-American community reached a watershed. For while Benjamin Mays and other pre–Black Power theologians put white Christianity on trial, Elijah Muhammad and radical Black Power advocates put integrationist Negro Christianity on trial. How did black pastors respond to the mounting crisis of faith in the African-American community? We turn to this question in the next chapter on the emergence of Black Power and the response of the black church.

PART TWO

1966-1995

CHAPTER 3

Black Power and Christianity

The NCBC and Albert Cleage as Defenders of the Faith

The "Negro Church" that Frazier wrote about no longer exists. It died an agonized death in the harsh turmoil which tried the faith so rigorously in the decade of the "Savage Sixties," for there it had to confront under the most trying circumstances the possibility that "Negro" and "Christian" were irreconcilable categories. The call to full manhood, to personhood, and the call to Christian responsibility left no room for the implications of being a "Negro" in contemporary America. With sadness and reluctance, trepidation and confidence, the Negro Church accepted death in order to be reborn. Out of the ashes of its funeral pyre there sprang the bold, strident, self-conscious phoenix that is the contemporary Black Church.

—C. Eric Lincoln, 1973

It was the destiny of black preachers and their churches to rise or fall with the masses. The masses were hurting and were determined to bring an end to their misery by whatever means possible. They were demanding the imposition of power . . . and there was justification enough in theological and ethical considerations for the black church to follow them. Perhaps in following, it would, once again, earn the right to lead.

—Gayraud S. Wilmore, 1979

Black Power made a dramatic impact upon African-American churches in the late 1960s and early 1970s. Indeed, the urban rebellions that swept across the country between 1963 and 1968 reflected the mounting frustration of African-American youth, who were deeply alienated from the mainstream of American life. During these turbulent years young African-Americans, especially in the ghettos of the urban North, quickly turned away from the ideologies of integration and nonviolence and toward the philosophies of black nationalism and self-defense. Also important for understanding the emergence of Black

Power, however, is the frustration African-American youth directed toward the black church—an institution they considered unresponsive to their radical, nationalist consciousness. Certainly, the nationalist teachings of Elijah Muhammad and Malcolm X had a profound impact on the younger, more militant leaders of the civil rights movement. Elijah Muhammad's claim that "Christianity is the white man's religion" influenced many African-Americans' perception of Christianity and the black church. As Gayraud Wilmore noted:

> Many Blacks, young and old, would not follow Malcolm into the Nation of Islam, but believed he spoke the truth about Christianity being a religion for White people. Once they were convinced of this, no traditional Negro Christian evangelicalism could satisfy their religious needs and hold them within the Black Christian church.[1]

Indeed, the relentless critique of the Nation of Islam and the emergence of Black Power caused "the credibility of the Christian faith to be severely tested" in black ghettoes across the nation.[2] Increasingly, young African-Americans began to view the black church as an "Uncle Tom" institution that was irrelevant to the concerns of youth during a new age of Black Power and black pride. Christianity was on trial in the African-American community. If it was to be acquitted of the charges, then black preachers and theologians would have to reinterpret the gospel so that it spoke to the specific needs of young people who were tired of the "love your enemy," nonviolent Christian ethics of pre–Black Power religious leaders. In fact, this generational debate over the efficacy of Christianity as an instrument of social change signaled the end of the integration-oriented civil rights movement. What factors contributed to this change, and how did it influence African-American religious thought?

In this chapter I examine the rise of Black Power and the prophetic response of clergy who embraced the challenge of creating a new black theology. The National Committee of Negro Churchmen, which began as an ad hoc group in July 1966, acted as apologists for Christianity at a time when *Christian* and *Black* appeared to be a contradiction in terms. The latter part of the chapter analyzes the ministry of Albert Cleage, the most radical clergy spokesman of the new black theology. Cleage developed a black Christian nationalism that responded to Elijah Muhammad's critique by interpreting Jesus as a revolutionary Black Messiah sent to lead his people in the fight against white oppression. While there are significant differences in the perspectives of the NCBC and Albert Cleage, no discussion of Christianity in the post–Black Power era can ignore the important contribution they made to the black church and community.

CHRISTIANITY, AMERICA, AND BLACK POWER

The Road to Black Power: 1966, the Pivotal Year

At the conclusion of the James Meredith "March against Fear," Floyd McKissick (who had just replaced James Farmer as leader of the Congress of Racial Equality) said, "1966 shall be remembered as the year we left our imposed status of Negroes and became Black Men . . . when black men realized their full worth in society—their dignity and their beauty—and their power.[3] In many ways, this remark accurately describes the repercussions of Black Power in the African-American community. Unfortunately, its male exclusive language also reflects the blatant sexism that characterized the movement and the subsequent development of black theology.[4] Yet, McKissick's prediction regarding the historical significance of 1966 must be interpreted in light of important events that led up to the historic Meredith march.

Mississippi and Alabama were known throughout the South as bastions of white supremacy and racial violence. Black people knew them as places of fear, intimidation, murder, and repression. Ironically, these two states were also the birthplaces of a new radical consciousness within the ranks of the southern civil rights movement known as the mood and spirit of Black Power. When James Meredith entered the University of Mississippi in 1962, he helped to set in motion a series of events that would change the course of race relations in America. The cry of Black Power that was raised four years later in Greenwood, Mississippi, simply gave expression to the rising spirit of courage, frustration, and anger that was filtering from the North (Malcolm X) into the hearts of young African-Americans throughout the South. Young blacks in Mississippi expressed their rage on a march through downtown Jackson after Medgar Evers, the courageous leader of the local National Association for the Advancement of Colored People (NAACP) branch, was assassinated in the driveway of his home in June 1963. Three months later, just weeks after the historic March on Washington, four little girls were killed when the Sixteenth Street Baptist Church in Birmingham, Alabama, was bombed by a group of white terrorists. Many young blacks were no longer willing to accept Martin Luther King's rhetoric about the redemptive quality of unearned suffering. Instead of seeking to love their enemies, they were prepared to follow the other biblical mandate: "eye for an eye, tooth for a tooth."[5]

Then in the summer of 1964, Fannie Lou Hamer and other political organizers of the newly formed Mississippi Freedom Democratic Party (MFDP) were defeated in their efforts to be seated at the Democratic National Convention in Atlantic City, New Jersey.[6] The national party's refusal to recognize the MFDP as the authentic democratic party of the state caused bitter disillusionment among young activists in the Student Nonviolent Coordinating Committee (SNCC), who had labored hard on voter education and registration campaigns in rural Mississippi.[7]

In the wake of this frustrating defeat, Stokely Carmichael and several other SNCC activists went to Lowndes County, Alabama, to work with local political organizers who were attempting to mobilize the African-American community. Well known for its history of violence, Lowndes County received national attention after the 1965 murder of Viola Liuzzo, a white housewife from Detroit who had volunteered as a driver in the Montgomery to Selma March. Inspired by Martin Luther King's presence in Alabama, John Hulett and some twenty others created the Lowndes County Christian Movement for Human Rights in March 1965.[8] After the passage of the 1965 Voting Rights Act, SNCC activists worked along with this grassroots leadership to organize a county-wide political party known as the Lowndes County Freedom Organization (LCFO); it was founded in March 1966. Interestingly enough, the new organization chose the black panther as its symbol, because its members knew that illiterate blacks would certainly know the difference between a rooster (symbol of the white Democratic party), an elephant (symbol of the Republican party), and a black cat.[9]

Indeed, these courageous political organizers faced an enormous task. Although blacks represented 80 percent of the population in the county, brutal violence and intimidation kept them locked out of any significant political and economic power.[10] After much work, the LCFO held a nominating convention and competed against the local white Democratic party in the November elections. Although their candidates lost (some registered blacks voted for the white candidates), it was a moral victory for African-Americans, who voted in the county for the first time since Reconstruction. Carmichael and Charles Hamilton captured the significance of the election:

> November 8, 1966, made one thing clear: some day black people will control the government of Lowndes County. For Lowndes is not merely a section of land and a group of people, but an idea whose time has come.[11]

While the events in Lowndes, Alabama, were unfolding another significant turning point in the freedom struggle occurred along U.S. Highway 51 in Mississippi. On June 5, 1966, James Meredith set out to march from Memphis to Jackson to dramatize "the overriding fear" that affected the everyday lives of blacks in Mississippi and throughout the deep South. The very next day Meredith was shot down by a sniper. When Martin Luther King, Jr. (representing the Southern Christian Leadership Conference), Roy Wilkins (the NAACP), Whitney Young (the National Urban League) and the younger leaders Stokely Carmichael (SNCC)[12] and Floyd McKissick (the Congress of Racial Equality, CORE) vowed to continue the march on his behalf, the stage was set for a clash of generations and ideologies.[13]

Disillusioned with white liberals and influenced by black nationalism, Carmichael and McKissick wanted to exclude whites from the march. They believed it was time for blacks to take control of their own destiny without the presence and influence of whites, whom they now encouraged to work against institutional racism and injustice in their own communities. Moreover, Carmichael and McKissick insisted on the right of marchers to defend themselves in the event of violent attacks and intended to issue sharp criticism of the Johnson administration. Roy Wilkins and Whitney Young (the two oldest civil rights leaders involved) were greatly disturbed by the proposals of the younger Carmichael and McKissick and consequently withdrew their support from the march. Although King was able to negotiate with the leaders of SNCC and CORE to ensure that the march remain interracial and nonviolent, he was not able to stem the growing tide of disillusionment concerning integration and nonviolence as viable goals of the black freedom movement.[14]

After the first stage of the march, King asked the young activists why they refused to sing the "black and white together" stanza of "We Shall Overcome." Their reply reflected their determination to change the course of the civil rights movement:

> This is a new day, we don't sing those words anymore. In fact, the whole song should be discarded. Not "We Shall Overcome," but "We Shall Overrun."[15]

Therefore, when Stokely Carmichael and Willie Ricks raised the cry of Black Power on June 16, 1966, the integration-oriented civil rights movement came to a screeching halt. Although King supported the call for racial pride and increased political and economic power, he believed the Black Power slogan had negative connotations of violence, domination, and hatred. Fearful that the slogan would confuse white allies and isolate the Negro community, King advocated the use of alternative slogans such as "black consciousness" or "black equality." The brunt of his argument was as follows:

> No one has ever heard the Jews publicly chant a slogan of Jewish power, but they have power. Through group unity, determination and creative endeavor, they have gained it. The same thing is true of the Irish and Italians . . . This is exactly what we must do. We must use every constructive means to amass economic and political power. This is the kind of legitimate power we need.

We must work to build racial pride and refute the notion that black is evil and ugly. But this must come through a program, not merely through a slogan.[16]

King was unsuccessful in his attempt to get SNCC leaders to abandon the Black Power slogan. The slogan spread like wildfire across the nation, and the white news media used it to sensationalize the ideological division in the leadership of the civil rights movement. After the Meredith March, the spotlight of national attention turned away from Martin Luther King and the ideology of integration to focus on Stokely Carmichael and the concept of Black Power. It did not take long for integrationist leaders such as Roy Wilkins and Whitney Young to repudiate Black Power as black separatism and racism in reverse. Leaders of the National Baptist Convention, meeting in Chicago in the summer of 1966, were also quick to denounce the Black Power slogan.[17] Meanwhile, Black Power advocates sought to clarify the concept via press conferences, pamphlets, newspaper articles, books, and television appearances. In their book *Black Power*, Stokely Carmichael and Charles Hamilton explained that the concept had nothing to do with black hatred or racism, but was rather a call for black people to consolidate their economic and political resources in order to acquire power. It was a call for unity and a sense of community wherein black people would be proud of their heritage and reject the racist institutions and values of American society.[18]

Notwithstanding attempts to clarify it, Black Power had more of a revolutionary spirit than a specific political or economic program to recommend. It was, moreover, a radical critique of the integrationist, nonviolent civil rights movement and its Christian foundation. Militant SNCC activists rejected the notion that prayer, love, nonviolence, and redemptive suffering could ever produce freedom for black people. Having seen too many blacks beaten senseless while the FBI stood by and took notes, SNCC activists grew weary of appeals to the moral conscience of the nation. They pointed out that bullets had no morals, "and white folks had plenty more bullets than they did conscience."[19] Gradually, these young but seasoned freedom fighters became convinced that a new approach was needed to confront the brutality of white racism. More than anyone else, Julius Lester captured the feelings of these young revolutionaries:

We used to sing "I Love Everybody" as we ducked bricks and bottles. Now we sing "Too much love, too much love, Nothing kills a nigger like Too much love." We know, because we still get headaches from the beatings we took while love, love, loving. We know, because we died on those highways and in those jail cells, died trying to change the hearts of men who had none. We know, those of us who're twenty-three and have bleeding ulcers. We know, those of us who'll never be quite right again. We know that nothing kills a nigger like too much love.[20]

Many of the young civil rights activists who converted to Black Power also began to question the assumption that nonviolence was the only Christian means of struggle. Could one lay claim to the Christian faith and also *reject* nonviolence? Julius Lester, himself the son of a minister, not only rejected nonviolence but seemed to advocate retribution:

The race war, if it comes, will come partly from the necessity for revenge. You can't do what has been done to blacks and not expect retribution. The very act of retribution is liberating, and perhaps it is no accident that the symbolism of Christianity speaks of being washed in Blood as an act of purification.[21]

Indeed, the rhetoric of young Black Power militants called for a road to freedom that involved "*preying* not praying," and "*swinging* not singing." Many of them labelled Martin Luther King and other ministers as "Rev. Sambos," while others repudiated Christianity altogether as "the white man's religion." The rhetoric of violence replaced the traditional Christian emphasis on patience and redemptive suffering. It was in this context that a small group of clergymen from across the nation rallied to the defense of the Christian faith by seeking to reinterpret it in light of Black Power.

THE NATIONAL COMMITTEE OF BLACK CHURCHMEN: DEFENDERS OF THE FAITH

By the end of 1966 young activists had succeeded in making Black Power the litmus test of authentic black leadership. Those who rejected the concept (i.e., Roy Wilkins and Whitney Young) were labelled Uncle Toms, while those who supported it were regarded as legitimate leaders. Dr. Nathan Hare, a Black Power advocate and professor of sociology at Howard University, claimed that the Black Power slogan had "the capacity for separating the black sheep from the colored goats among Negro leaders."[22] Using this criterion, the National Committee of Negro Churchmen (changed to National Committee of Black Churchmen in 1968) must be considered black sheep, or legitimate black leaders in tune with the feelings of the masses. Not many weeks after the cry of Black Power was raised on the Meredith March, this ad hoc group of black clergymen issued a statement in support of the controversial new slogan.

Under the leadership of Dr. Benjamin F. Payton, executive director of the Commission on Religion and Race of the National Council of Churches (NCC), the NCNC was organized as an informal, ad hoc committee in July 1966. An initial meeting was held at the Interchurch Center at 475 Riverside Drive in New York City, followed by subsequent meetings at Bethel AME and Mother Zion AMEZ churches in Harlem. This gathering of ministers sought "to speak a word of clear analysis" in the confusion and chaos surrounding the advent of Black Power, and intended to mobilize radical ministers in the North as King had done in the South a decade earlier with the Southern Christian Leadership Conference. By the end of July the group had raised $10,000 for a full-page advertisement in the *New York Times* and had garnered the support of some of the most prominent African-American ministers in the country.[23]

Mediating Two Traditions: The July 31, 1966, Statement

The Black Power statement that appeared in the July 31, 1966, edition of the *New York Times* marked an important turning point in the history of the civil rights movement and the black church. By endorsing the call for Black Power, the NCBC moved away from the primary emphasis on interracial reconciliation as defined by Benjamin Mays, Howard Thurman, and Martin Luther King, Jr., and toward a new interpretation of Christian faith that focused on *blackness* and *power*. By pointing out the limitations of the integration-oriented civil rights movement and articulating a theological justification for Black Power, the NCBC laid the foundation for contemporary black theology.

The Black Power statement of July 31, 1966, initiated the development of a fresh theological consciousness that separated radical black Christianity from the religion of white churches. Although the NCBC clergy still expressed a concern for the beloved community of interracial fellowship envisioned by Benjamin Mays, Howard Thurman, and Martin Luther King, Jr., they also took a lesson from Elijah Muhammad and Malcolm X:

> We must first be reconciled to ourselves lest we fail to recognize the resources we already have and upon which we can build. We must be reconciled to ourselves as persons and to ourselves as a historical group . . . As long as we are filled with hatred for ourselves, we will be unable to respect others.[24]

The NCBC clergy did not abandon the concern for reconciliation so strongly expressed by pre–Black Power religious thinkers. They too believed in the oneness of humanity, proclaiming that "we and all Americans are one." But influenced by the mood and spirit of Black

Power, they were especially careful to repudiate any assumption that their concern for reconciliation was motivated by fear. The clergy emphatically stated that their concern for reconciliation was not based on any fear as a minority group comprising only 10 percent of the American population. Noting that African-Americans were already painfully aware of the awesome power wielded by the 90 percent majority, the NCBC clergy declared:

> We do not need to be threatened by such cold and heartless statements. For we are men, not children, and we are growing out of our fear of that power, which can hardly hurt us any more in the future than it does in the present or has in the past.[25]

Nor was concern for reconciliation based on the fear that not to do so would jeopardize the gains of the civil rights movement; those victories did not fundamentally change the lives of the masses of blacks, particularly in the urban North. Instead, the NCBC argued that the acquisition of Black Power was a precondition for any meaningful reconciliation between blacks and whites. The emphasis on the achievement of institutional group power instead of the attainment of individual constitutional rights demonstrates the discontinuity between the NCBC position and that of pre–Black Power religious thinkers. However, the NCBC's firm belief that Black Power must lead to more effective participation "at all levels of the life of our nation" (integration), shows that there is also continuity between pre- and post–Black Power religious thought.

Vincent Harding's analysis of NCBC documents validates the claim that the organization served as a bridge linking pre– with post–Black Power African-American religious thought. Harding observed that while early NCBC documents used the radical rhetoric of the Black Power movement, the substance of their statements was basically consistent with the integrationist stance of Benjamin Mays and Martin Luther King.[26]

To be sure, the NCBC reminded America that it needed its black citizens, just as Benjamin Mays and others did in the months before and after World War II. But the NCBC clergy insisted that the pursuit of power, not reconciliation or interracial harmony, must be the fundamental basis of the African-American freedom struggle. Although some pre–Black Power religious thinkers identified the issue of power relationship (as opposed to race prejudice) as the major source of racial tension in the 1940s, the dominant ideology that shaped the civil rights movement was integration, not the celebration of blackness and the attainment of group power.[27] By emphasizing power instead of Christian love and interracial harmony, the NCBC signaled an important shift in African-American religious thought. Considered "ecclesiastical renegades, denominational radicals and mad preachers,"[28] the NCBC clergy poignantly stated the case for Black Power:

> The fundamental distortion facing us in the controversy about "black power" is rooted in a gross imbalance of power and conscience between Negroes and white Americans.

Noting the widespread assumption that whites are justified in getting what they want through the use of power, while blacks are limited to appeals to conscience, the NCBC clergy put their finger on the heart of the problem:

> As a result, the power of white men and the conscience of black men have both been corrupted. The power of white men is corrupted because it meets little meaningful resistance from Negroes to temper it and keep white men from aping God. The conscience of black men is corrupted because, having no power to implement the demands of conscience, the concern for justice is transmuted into a distorted form of love, which in the absence of justice, becomes chaotic self-surrender. Powerlessness breeds a race of beggars. We are faced now with a situation where conscienceless power meets powerless conscience, threatening the very foundations of our nation.[29]

The statement criticized the white church and its clergy for attacking the concept of Black Power and argued that there can be no authentic interracial fellowship until blacks achieve political and economic power. The clergy also urged the leaders of America to make the rebuilding of the inner cities the nation's first priority, and to create equal opportunity for blacks in employment, education, and housing. Although they deplored "the violence of riots," they interpreted them as the expression of God's judgment "upon our nation for its failure to use its abundant resources to serve the well-being of people, at home and abroad."[30]

But most important, the NCBC clergy addressed the black community. As James Cone observed, never before in the history of the African-American church had a group of pastors so frankly and publicly engaged in radical self-criticism. Indeed, their prophetic self-criticism was "a revolutionary step" toward making the black church more faithful to the liberating gospel of Jesus Christ.[31] Like Benjamin Mays and Elijah Muhammad, the NCBC clergy criticized the otherworldly character of the black church. To be sure, this criticism, made by Christian integrationists and non-Christian nationalists alike, is a major characteristic of African-American religious thought before and after Black Power. The July 1966 statement reiterated this well-known critique:

Too often the Negro church has stirred its members away from the reign of God in this world to a distorted and complacent view of an otherworldly conception of God's power. We commit ourselves as churchmen to make more meaningful in the life of our institutions our conviction that Jesus Christ reigns in the "here" and "now" as well as in the future he brings upon us.[32]

This type of self-criticism was a recurring theme in early NCBC published statements. No doubt the scathing nationalist critique of Christianity made by Elijah Muhammad and Malcolm X compelled the NCBC clergy to confront publicly the weaknesses of the black church. That is why I argue that one cannot understand the rise of the NCBC and the subsequent development of black theology without seeing how the nationalist critique of Christianity, which was widely embraced by young Black Power advocates, forced African-American pastors and theologians to rally to the defense of biblical Christianity. The prophetic leaders of the black church, especially in the ghettoes of the urban North, knew that if they did not respond immediately to the charges made by the black nationalists, they would not be able to minister effectively in their communities.

The Impact of the NCBC on the American Churches

The dynamism of the Black Power movement provided the black clergy with a sense of urgency as they sought to preserve the credibility of the Christian faith in the wake of the black revolution. The NCBC ministers in the white denominations did not care if their white colleagues criticized them for embracing what they considered the "un-Christian" secular ideology of Black Power. Likewise, radical ministers in the historically black denominations were also determined to move beyond the traditional conservative stance of their respective church hierarchies. Indeed, African-American pastors in both white and black denominations were united in their determination to respond creatively to the challenge of Black Power.

Therefore, the NCBC members who attended the September 1967 Conference on the Church and Urban Tensions sponsored by the NCC (Washington, D.C.) did not hesitate to demand that black and white delegates form separate caucuses for reflection on the urban crisis facing the nation. For three days the black and white delegates met in separate rooms, reuniting only in the final plenary session to share their respective statements on the church and the urban crisis.[33] The African-American delegates did not worry about offending the white, liberal clergy who attended the conference; they were concerned about black liberation, which according to Gayraud Wilmore included "the freedom not to be conditioned by the feelings of White brothers and sisters who needed them for the sake of their own injured consciences."[34]

As in the Black Power statement issued one year earlier, the NCBC clergy gladly embraced the challenge Black Power presented to the African-American church. In a very real sense, they acknowledged that there was a measure of truth in the nationalist claim that "Christianity is the white man's religion." They confessed that the contemporary black church had failed to "celebrate, preserve, and enhance the integrity of Blackness under the Lordship of Christ" in the tradition of the historic black church. Instead of quickly dismissing Elijah Muhammad's nationalist critique, these African-American clergy openly confessed their apostasy and admitted their complicity in the oppression of their own people:

> We confess that in recent times we have not lived up to our heritage . . . Rather we have fallen prey to the dominance of White Society and have allowed the truth, meaningfulness and authenticity of the Black Church to be defamed by our easy acceptance of its goals, objectives and criteria for success. Therefore, the Black Church has unwittingly become a tool for our oppression, providing an easy vehicle for escape from the harsh realities of our own existence.[35]

The black delegates at the 1967 NCC conference were simply expressing what many in their communities already knew. But the significance of their statement is that instead of remaining silent about this painful reality, they *publicly* acknowledged their guilt. Perhaps they were motivated by the biblical idea that those who claim to be sinless are liars, and that confession is the precondition for meaningful repentance (1 Jn 1:8-10). With humility and sincerity, they faced the possibility that their words of confession were too little and too late:

> Since as Black Churchmen we find ourselves in the unenviable role of the oppressor, we are in real danger of losing our existence and our reason for being, if indeed we have not already lost them.[36]

But just as early Christians rejoiced in the assurance that God forgives penitent sinners, the African-American clergy gladly interpreted Black Power as the means by which God will restore the black church:

> We rejoice in the Black Power Movement, which is not only the renewed hope for Black People, but gives the Black Church once again, its reason for existing. We call upon Black Churchmen everywhere to embrace the Black Power Movement, to divest itself of the traditional churchly functions and goals which do not

respond to the needs of a downtrodden, oppressed and alienated people.[37]

The black clergy's insistence on separate caucuses at the September 1967 NCC conference and the honest self-criticism of their statement were clear manifestations of the impact Black Power had had on their consciousness. They knew all too well that Christianity was on trial in their communities, and that radical changes were necessary if the black church was to fulfill its divine mission to be an agent of liberation (Lk 4:18-19). To that end, the ad hoc committee of African-American clergy met in Dallas, Texas for the purpose of establishing a permanent organization (October 1967). Within a year black caucuses were established in nine major white denominations.[38]

African-American pastors in white denominations were especially sensitive to the nationalist charge that black preachers were representatives of "the white man's religion." Consequently, they were even more determined to confront racism in their denominations and to advocate a theological perspective that embraced Black Power. Indeed, the growing disillusionment with white America that caused young blacks to embrace Black Power was the same sense of frustration that led black pastors in white denominations to be the first advocates of black theology. According to Gayraud Wilmore, this growing black consciousness in the African-American religious community—reflected in the formation of black caucuses in white denominations and initial efforts to articulate a black theology—was "directly traceable" to the action of the black delegates at the September 1967 NCC conference in Washington, D.C. Wilmore explained the significance of these developments in this way:

It was the most dramatic demonstration of the influence of the black power movement within the precincts of the American religious establishment. It inaugurated an era of confrontation and negotiation between blacks and whites unprecedented in the twentieth-century church.[39]

The NCBC played the most decisive role in this movement toward Black Power. It helped to bridge the gap between pre– and post–Black Power African-American religious thought, and it laid the foundation for the subsequent development of a distinctively black Christian theology of liberation. No doubt the organization was well aware of the pivotal role it played. Describing the black clergy that comprised the NCBC, Leon Watts writes:

We found ourselves regarded as the true "outsiders": neither fish nor fowl; not really the enemy, but not really the recognized ally to the Black community. Standing between us and the Black community was "white Christianity" which we allegedly represented. That impression needed to be corrected post haste.[40]

With the assistance of religious scholars and theologians such as James Cone, Henry Mitchell, Gayraud Wilmore, J. Deotis Roberts, and Preston Williams, the NCBC began to confront the charge that black clergy were representatives of white Christianity. Through the work of its Theological Commission, established at the 1967 Dallas convocation and chaired by Gayraud Wilmore, the NCBC initiated the development of a theological perspective on the Christian faith that emphasized liberation as the essence of the gospel. Moreover, unlike the pre–Black Power religious thought, which embraced integration and minimized the significance of race, the nascent theological perspective of the NCBC celebrated blackness and made it into a central theological category.[41] The creation of a fully developed black theology became one of the NCBC's major concerns, dominating the discussion at the October 1968 convocation in St. Louis.[42] The following summer in Atlanta, the organization issued a statement on black theology, defining it as a theology of black liberation that

> seeks to plumb the black condition in the light of God's revelation in Jesus Christ, so that the black community can see that the gospel is commensurate with the achievement of black humanity.[43]

Notwithstanding its limitations,[44] the NCBC's creative response to the challenge of Black Power helped regain the credibility of Christianity in urban black communities across the nation. It was this potential to make Christian faith relevant to the liberation of the oppressed that caused excitement and activity in the black religious community in particular and American Protestantism in general.

NCBC leaders such as Metz Rollins (the organization's first executive director and currently pastor of St. Augustine Presbyterian church in the Bronx) proclaimed the "coming of age" of the black church. Rollins declared that the black church, having learned from the community's emphasis on Black Power and black consciousness, "has matured in an acute awareness of its own unique gifts, its own peculiar understanding of the Gospel of Jesus Christ, and a new appreciation of its own hallowed and tortured history."[45] Convinced that this revitalized black church will benefit the entire Christian community, Rollins articulated what he and others understood to be the messianic role of the black church:

> This new stance of the black church, this coming of age, is a healthy development on the American church scene. Black churchmen

have much to contribute out of their background of suffering and oppression to the life of the whole church. Their statements on pressing contemporary issues will bring a new understanding of what it means to be faithful to Jesus Christ in times like these.[46]

Indeed, it was this same conviction that led Leon Watts to proclaim:

The National Committee of Black Churchmen is not an ecumenical organization alongside others . . . It may save Christianity in the Western world by giving it back to the people.[47]

Yet the NCBC was not alone in its response to Black Power. There were other important voices that also sought to save Christianity, if not for the entire Western world then certainly for that segment of the African-American community that had already abandoned the faith.

THREE CHARACTERISTICS
OF NASCENT BLACK THEOLOGY

Inspired by the prophetic response of the NCBC, other African-American clergy began to address the implications of Black Power for the black church and its theology. Like the NCBC statements, these early commentaries on Black Power lift up three recurring themes: 1) Black Power demands a prophetic internal critique of the black church; 2) Black Power is a necessary step toward a more just society and a renewed American church; and 3) Black Power is consistent with biblical Christianity.

Prophetic Internal Critique

Aware that the nationalist critique of Christianity was widely accepted by many in the African-American community, prophetic black clergy leaders responded by subjecting the black church to radical, internal self-critique. Basically, they sought to defend biblical Christianity by confessing that they had failed to practice it in their churches. By accepting the legitimacy of some aspects of the nationalist argument, black preachers were essentially asking young African-Americans to give Christianity and the church a second chance. The use of this strategy proved to be an effective defense at a time when many militant young people believed that it was impossible to be fully black and Christian at the same time.

In 1968 the Philadelphia Council of Black Clergy issued an important statement that reflected this type of self-criticism. In their paper, entitled "Black Religion—Past, Present, and Future," the Philadelphia clerics acknowledged that the contemporary African-American church had abandoned its historic commitment to black liberation. Contrary to the ministry of Jesus and the bold leadership of nineteenth-century black ministers like Rev. Henry Highland Garnet, the contemporary black church had been lulled to sleep by "the illusory promise of integration." The Philadelphia clergy called on the black church and community to reject "the mythology of the American dream for the truth of the Afro-American experience," and to incorporate the spirit of black pride into their ministry and theology:

> Black Churchmen, consciously Black and consciously Christian, in swelling numbers are attesting to the bankruptcy of integration as a religious option. They call upon their Black brothers to repudiate both the symbol and the substance of the white man's integration; to disavow, in the conduct of their faith and in faithfulness to their people, the sanctity of whiteness.[48]

Moreover, the Philadelphia clergy argued that the aims of Black Power are consistent with the ministry of Jesus Christ. Since Jesus—the source and norm of authentic Christian faith—directed his ministry to the poor and downtrodden, the black church must make the liberation of the oppressed its primary concern. Aware of the oppressive role institutional Christianity has played in the African-American experience, the Philadelphia clergy reminded the black church that its "commitment is to Christ and not to Christianity," and that Christ was a revolutionary figure dedicated to the eradication of exploitative and oppressive systems.[49]

Calvin Marshall, an NCBC leader and pastor of Varick Memorial AMEZ Church in Brooklyn, New York, also offered a prophetic internal critique of the black church. Marshall confessed that his denomination had failed to live out its historic commitment to black liberation in the tradition of Harriet Tubman, Sojourner Truth, and Frederick Douglass, all members of the AMEZ church. Instead of immersing itself in the black liberation struggle, the church had dedicated itself to the preservation of the status quo:

> Being accepted by the National Council of Churches meant more to her (AMEZ church) than being accepted by the people of the black ghetto. Trips to the Holy Land became more important than trips through the streets of her impoverished neighborhoods— to see, to feel, to hear, and to taste the plight of her people.[50]

Like the Philadelphia clergy, Marshall reminded the black church that Jesus was a radical leader who confronted the religious, political, and social systems that oppressed the poor. Claiming that the contemporary black church had reduced the significance of Jesus' death to the ritual of "breaking bread and sipping wine," Marshall expressed a radical perspective that challenged the conservative christology of the black church:

> We are able to talk about the crucifixion of Christ without really understanding that here was a radical, a revolutionary who was put to death for treason. Christ was an anarchist pure and simple. Christ was a Malcolm X.[51]

Perhaps the most frank expression of prophetic internal critique was made by the Black Methodists for Church Renewal (the black caucus of the United Methodist Church established in Cincinnati, Ohio, in February 1968). This group of clergy and lay leaders began their statement with a confession that clearly demonstrates the effect of Black Power on their consciousness. The Black Methodists confessed that they had too often denied their blackness and consequently alienated themselves from many in the African-American community. They admitted their failure to play a significant role in the black revolution, and confessed that "we have been too comfortable in our 'little world,' too pleased with our lot as second-class citizens and second-class members of the Methodist Church."[52]

The Black Power Path to Genuine Integration

In addition to engaging in prophetic self-criticism, black theologians maintained that Black Power was not a call for permanent separation, but rather a necessary step toward a truly integrated American society. Contrary to those who feared Black Power entailed a repudiation of the beloved community, African-American church leaders claimed that it would actually lead to improved race relations.

Episcopal clergyman Nathan Wright, Jr.—who served as executive director of the Department of Urban Work for the diocese of Newark, New Jersey, and chaired the National Conference on Black Power, July 20-23, 1967—was one of the first leaders clearly to articulate the positive theological implications of Black Power. For Wright, the call of Black Power was essentially a religious opportunity for black people to fulfill the divine purpose of human growth. Furthermore, he argued that "power is basic to life" and is therefore necessary if "life is to become what God destined it to be."[53] But because African-Americans have been systematically oppressed by a white racist society, they have not fully exercised their God-given power to contribute to the life of the nation. Consequently, Wright argued that "Black Americans must be determined to use for their own good, and for the good of the nation as a whole, the latent power of their ethnic numbers."[54]

As Wright saw it, the civil rights movement emphasized what African-Americans are due, while Black Power focuses on what black people are capable of giving to themselves and their country. For him, Black Power is a call for self-sufficiency and independence, the same qualities other ethnic groups marshalled "to thrust themselves into the mainstream of American life."[55] Far from leading to black separatism, Black Power is a necessary step toward genuine integration:

> Black power in terms of self-development means that we want to fish as all Americans do in the mainstream of American life.[56]

For Wright, Black Power is not a call for blacks to hate whites; rather, it is a creative force that is vital to the peace and growth of the entire nation. Accordingly, Wright concluded, "It is only as white men see in Black Power a mirror of the abuse of white power that they are frightened."[57]

Rev. Thomas Kilgore, Jr., past president of the American Baptist Convention and pastor emeritus of the Second Baptist Church in Los Angeles, also responded positively to the emergence of Black Power. Like Nathan Wright, Kilgore believed that the concept of Black Power would strengthen the black community and lead to the revitalization of American religion as a whole. Convinced that "the black church must win young blacks to Christianity," Kilgore embraced the new emphasis on Black Power and black pride. Although he maintained a strong belief that the true nature of the faith "rises above 'white church' and 'black church,'" Kilgore argued that separate black organizations like NCBC are needed to help the black church minister more effectively to the specific needs of the African-American community. Therefore, he applauded efforts to develop a relevant Christian theology in light of the black experience and challenged the black church to build upon its strength by developing coalitions with community organizations that will foster black educational, economic, and political development.[58]

Like other clergy during the period, Kilgore believed that a revitalized black church would lead to the renewal of the American church as a whole. As he saw it, "the larger segment of the American church is faint and about ready to die, and deliverance must come from somewhere." Convinced that ecumenical bodies such as the National Council of Churches and the Consultation on Church Union were incapable of leading to the renewal of the church in America, Kilgore proclaimed:

> Renewal will come when black Americans and the black church move from many vantage points into the mainstream of American life and turn it upside down and set it on fire.[59]

What did the black church have to offer the white church and society? Kilgore believed that the black church could "lead their white brothers to religious relevance"; bring life to the "rigid and joyless" worship experience in the white church; help liberate whites from the demons of racism; and (considering the impending defeat in Vietnam) teach America about the meaning of suffering, defeat, and redemption.[60]

Kilgore's analysis of Black Power and Christianity demonstrates the important link between African-American religious thought before and after Black Power. Like NCBC and black caucuses in white denominations, Kilgore took the best of the integrationist vision and combined it with a perspective on Black Power that was consistent with the universalism of the Christian faith. Consequently, he embraced the new emphasis on black pride, while maintaining that

> the true measure of authentic blackness is not to be black and proud in the context of all-blackness, but rather to affirm the validity of blackness and manhood in the context of the total society.[61]

Ever mindful to preserve the integrationist vision of the beloved community, Kilgore concluded that as black and white Christians work together to renew the American church, "we may all come to understand that we are human first, racial or ethnic groups second, and have national and religious ties, lastly."

The Black Power Path to Genuine Christianity

The early defenders of black theology insisted that a creative interpretation of Black Power was a necessary prerequisite for the theological reconstruction of Christianity in the African-American community. For them, the acceptance of Black Power and black culture was indispensable if the African-American church was to have any relevance and credibility whatsoever in black ghettos throughout the nation. At the same time they assured skeptics that a distinctively black interpretation of the faith would not distort the essence of the gospel. On the contrary, they claimed that a black theological perspective would ultimately enhance black Christians' awareness of the universality of the faith.

Two noteworthy essays by Henry Mitchell and Gayraud Wilmore are representative of this position. In a 1968 article entitled "Black Power and the Christian Church," Mitchell argued that African-American pastors and seminarians need to have a better appreciation of the distinctive quality of black religious culture—its music, preaching, worship style, and theology—if they are ever to correct the widespread perception among younger blacks that Christianity is the white man's religion. Ironically, black colleges and seminaries contributed to this false notion by failing to teach the uniqueness of black Christianity and neglecting the scholarly investigation of the African-American religious tradition.[62]

Mitchell makes the point that black churches that accentuate white culture while deemphasizing the uniqueness of their own religious heritage ("white-culture black churches") must either embrace the vibrant African-American religious tradition or "join the white churches in a slow, inexorable march to a common grave."[63] From the courageous struggle against injustice to the therapeutic value of its worship experience, black religion has made a tremendous contribution to the "psychic wholeness and firm identity" of the African-American community. That is why, Mitchell concludes, "black religion is the only means of reaching, helping and saving the vast majority of black people, both here and hereafter."[64]

Like Mitchell, Gayraud Wilmore believed that the black church had to immerse itself in African-American culture before it could make its full contribution to the wider ecumenical movement. In "The Case for a New Black Church Style," published in 1968, Wilmore warned the church that if it is to continue as a viable institution in the black community it will have to "end its basic conformity to European theological traditions and Anglo-Saxon structures of value" and revive its historic commitment to black culture and black liberation.[65]

Like the other early defenders of black theology, Wilmore claimed that an emphasis on black culture would enhance rather than detract from black Christians' awareness of the universality of the faith:

> The problem of the whitenized black churches today is how to recover their own self-respect by demythologizing the white cultural bag through which the faith was transmitted to them and in which they have curled themselves up so comfortably. In doing so they may discover that the essence of the Christian faith not only transcends ultimately the ethnocentric culture of the white man, but that of the black man as well; that this Christ, in whom there is neither Jew nor Greek, bond nor free, is also neither black nor white.[66]

The African-American pastors and theologians who responded positively to the emergence of Black Power concurred with Black Power advocates that black people must learn to love themselves before they can properly love others. That is why they did not perceive the acceptance of Black Power as a retreat from the universalism of the Christian gospel, but rather a necessary corrective to the "idol of Integration" and its negative impact on the African-American community.

Vincent Harding aptly described this position in his seminal essay "The Religion of Black Power":

> Perhaps we were urged towards an identification with mankind-at-large (often meaning white mankind) before we had learned to identify with our black neighbors. It is likely that our humanity really begins in the black ghetto and cannot be rejected there for an easier, sentimental, white-oriented acceptance elsewhere.[67]

Referring to the apostle Paul's personal testimony in Philippians 3:1-8, Harding declared that African-Americans must also affirm their racial and cultural heritage before they can "count it as dung" for the sake of a broader universal human family.[68] Accordingly, he claimed that Black Power's strong emphasis on self-love (the dominant theme in the new "gospel of Blackness") is not a retreat from Christian universalism, but simply the realization that African-Americans "must love their communities in order to love the world."[69]

In fact, Harding saw in the concern of Black Power advocates for the oppressed non-white peoples of the Third World (the majority of the world's population), a universalism as broad as that found in most Western religious traditions. Considering Jesus' own radical commitment to liberate the victims of injustice, Harding reasoned that Black Power's unambiguous identification with revolutionary movements in the Third World "actually brings Black Power into the orbit of a universality more authentic than the largely parochial sentiments of a Judeo-Christian western commitment."[70] Indeed, Harding asked a provocative question:

> Is it not possible that a universalism based on suffering, struggle, and hope is more vital than some vague identification based on common links to a possibly dead Creator-Father?[71]

Noting the failure of most African-American pastors to support publicly revolutionary movements in the Third World, Harding characterized the black church hierarchy as being "no more Christian than its white counterpart on such issues." As he saw it, this position (or lack thereof) reinforced the negative perception of Christianity in the black community:

> Should the sense of solidarity with the exploited peoples grow to major proportions in the Afro-American communities, it may well prove impossible for such religious leaders to hold on to their already shaky grounds.[72]

But the African-American clergy who responded creatively to the challenge of Black Power interpreted it as God's divine judgment on a racist American society and an impotent Christian church. Just as Elijah Muhammad and Malcolm X proclaimed Allah's judgment on white America, prophetic African-American Christian clergy declared that God had chosen the vehicle of Black Power to deliver the divine verdict against American Christianity. As Vincent Harding saw it, the hypocrisy of white Christianity—its involvement in the enslavement and oppression of African-Americans and its participation in the exploitation of third-world nations—was itself largely responsible for the emergence of Black Power. Accordingly, he described Black Power as "a repudiation of the American culture-religion that helped to create it and a quest for a religious reality more faithful to our own experience."[73] For Harding, Black Power is God's judgment on American Christianity for turning "the universal Christ into an American mascot, a puppet blessing every mad American act," from the genocide of the Native Americans to the bombing of Hiroshima:

> It may be that America must now stand under profound and damning judgement for having turned the redeeming lover of all men into a white, middle-class burner of children and destroyer of the revolutions of the oppressed.[74]

Prophetic African-American clergy reminded the American church that the Bible itself records God's proclivity to judge God's people in ways the community least expects. Since God is the same yesterday, today, and tomorrow, God's method of dealing with humanity is consistent throughout time. Just as the Hebrew scriptures narrate God's use of floods, famines, and rival nations like Babylon to judge the people of Israel, the contemporary racial climate in America indicates that God has chosen Black Power as a modern-day vehicle of divine judgment. The words of the Rev. John Hurst Adams, now a bishop in the A.M.E. church, are representative of this position:

> Black Power . . . must be discerned as a *Sign of Our Time*. It is the sign of the Judgement of God upon us . . . Unable to find servants and prophets for his task within the Church, God has acted again in History, as he always does, to warn, chasten, and recall his people from idols made in their own image. The Idolatry of whiteness is being questioned by God and History.[75]

In sum, the African-American clergy who responded positively to the emergence of Black Power claimed that a responsible interpretation of the concept was not a retreat from the ultimate goal of the beloved community envisioned by Martin Luther King, Jr., and other pre–Black Power religious thinkers. To the contrary, they insisted that Black Power was a necessary prerequisite to genuine integration. By claiming that Black Power was a means to a truly integrated society, these African-American clergy played an important political role in the transition from civil rights to Black Power.

While mediating between civil rights and Black Power, integration and nationalism, prophetic African-American clergy also sought to defend biblical Christianity from the oft-repeated nationalist critique that "Christianity is the white man's religion." Indeed, their efforts to reconcile the particularity of blackness and the universality of the gospel laid the foundation for the subsequent development of black theology. The African-American clergy who responded positively to the challenges of the black revolution preserved the best of pre-- Black Power religious and political thought in the midst of rapid so- cial and cultural change. That is why James Cone, borrowing Paul Tillich's self-designation, described the early defenders of black the- ology as

> theologians "on the boundary" between integration and separa- tion, nonviolence and self-defense, "love our white enemies and love our black skins." They refused to sacrifice either emphasis; they insisted on the absolute necessity of both.[76]

But if there was one early interpreter of black theology who defi- nitely crossed "the boundary," it was the Rev. Albert B. Cleage, Jr., the controversial pastor of Shrine of the Black Madonna in Detroit. No discussion of the emergence of Black Power and the response of the church would be complete without an analysis of the significant role he played as a critic and defender of the faith.

CHRISTIANITY, ALBERT CLEAGE, AND THE BLACK MESSIAH

Like the other radical African-American clergy discussed in this chapter, Albert Cleage was keenly aware that Christianity was on trial in the black ghettos of the nation. Cleage was active in the early devel- opment of the NCBC, and his book of sermons, *The Black Messiah*, published in the fall of 1968, sparked a great deal of excitement about the prospects of developing a radical black theology.[77] Like the NCBC clergy, Cleage proclaimed that the black church had failed to make the gospel relevant to the community's quest for Black Power and black consciousness. But Cleage's criticism of the African-American church cut much deeper than that of any of his contemporaries. More than anyone else, Cleage was determined to expose what he considered the underlying *theological* reasons for the black churches' failure to be more involved in the African-American liberation struggle.

According to Cleage, the black church "must face the simple fact that its basic problem is a theological one," namely, its fanatic adherence to the classical doctrine of the atonement. Essentially, Cleage argued that the African-American church was not actively involved in the black revolution because its theology of "individualistic otherworldly salvation" was not designed to encourage physical participation in movements for social and political change. Consequently, he called the black church a "counterrevolutionary" institution that will never be of service to the liberation struggle until it abandons its individualistic otherworldly conception of salvation.[78]

At first glance it might appear that Cleage's criticism of the black church is no different from the otherworldly critiques made by pre– and post–Black Power Christian thinkers (Benjamin Mays and the NCBC clergy). But it is important to note that Cleage was not simply criticizing the church for *overemphasizing* otherworldly salvation and downplaying the need for social and political change. Rather, Cleage insisted that the classical doctrine of the atonement (an emphasis on the salvation of the individual believer by faith in Jesus' sacrifice on the cross) must be discarded *altogether,* because it cannot inspire an oppressed people to struggle collectively for their social, political, and economic salvation on earth.

Instead of a gospel of *individualistic other*worldly salvation, Cleage preached a gospel that emphasized the liberation of the black *community* in the *present* world. Convinced that "everything about traditional Christianity is false," he developed a radical black Christian nationalism based on the theological premise that "nothing is more sacred than the liberation of black people."[79] What factors shaped Cleage's views and helped to make him a pivotal figure in the early development of black theology?

Biographical Sketch

Albert Cleage was born on June 13, 1911, in Indianapolis, Indiana. The fact that his father became a prominent physician in Detroit meant that Albert and his siblings did not face the poverty and racial oppression that Benjamin Mays, Howard Thurman, and Elijah Muhammad encountered growing up in the deep South. However, a brief examination of Cleage's career will show that his relatively secure socio-economic position did not desensitize him to the plight of the black masses.

A graduate of Wayne State University and Oberlin School of Theology, Cleage began his ministry at the Chandler Memorial Congregational Church in Lexington, Kentucky, in 1943. While there he received an invitation to become an interim co-minister at the Church for the Fellowship of All Peoples in San Francisco until Howard Thurman arrived from his position as Dean of the Chapel at Howard

University. Cleage served the interracial church until July 1, 1944. More than two decades later he described the famous congregation as "a contrived, artificial affair":

> The whites who came, came as sort of missionaries. They wanted to do something meaningful, but this was not really their church. The blacks regarded it as experimental too, or were brainwashed to think it was something superior.[80]

Moreover, Cleage characterized Dr. Alfred G. Fisk as a "well-meaning" man who nevertheless shied away from issues involving tension, conflict, and power:

> He talked of the glorious fellowship washed in the blood of the Lamb; I talked about hell on the alternate Sundays. He felt upset about my preaching, but didn't want to raise racial tension in his heaven.[81]

While in San Francisco, Cleage was called to the pastorate of the historic St. John's Congregational Church in Springfield, Massachusetts. His ministry there was oriented toward the development of a vibrant youth program and active community service. Cleage was on the Executive Board of the local NAACP, served as chair of its housing committee, and fought for equal employment opportunities for blacks. His work at St. John's proved to be valuable experience for his most challenging appointment, the pastorate of Central Congregational Church in Detroit. What was the nature of Cleage's ministry in Detroit, and how did Central Church become Shrine of the Black Madonna?

Cleage arrived in Detroit in 1951 and quickly became involved in every major civic issue ranging from housing discrimination to community control of local school boards. By the early 1960s he had earned a reputation as a radical political activist who articulated a brand of black nationalism similar to that found in Elijah Muhammad's Nation of Islam. In addition to his many public appearances around the city, Cleage expounded his political views in the *Illustrated News*, a bi-weekly newsletter he co-founded and edited. His blunt language and uncompromising commitment to black liberation caused many observers to label him "fiery and controversial," two adjectives often used to describe Malcolm X. Indeed, Cleage's theology of Black Christian nationalism was influenced by the social and political views of his friend "Brother Malcolm," as he called him.

Even during the height of the civil rights movement, Cleage preferred Malcolm's "pragmatic realism" to Martin Luther King's "mystical kind of idealism," which, for him, had no "roots in objective reality."[82] Although he respected King, Cleage believed the former's commitment to theological liberalism blinded him to the radicality of human evil. As he saw it, King's belief that nonviolence and redemptive suffering were the best methods to achieve black liberation demonstrated a basic lack of understanding concerning the nature of power and how it functions in society. Influenced by Reinhold Niebuhr's *Moral Man and Immoral Society*, Cleage explained his critique of Dr. King:

> We've got to make sure the definitions of human nature and society are both sound. If they are not sound, then your whole revolution gets off the track. This was the problem of Dr. King. He was not realistic. You can hope for change, but it must be predicated on reality, not what we dream of. It must be based on people—and their nature—rather than dreams.[83]

It was Cleage's disenchantment with King and the mainline civil rights movement that set the stage for his first meeting with Malcolm X. In June 1963 Cleage worked with the Rev. C. L. Franklin and other members of the Detroit Council for Human Rights (DCHR) to organize the Detroit Freedom March in support of Dr. King and the Southern civil rights movement. Although Cleage criticized King for failing to relate his "dream" to the harsh realities of life in the urban ghettos of the North, he agreed to lead the DCHR's efforts to organize a Northern Christian Leadership Conference after the mold of King's SCLC.[84] But when Cleage invited Conrad Lynn and William Worthy of the Freedom Now Party (a black independent political party of which Cleage was Michigan state chairman) to attend the exploratory Northern Leadership Conference scheduled for November 9-10, 1963, the Rev. C. L. Franklin, chairman of the DCHR, objected to what he considered the "extremist" (i.e., repudiation of nonviolence) and "communist" influence of the Freedom Now Party:

> The Detroit Council for Human Rights wants Freedom Now!— but not with or through the Freedom Now Party. I am not in disagreement with the goals and aspirations of the Freedom Now Party, the Black Muslims, or any other black national group. Rather, I am not in agreement with the means to obtain these goals of political power, economic security, and human dignity for all people ... the DCHR does not court the attendance of Communists or the left wing element.[85]

Cleage refused to accept the "arbitrary limitations" imposed by C. L. Franklin and resigned from his position as chair of the Northern Leadership Conference planning committee. He subsequently joined with members of GOAL (Group On Advanced Leadership) to organize a

Northern Negro Grass Roots Leadership Conference to be held in Detroit at the same time as the more conservative DCHR-sponsored meeting. The two-day Grass Roots conference conducted workshops on key issues including political action, jobs, and self-defense, and culminated with a large public rally at the King Solomon Baptist Church. William Worthy of the Freedom Now Party, Cleage, and others addressed the rally, but the main attraction and featured speaker of the gathering was none other than Malcolm X.

Although Cleage had followed the media coverage of Malcolm and the Nation of Islam, this was his first opportunity to meet Malcolm in person. Several years later he reflected on the encounter:

> At the Grass Roots Conference I heard his best speech, and it was an amazing experience. I spoke just before Brother Malcolm and I was surprised to see that we spoke from the same basic position and projected the same basic conclusions, even though we had not talked together before and had developed our positions independently.[86]

Malcolm's "Message to the Grass Roots" speech was a scathing critique of the mainline civil rights movement and a call for blacks to control the social, political, and economic destiny of their own community. Throughout his ministry and political activity in Detroit, Cleage held the same basic belief that black liberation will not be realized by the attainment of individual civil rights, but rather by the achievement of group power enabling African-Americans to shape and control their own communities. In fact, Cleage echoed the black nationalist philosophy of Brother Malcolm when he asserted that

> Black people do not only want equal rights granted by a powerful dominant white group. Black people want the power to control their own destiny, to define their own identity and condition.[87]

Following the Grass Roots conference, Cleage and Malcolm appeared on the same platform on several more occasions. Cleage was especially grateful for Malcolm's public expression of support for his ministry.[88] But a segment of the leadership of Central Church was not enthused about its pastor's relationship with Minister Malcolm X. In April 1964 a group of church leaders, including trustees, deacons, and charter members, petitioned the Church and Society Committee of the Detroit Metropolitan Association of Congregational Churches to investigate the nature of Cleage's preaching. The group of dissatisfied members complained that Cleage preached hatred of whites, endorsed black nationalism, repudiated integration and nonviolence, and associated with "extreme militant leadership such as Malcolm X."[89] In June, Cleage appeared before the committee and defended his acceptance of black nationalism as consistent with the teachings of Christianity. Concerning the charge that he associated with "extreme militant" leaders, Cleage sarcastically urged the white committee members to invite Malcolm to their churches:

> You ought to have Malcolm to your churches. He's better than the stuff they get. He would come. I would say hurry up and get him here, he could do you so much good.[90]

Despite the tension-filled meeting, the committee voted to acquit Cleage, who thereafter removed from office those church leaders who brought the complaint against him. With the emergence of Black Power two years later and the Detroit rebellion of 1967, the older and more conservative members of Central Church began to leave of their own accord. As young black militants who had little or no respect for Christianity or the black church began to swell the ranks of Cleage's church, the transition from Central Congregational to Shrine of the Black Madonna was well under way. On Easter Sunday, March 26, 1967, Cleage unveiled the large mural of the Black Madonna holding the infant Jesus and announced the formation of the Black Christian Nationalist Movement.

From Slave Christianity to Black Christian Nationalism

One cannot fully understand Cleage's theology without seeing him in relation to Elijah Muhammad's Nation of Islam. Cleage liked the nationalist focus of the Black Muslims and respected their ability to reform the lives of troubled youth who had become involved with drugs, alcohol, and crime. But Cleage also realized that the masses of African-American youth would neither accept the Puritan ethic of the Nation of Islam nor completely renounce the Christian heritage of their parents and grandparents. He therefore sought to develop a Black Christian Nationalist movement that fused the black nationalism of Elijah Muhammad and Malcolm X to an African-American Christian base.

Furthermore, Cleage knew that if the black church was to have any relevance in the age of Black Power and black consciousness, it would have to address key themes and issues raised by Elijah Muhammad. One such issue was the black community's widespread acceptance of the Nation of Islam's counter-racist claim regarding black superiority and white inferiority. Having heard elementary-school children expound the inherent subhumanity of the white race, Cleage observed that many African-Americans believed the Yakub myth without even knowing its origin. Moreover, the myth's influence on the poetry and creative writing of artists such as Imamu Amiri Baraka, Don Lee, Sonia Sanchez, and Nikki Giovanni led Cleage to assert that Elijah Muhammad has "exerted a phenomenal influence upon the thinking of Black people during the past fifty years."[91]

Cleage believed the Yakub myth helped African-Americans affirm their humanity and break their identification with white society. Since blacks were "brainwashed," "indoctrinated," and "programmed" to elevate white culture and devalue their own, Cleage reasoned that the Yakub myth provided an important bridge to black independence. But despite these positive benefits, Cleage believed the myth gave African-Americans a false understanding of their own humanity and obscured the fundamental reasons behind black oppression. Like the pre–Black Power Christian integrationists, Cleage accepted the biblical claim regarding the essential unity of the human family. But whereas Mays, Thurman, and King leaned toward a liberal theological anthropology, Cleage emphasized a neo-orthodox position similar to that of Reinhold Niebuhr and Paul Tillich:

> The white man—even though he acts as a beast, and certainly he does—is not subhuman or nonhuman, and the Black man, though he accepts all of the indignities heaped upon him by the white man, is not an angel . . . The Black man and the white man must be understood in terms of the universal will to power . . . White people have been ruthless in their use of power. Under the same circumstances the Black man will act in the same way.[92]

According to Cleage, white society is corrupt because it pursues an individualistic concept of power. Likewise, he observed that "even as black men scramble after individual power they become bestial."[93] Therefore, Cleage presented his theology of Black Christian Nationalism as a safeguard against "the dehumanizing effects of white individualism." Unless black people "learn to bury their individualism in the life of the Black Nation," he argued, they will succumb to the same demonic forces that have corrupted whites.

Cleage was especially concerned about the individualism that pervaded the theology of the black church. As stated earlier, he believed the counterrevolutionary "slave theology" of the black church—specifically its emphasis on individualistic otherworldly salvation—was one of the biggest stumbling blocks to black liberation. Basically, Cleage reiterated Elijah Muhammad's analysis of the negative impact white Christianity had on the slave community. Like Muhammad, he argued that slave Christianity was characterized by its emphasis on the whiteness of Jesus and God; the preaching of individual salvation as an escape from the harsh realities of slavery; and a focus on petty moral prohibitions against fornication, playing cards, smoking, and drinking. However, unlike Elijah Muhammad, Cleage did acknowledge that slaves took the Christianity preached by their masters and turned it into an instrument of survival. As he saw it, the slaves' emotional religious services offered an escape from the brutality of slavery and gave them hope for a better life in the next world.[94]

Although aspects of slave Christianity enabled blacks to survive extreme oppression, Cleage believed it perpetuated a Western individualism that undermined the collective struggle of the African-American community. Accordingly, he maintained that the slave theology of the "old-time black church," which teaches blacks to wait for God to save them in the next world instead of using their God-given power to change their present plight, must be discarded post haste. In its place must emerge a "new-time black church" with a radical black theology that meets the needs of the black revolution. Cleage emphasized the urgency of the task at hand:

> This is a moment of decision for the self-conscious part of the black church. There are some black churches which are irrelevant. They still jump up and down and cross the Red Sea every Sunday. But there aren't many of those left. They are relics. Dinosaurs. The new church that is coming into being is made up of pastors and congregations who realize they've got to minister to the real needs of the ghetto—the need for black identity and consciousness.[95]

For Cleage, the formulation of a black christology was an important part of the community's quest for a new black identity. Like the NCBC clergy, Cleage knew that the black church "must recapture the loyalty of African-American youth if it is to be significant in the black revolution."[96] Moreover, he developed his black theology in response to Elijah Muhammad's charge that "Christianity is the white man's religion," as did the other radical clergy discussed in this chapter. But Cleage's reinterpretation of Christianity went far beyond that of the NCBC. He refuted claims about the inherent whiteness of Christianity by interpreting the historical Jesus as a Black Messiah who worked to rebuild the Black Nation of Israel and liberate it from white Roman oppression.

Ever vigilant to expose the lie about a white Jesus with blond hair and blue eyes, Cleage argued that "Jesus was a Black Messiah born to a black woman." Cleage rejected the doctrine of the incarnation, proclaiming, "We are not talking about God the Father. We are concerned here with the actual bloodline."[97] In fact, he traced the genealogy of Jesus to prove his claim that Jesus was of African ancestry:

> When I say Jesus was black, I'm not saying, "Wouldn't it be nice if Jesus was black?" or "Let's pretend Jesus was black" or

"It's necessary psychologically for us to believe that Jesus was black." I'm saying that Jesus WAS black. There never was a white Jesus.[98]

Thus, Cleage defended Christianity from Elijah Muhammad's attack by raising the counter-claim that "Christianity is essentially and historically a black man's religion."[99]

According to Cleage, Jesus was a black nationalist leader whose mission was similar to that of Malcolm X. As he saw it, both men "tried to bring black people together, tried to give them a sense of purpose, and to build a Black Nation."[100] In fact, Cleage understood Jesus as the leader of a revolutionary movement, not an organizer of churches. As he saw it, "Jesus didn't spend his life waiting to be crucified." Instead, he devoted his life to two important tasks: organizing the Black Nation to fight against Roman rule, while preaching against the spirit of individualism that corrupted his people—many of whom "were willing to sell out the Nation for personal gain."[101]

In Cleage's view, it was the apostle Paul who distorted the original teachings of the Black Messiah and caused "the tremendous confusion in Christianity." After the death of Jesus, Paul corrupted his teachings with pagan concepts from Greco-Roman philosophy to meet the religious needs of white Gentiles. According to Cleage, Paul "went out organizing Churches from city to city, changing the religion *of* Jesus to a religion *about* Jesus." Paul's new religion *about* Jesus emphasized a resurrection faith that promised eternal life to individuals who believed that Jesus' sacrificial death on the cross atoned for their sins.[102] However, for Cleage, Paul's new gospel had nothing to do with nationalist teachings of Jesus, the Black Messiah. Ironically, Cleage observed, "Jesus was distorted by the institution that was set up in his name":

The Apostle Paul . . . set up Churches everywhere and said, "This is Christianity. All of you who follow after Jesus, come right on in here." And then he changed the whole thing around. No longer was it building a Nation, it was tearing down a Nation. It was leading people right back to the same old individualistic kind of thing which Jesus had fought against all of his life. In the name of Jesus they created a new kind of individualism.[103]

For Cleage, the urgent task of the African-American church is to recover the original teachings of the Black Messiah and apply them to the black revolution. He urged black churches to repudiate the individualistic emphasis of white evangelicalism and realize that the God of the Bible (for Cleage, the Old Testament and the synoptic gospels) was concerned about the salvation of the Nation in the present world, not the salvation of individuals in heaven. Put succinctly, Cleage argued that "the group concept is historic Christianity. Individualism is slave Christianity."[104]

Indeed, just as Elijah Muhammad warned those blacks who refused to join the Nation of Islam that they would be destroyed along with white America, Albert Cleage presented Black Christian Nationalism as the only road to salvation for the African-American community:

> There is no real Black liberation movement in America today apart from Black Christian Nationalism . . . Today we represent only a small minority of Black people, but a minority that is disciplined and totally committed. Black individuals are going to be destroyed. Only Black people who are willing to accept total commitment to a philosophy, a program, and a discipline, and come into the Black Nation can hope to survive.[105]

Finally, although Cleage and the NCBC clergy reached very different conclusions about the essential nature of Christianity, they both embraced their roles as defenders of the faith at a time when it was increasingly unpopular to be young, black, and Christian. While other radical clergy might not have shared Cleage's understanding of Jesus as a revolutionary nationalist descended from Black Africa, they certainly supported his efforts to link the message of Black Power with the liberating gospel of Jesus.

Cleage's ministry demonstrates that the black theology of the late 1960s emerged in the churches as pastors sought to respond to the challenge of Black Power. As Gayraud Wilmore observed, it was pastors like Cleage, "who were preaching every Sunday in the ghettos of the nation," who "hammered out the first tenets of a Black Theology on the anvil of their experience."[106] If Cleage and other radical clergy in the NCBC are credited with outlining the first tenets of black theology, then James Cone must be recognized as the pioneering figure in the development of a systematic theology of black liberation. No other person had a more decisive impact in shaping the black theological agenda. We turn now to an examination of the significant role he played in the ongoing trial of Christianity in the African-American religious experience.

CHAPTER 4

Christianity and Black Power

James Cone's Role in Reinterpreting the Faith

The Rev. Albert Cleage of Detroit is one of the few black ministers who has embraced Black Power as a religious concept and has sought to reorient the church-community on the basis of it. The Black Muslims, through allegiance to Islam, have demonstrated more than any existing black religious community, the relationship between religion and the suffering of black people. It is time for black Christian theologians to begin to relate Christianity to the pain of being black in a white racist society, or else Christianity itself will be discarded as irrelevant in its perverse whiteness. Christianity needs remaking in the light of black oppression.
—James H. Cone, 1969

My very good friend Dr. James H. Cone is undoubtedly a most interesting and meaningful Black theologian. His task is certainly not an easy one. He is our apostle to the Gentiles. He drags white Christians as far as they are able to go (and then some) in interpreting Black theology within the established framework which they can accept and understand.
—Albert B. Cleage, 1972

For what reason had God allowed a poor black boy from Bearden to become a professional systematic theologian? . . . I could not escape the overwhelming conviction that God's Spirit was calling me to do what I could for the enhancement of justice in the world, especially on behalf of my people. It seemed to me that the best contribution I could make was to uncover the hypocrisy of the white church and its theology . . . I felt that God must have been preparing me for this vocation, that is, the task of leveling the most devastating black critique possible against the white church and its theology.
—James H. Cone, 1982

More diligently than any other person, James Cone sought to rein-terpret the spectrum of Christian theology in light of Black Power. Driven by a sense of prophetic urgency given to those with a divine mission, Cone was relentless in his efforts to develop a systematic, black theology of liberation that was both fully *black* and fully *Christian*. As the biblical prophet Jeremiah characterized his call to preach as "a fire shut up in my bones" (20:9), this militant twentieth-century prophet was gripped by a theological calling that consumed his entire being. Like Albert Cleage and the radical NCBC clergy, Cone knew that Christianity was on trial in the African-American community. His pas-sionate commitment to reinterpret the gospel in light of black oppres-sion, therefore, was largely inspired by the pressing need to defend biblical Christianity from the nationalist critique of Elijah Muhammad and secular Black Power advocates who dismissed Christianity as an irrelevant, white religion designed to oppress African-Americans.

Indeed, Cone's desire to relate the Christian gospel to the African-American freedom struggle linked him to the pre–Black Power thought of Benjamin Mays, Howard Thurman, and Martin Luther King, Jr. Their shared commitment to black liberation is the most basic common de-nominator between African-American religious thought before and after Black Power. But Cone's emphasis on blackness as a theological con-cept; his vehement attacks on the theological bankruptcy of white Chris-tianity; and his refusal to accept nonviolence as the *only* Christian means of struggle separated him from the theology of his predecessors. Given the similarities and differences between the theologies of James Cone and pre–Black Power religious thinkers, it is appropriate to ask what role the former played in the ongoing trial of Christianity before the court of African-American opinion. However, one cannot fully appre-ciate the distinctive nature of Cone's contribution without first seeing him in relation to older African-American religious scholars who ques-tioned the viability of efforts to develop a black theology in the late 1960s and early 1970s.

IS THERE A "BLACK THEOLOGY?": THE MISGIVINGS OF PRE–BLACK POWER RELIGIOUS THINKERS

In the previous chapter we examined several early responses to the emergence of Black Power by radical African-American clergy in the NCBC. Through the work of its Theological Commission, the NCBC demonstrated that a relevant, black perspective on the Christian faith was mandatory for the rehabilitation of Christianity in the African-American community. But not all African-American religious thinkers were enthused about the urgent call for a "black theology." Some older scholars who had reached the peak of their careers before the rise of

Black Power were disturbed about the new emphasis on blackness, and viewed it as a distortion of the universality inherent in the Christian message.

This skepticism about the viability of black theology was addressed at the twenty-sixth annual meeting of the prestigious Institute of Religion at Howard University. The theme of the May 1969 conference was "The Black Revolution: Is There a Black Theology?" Frank T. Wilson (an executive of the United Presbyterian Church in the U.S.A. and former dean at Lincoln University and Howard University School of Religion) and Richard I. McKinney (professor of Philosophy at Morgan State College) expressed views that were representative of the misgivings most pre–Black Power religious thinkers had concerning the emergence of black theology. Significantly, these two thinkers had participated in the Institute's ongoing discussion of "The Christian Imperative in Race Relations" in the early 1940s.

Frank T. Wilson wrote the guest editorial for the papers of the conference, which were published in the summer of 1969. Concerned that the term *black theology* "has become cliche even before its substance could be attested or its basic character verified," Wilson emphasized the need for an objective analysis of this new religio-cultural phenomenon. Moreover, Wilson reasoned that since the Institute was established to provide a forum for addressing the relation of the church, theology, and social ethics to aspects of the human experience in contemporary national and international issues, the decisive impact of Black Power on the study of religion warranted further investigation. No doubt, Wilson also felt the need to justify the Institute's deliberations on black theology to those who might view such discussion as an abdication of the group's original mission. He reminded such persons that

> the Institute is being faithful to an historic commitment as it provides means and instrumentality for burrowing into a subject that is surrounded by many question marks. The timeliness of this venture is underscored by rumblings from diverse "pilgrim bands" whose quest for identity is essentially a quest for meaning.[1]

Certainly Wilson's desire to engage in an objective discussion about the prospects of a black theology is praiseworthy. Like the NCBC clergy, he recognized that there is a wealth of material in the African-American religious experience that merits serious theological study. Furthermore, he knew that African-American scholars in the field of religion gravitated to the biblical, historical, and social-ethical disciplines, and that "theology of any kind has been low in scale of professional choice or scholarly interest."[2] But despite his claims to objectivity, it is evident that Wilson, like other African-American religious scholars of his generation, was negatively predisposed to the concept of a *black* theology.

Basically, Wilson questioned the validity of attaching ethnic labels to theology and issued a warning to those in the religious and academic communities who "jump onto many kinds of bandwagons in the effort to identify with the ascendant ideology, strategy or terminology of the time."[3] But Wilson did not acknowledge that his own commitment to the integration "bandwagon" shaped his approach to the concept of a distinctive black theology. That is why he made an important distinction between theological reflection on the black experience, on the one hand, and "black theology" as a "peculiar ethnic phenomenon" on the other. For Wilson, the former is legitimate because it has the potential to "bring fresh and invigorating insights into the ageless quandary about the nature and destiny of man and the relation of God to the whole human enterprise"; while the latter is dangerous because it implies an erroneous attempt "to draw circles around culturally induced modes of expression and to treat these as 'life forms' or 'thought forms' devoid of elements of universality." Based on these initial observations, Wilson reached the tentative conclusion that the excitement about black theology is essentially a "call . . . for Black theologians and not for a generically unique Black Theology."[4] Nevertheless, Wilson believed the Institute's participation in the current discussion about black theology could help to "focus more precisely the direction of the inquiry" and "sharpen the tools for careful probing." In addition, he believed the deliberations called for rational minds and "sensitive spirits" capable of leading the African-American religious community beyond the shallowness of nationalist rhetoric to the real substance of universal theological concern. Therefore, Wilson maintained:

> The Institute of Religion has joined the conversation at a most propitious moment. In such a venture there must be sensitive spirits, as well as competent scholars, who will be alert to the hazards of ethnic pride and aware of the temptation toward a kind of glorified chauvinism.[5]

Professor Richard I. McKinney shared the concerns of Frank T. Wilson and other pre–Black Power religious thinkers. Like other African-American scholars of his generation, McKinney acknowledged the legitimacy of the current search for racial identity and interpreted the call for a black theology as a byproduct of this larger social movement. Given the widespread feeling of inferiority and self-hatred that has affected generations of African-Americans, McKinney saw the proposals for a distinctive black theology as a manifestation of "the search for certain psychological needs and goals of Black people":

> Everywhere we are reminded of the search for racial identity, and it is clear that there are certain Blacks who are in need of this.

If a black man, lacking the sense of ultimate significance, is persuaded that there is a theology especially for him, he will probably experience an inner uplift . . . The plea for a Black Theology, therefore, is calculated to inspire a new sense of dignity, self-respect, and personal significance among Black people.[6]

Beyond this psychological motivation, McKinney also realized that nascent black theology emerged as a protest against the hypocrisy of white Christianity. Aware that "much of the traditional theological and ethical emphases of Whites" has ignored the problem of black oppression, McKinney confirmed the need to expose and correct racist distortions of the gospel:

To the extent that the preachments of the dominant White group in America have emphasized and/or supported racial or class exclusiveness, a need for calling attention to this omission is easily recognized.[7]

However, for McKinney, the issue was not whether the African-American religious community should challenge the racist character of white Christianity; scholars like Benjamin Mays and George Kelsey had already demonstrated the need for this theological critique. Rather, the concern voiced by McKinney, Wilson, and other integrationist thinkers was whether the concepts of a "Black Christ" and a "Black Theology" were legitimate responses to the sins of white Christianity. In other words, McKinney raised the moral question, "Do two wrongs make a right?" What will keep black theology from being "the substitution of one racism for another, this time clad in the respectable gowns of academe?"[8]

Just as Martin Luther King, Jr., believed the negative connotations of the Black Power slogan (domination, violence, and hatred) jeopardized his vision of the beloved community, McKinney believed the term *black theology* implied that God is "primarily pro-Black" and distorted the ideal of universality embodied in the life and teachings of Jesus. Like Benjamin Mays, McKinney referred to the parable of the Good Samaritan to prove that "Jesus was much more concerned with justice than with race."[9] And even if it is probable that Jesus had dark and not white skin, McKinney argued, this had no bearing whatsoever on the essence of his message. Therefore, a theological position that emphasizes the blackness of Christ not only distorts the significance of Jesus' life, but also polarizes American society in general and the Christian community in particular:

The term "Black Theology" . . . is calculated to alienate non-Blacks from Blacks. American society is polarized enough as it is. To have one group of Christians promoting primarily the supposed "blackness" of Christ is to foster division in the "body of Christ" that will require a long time to heal.[10]

Because of these liabilities, McKinney concluded that "Black Theology" had the potential to do more harm than good. Instead of inventing "way out ideologies" to effect social transformation, McKinney urged African-American theologians to work for change "within the context of a close adherence to the essence of the Christian message as we find it in the record of Jesus' life and teachings."[11] What McKinney did not acknowledge was that his interpretation of "the essence of Christianity" was conditioned by his own commitment to the ideology of integration. Consequently, McKinney and other pre–Black Power religious thinkers emphasized the ideal of universality as the central theme of Christianity. That is why most pre–Black Power theologians insisted that the concept of black theology was viable *only* if its "basic thrust"

is in the direction of an increased awareness of all people, Blacks and Whites alike . . . without, at the same time, doing violence to the concept of a universal God and of a Jesus who is concerned for all humanity.[12]

CHRISTIANITY, LIBERATION, AND THE EMERGENCE OF JAMES CONE

While pre–Black Power thinkers emphasized *universality* as the essence of the gospel, James Cone accentuated *liberation* as the "basic thrust" of the Christian message. Just as the NCBC clergy underscored the need for the black church and community to shift its emphasis from love (as defined by Martin Luther King, Jr., and the civil rights movement) to power (as defined by Stokely Carmichael and the Black Power movement), James Cone stressed the importance of shifting the emphasis in African-American theological discourse from universality to liberation.

To be sure, many of Cone's critics believed his unyielding commitment to black liberation compromised his allegiance to the universal nature of the gospel. Though Cone was aware of the misgivings voiced by pre–Black Power thinkers, he was not interested in preserving the universality of Christianity at the expense of black liberation. Therefore, he let nothing soften his radical call for the "complete emancipation from white oppression by whatever means black people deem necessary."[13] While Cone insisted that black theology was Christian theology, and therefore consistent with the universality of the gospel, it is clear that the ideal of universality was not the theological norm that guided his work. On the contrary, Cone wrote during the height of the black revolution, and he knew that African-American youth would discard Christianity altogether if theologians did not begin to relate the gospel to "the pain of being black in a white racist society." Therefore, he contended that universality was an unacceptable norm for a radical black theology; if Christianity was to be a source of liberation and not enslavement, Cone argued, it needed "remaking in the light of black oppression."[14]

Whereas pre–Black Power thinkers believed the ideal of universality was the norm that legitimated African-American theological reflection, Cone advocated a theological methodology based on the black nationalist affirmation, "The fact that I am Black is my ultimate reality." Accordingly, Cone articulated his theological norm in opposition to the excessive universalism of pre–Black Power Christian thinkers:

> My identity with *blackness*, and what it means for millions living in a white world, controls the investigation. It is impossible for me to surrender this basic reality for a "higher, more universal" reality. Therefore, if a higher, Ultimate Reality is to have meaning, it must relate to the very essence of blackness.[15]

Clearly, there are important methodological differences between Cone's approach to theology and that of his predecessors. As we shall see later in this chapter, even some of Cone's colleagues in the black theology movement objected to what they considered his uncritical acceptance of Black Power. However, one cannot fully grasp Cone's relation to pre–Black Power thinkers and the black theologians who criticized him, without first understanding how the formative factors in his development shaped his perspective on Christianity, racism, and black oppression.

Biographical Sketch

Like Benjamin Mays, Howard Thurman, and Martin Luther King, Jr., James Cone knew firsthand the humiliation of racial segregation and discrimination. Born on August 5, 1938, in Fordyce, Arkansas (and raised in Bearden), the reality of southern racism shaped Cone's theological consciousness just as it did his predecessors. But whereas Mays, Thurman, and King developed their theological views in dialogue with the political ideology of integration, Cone (forty-four years younger than Mays and thirty-eight years younger than Thurman) articulated his theology in dialogue with the political philosophy of black nationalism. This basic generational difference is the most fundamental reason for the sharp contrast in theological views. But it would be a mistake to conclude that Cone's militant perspective was a complete departure from the views of his predecessors. On the contrary, I believe an analysis of Cone's development will show the influence of Negro theologians on his thinking and provide important insights into the continuity that exists between pre– and post–Black Power religious thought.

Apart from the civil rights and Black Power movements, two foundational experiences shaped Cone's perspective on the relation between Christianity and racial injustice: his upbringing in Bearden, Arkansas, and six years of graduate theological training at Garrett Seminary-Northwestern University in Evanston, Illinois. Cone's introduction to Christianity at the Macedonia African Methodist Episcopal Church and his encounter with southern white racism were the first building blocks in his theological development. The fact that Cone first reflected on the meaning of the gospel in the context of racial segregation had a profound impact on his theological consciousness. Similarly, Cone's encounter with the racism of white professors at a *Christian* seminary in the North sharpened his awareness of the need for an interpretation of the gospel that took black oppression as its point of departure. Therefore, one cannot understand Cone's radical black theology without an understanding of how personal encounters with the racism of white Christians in the South and the North fueled his militancy and formed the existential basis for his scathing critique of white Christianity.

Like Benjamin Mays, Cone credits his parents and church for instilling in him a vibrant spirituality that reinforced his self-esteem and inspired him to resist white oppression. In *My Soul Looks Back* he calls his mother, Lucy Cone, "one of the pillars" of the church and "a firm believer in God's justice."[16] She taught her sons (Charles Jr., Cecil, and James) that their self-worth was not dependent on white society but rather bestowed by God who created all people equal. The faith Lucy Cone transmitted to her children enabled them to know that God is a "very present help in times of trouble." Thus, the spirituality of the black church that nourished Mays, Thurman, and King also sustained Cone in moments of crisis and despair.

While it was Cone's mother who taught him the importance of cultivating faith, it was his father who demonstrated how to fight white racism with tenacity and courage. Cone characterized his father as a proud man who practiced what he preached—namely, the need to confront white society from the position of strength and independence. Charlie Cone resisted the racist, southern practice of referring to black men and women as "boy" and "girl," and was prepared to fight any white person who used those terms in his presence. Similarly, Charlie Cone's unyielding commitment to economic and political independence explains why he refused to work for whites (even in financially difficult times) and rejected money from white politicians who wanted to post stickers on his property during election time. These actions, and others like them, taught James and his brothers that dignity and integrity are more important than money, and that one's commitment to the truth must not be compromised because of dependence on white society.[17]

The lessons James Cone learned from his parents had a profound impact on the content and style of his work, which he humbly regarded as "just dim reflections" of what his parents taught and lived.[18] They, along with the church and supportive black teachers from grade school through college, gave Cone all the tools he needed to excel in a racist society. Nevertheless, the young Cone struggled to interpret the meaning of Christianity in the context of black suffering. As young aspiring theologians, he and his brother Cecil wondered why a loving God would permit the continued oppression of blacks at the hands of whites, who, even more perplexing, also claimed an allegiance to the Christian faith. How could white Christians oppose school integration, exclude blacks from their churches, and yet claim to love God and Jesus Christ? Reflecting on the impact of this dilemma on his consciousness, Cone wrote, "The dual reality of white injustice and black faith, as a part of the structure of life, created a tension in my being that has not been resolved."[19]

Clearly, the theological questions Cone raised as a teenager were the same issues Negro theologians addressed throughout the 1930s and 1940s. As we have seen, the existence of segregation and the support it received from white churches formed the bases of their critique of American Christianity. It is also important to note that the values Cone learned from his parents, which continue to shape his ministry as a theologian, were repeatedly emphasized in the writings and speeches of Benjamin Mays, Howard Thurman, and their most famous protege, Martin Luther King, Jr. Just as Mays influenced King's decision to enter the ministry, King's commitment to racial justice reinforced Cone's emerging identity as a preacher of the gospel. Cone entered the ministry at the age of sixteen, preaching his first sermon on December 12, 1954. One year later, Martin Luther King was thrust into the national spotlight as the leader of the historic Montgomery bus boycott that launched the civil rights movement. A student at Shorter Junior College at the time, Cone followed the boycott closely in his role as reporter of current events at the daily chapel assemblies. Like other young ministers in the South, he was greatly influenced by King's dual commitment to academic excellence and social justice, and he acknowledged that "Martin King was my primary resource on how to think about the gospel and the black struggle for freedom." Indeed, King helped a generation of young ministers realize that "fighting for justice was as important as preaching the gospel on Sunday morning."[20]

As fate would have it, King's rise to fame had a profound impact on Cone's theological development in the 1950s, as did King's tragic death a decade later. The important point to underscore at this juncture, however, is that Cone's development as a young minister and theologian coincided with the emergence of Martin Luther King, Jr., and the civil rights struggle of the 1950s and 1960s. Significantly, the thinking of Mays and Thurman, which culminated in the ministry of Martin Luther King, is the same theological perspective that shaped the early thought of James Cone. Herein lies an important link between pre– and post–Black Power thought that must not be overlooked.

When Cone graduated from Philander Smith College and entered Garrett Seminary (Evanston, Illinois) in 1958, he encountered a northern, intellectual racism that tested his faith as much as the racism he encountered in the South. Like all black students who attended white seminaries before the rise of Black Power (and unfortunately even some today), Cone was discouraged from analyzing racism as a theological problem by white professors who viewed it as a political issue unrelated to serious reflection on the Christian gospel. Furthermore, throughout his six years of residence at Garrett-Northwestern (1958-1964), not one black author appeared on the required reading list for Cone's course of study. As he later observed, this form of racism "had profound effects on the self-esteem of black students" by suggesting that African-Americans had no intellectual contribution to make regarding an understanding of the gospel.[21]

It was in this context that Cone, the young seminarian, first heard Howard Thurman speak at the Rockefeller Chapel of the University of Chicago. Although he does not recall the specific content of Thurman's address, he remembers the event as "a breath of fresh air in a theological atmosphere defined by neo-orthodox and the death of God theologies." Years later he described the style and presence of Thurman as one who spoke "about Jesus as if he knew him as the friend next door":

> His style was slow, with many long pauses between words and sentences. His penetrating eyes made one feel that he saw the very depths of your soul. His presence was powerful, almost overwhelming and completely unforgettable . . . He made me think there was hope for me as a black theologian, struggling to make sense out of the gospel of Jesus in an environment that did not acknowledge my humanity.[22]

Despite the reassurance provided by Thurman's lecture and professors William Hordern and Phillip Watson (mentors who assured Cone of his ability to do Ph.D. work), Cone's graduate experience was as much a test of character as it was an academic challenge. As Garrett-Northwestern's first African-American doctoral candidate in systematic theology, Cone felt obligated to prove wrong those white professors who questioned his intellectual capability. In light of the odds against him, he experienced a tremendous feeling of accomplishment when he graduated with the Ph.D. degree in the spring of 1965. Having mastered the theology of Karl Barth, Emil Brunner, and Paul Tillich, he was now free to face the challenge of relating systematic theology to the black freedom struggle.

However, when Cone began his teaching career at his alma mater, Philander Smith College, he had a difficult time relating the study of systematic theology to the black experience. Consequently, he found himself in "an intellectual quandary" when faced with the responsibility of making theology relevant to the concerns of his young students. He later described his dilemma like this:

> What did Barth, Tillich, and Brunner have to do with young black girls and boys coming from the cotton fields of Arkansas, Tennessee, and Mississippi seeking to make a new future for themselves? This was *the* major question for me . . . The contradiction between theology as a discipline and the struggle for black freedom in the streets was experienced at the deepest level of my being.[23]

Cone's predicament was not easily resolved. The emergence of Black Power in the summer of 1966 further intensified his identity crisis as an African-American theologian with a doctorate in European theology. Was not Christianity, insofar as he studied it at Garrett-Northwestern, "the white man's religion," as Elijah Muhammad and other black nationalists had claimed? When Cone left Philander Smith and began teaching at Adrian College (Adrian, Michigan), he was forced to confront this question in a more decisive way.

The Impact of Black Power on James Cone

Isolated in a suburb of Detroit, Cone rejoiced when he read the NCBC statement on Black Power in July of 1966. Although he did not become a member of the organization until the spring of 1969, after the publication of his *Black Theology and Black Power*, he felt encouraged by efforts to relate Christianity to the more radical elements of the black liberation struggle. But the NCBC statement alone was not enough to resolve Cone's dilemma. Although he agreed with the NCBC interpretation of Black Power, he nevertheless felt that creative artists like Richard Wright, James Baldwin, Ralph Ellison, and Amiri Baraka offered a more substantive response to the problem of black oppression than African-American Christian thinkers.

Still frustrated by his inability to relate systematic theology to black oppression, Cone considered the possibility of returning to graduate school for a Ph.D. in literature. Had it not been for the Detroit "riot" of

July 1967 (which left thirty-six black people killed by gunfire from the Detroit police, state troopers, and national guardsmen) and the assassination of Martin Luther King, Jr., in April 1968 and the urban rebellions that followed, Cone might have become a quiet English professor instead of a radical black theologian who helped change the direction of twentieth-century African-American religious thought.[24] Interestingly enough, the Detroit rebellion that catapulted Albert Cleage into the theological and ecclesiastical spotlight also served as a catalyst for awakening within Cone a prophetic calling to relate systematic theology to the problems of the African-American church and community. Geographically located not far from one another, both Cleage and Cone were forced to meet the challenge of prophetic Christian leadership at a time when it was increasingly unpopular to be both black and Christian. Just as the 1966 Meredith March inspired the NCBC's Black Power statement, so the 1967 Detroit rebellion pushed both men to articulate a perspective on the Christian faith that embraced Black Power. Although Cone did not share Cleage's nationalist biblical interpretation, he did respect the latter's ministry as an example of what needed to take place in the realm of African-American theological discourse. That is why he wrote in *Black Theology and Black Power* that "the Rev. Albert Cleage of Detroit is one of the few black ministers who has embraced Black Power as a religious concept and has sought to reorient the church-community on the basis of it."[25] Indeed, the series of sermons Cleage preached in the wake of the Detroit uprising (published in 1968 under the title *The Black Messiah*) demonstrated his ability to relate Christianity to the plight of black people.

Like other early responses to Black Power, Cone's conviction that black theologians must begin relating the gospel to black oppression was a direct response to Elijah Muhammad's nationalist critique of Christianity as a white religion incapable of meeting the spiritual and political needs of the African-American community. In fact, in a statement often overlooked by interpreters of his theology, Cone credited the Nation of Islam and not the denominational black churches with having "demonstrated more than any existing black religious community" the need to make faith relevant to black suffering.[26] Thus, when Cone spoke of stripping the gospel of its "whiteness," and reinterpreting the Christian tradition in order to "destroy the influence of heretical white American Christianity,"[27] he was signaling the need for a prophetic response to the nationalist critique of Christianity.

While NCBC's Theological Commission was laying the groundwork for black theology, African-American students and religious scholars waged a war on white seminaries for excluding the black religious experience from the theological curriculum. Not surprisingly, black clergy, students, and professors in white denominations and institutions were acutely sensitive to this critique and therefore more determined than their colleagues in black institutions to prove that it was not true.

There can be no doubt that Charles Shelby Rooks (a 1953 graduate of Union Theological Seminary, New York, and Executive Director of the Fund for Theological Education from 1960 to 1974) was the most instrumental figure in coordinating efforts to make the study of African-American Christianity an integral part of theological education. In the fall of 1968 black seminarians from around the country gathered at Boston University to discuss the significance of the black church for theological education. Rooks and other leaders in the early development of black theology—including Albert Cleage, Vincent Harding, Nathan Wright, C. Eric Lincoln, and Benjamin Payton—addressed the conference, emphasizing the importance of relevant theological training to meet the specific needs of leadership in African-American churches and communities.[28]

More forcefully than anyone else, Rooks had been asking for several years how black seminarians could be adequately prepared for ministry in black churches if there were no courses on the history, theology, and sociology of the African-American religious experience? Furthermore, how could black students and professors be faithful to the spirit of Black Power if they failed to confront white seminaries that excluded the black experience from the theological curriculum? For the first time, the African-American theological community began to demand answers to these questions in a way it had never done before the rise of Black Power. In relentless fashion, Shelby Rooks brought these concerns to the attention of white and black seminary presidents and theological educators. In fact, Rooks and others were so deliberate in their efforts to reshape the seminaries that they became affectionately known as "the black mafia of theological education."[29] Indeed, the Boston conference provided an excellent opportunity for faculty and student leaders to organize and plan their attack on racism in the white seminaries. Rooks, who must have been considered "the Godfather" by those who used the mafia analogy, described the significance of the gathering:

> The meeting was important because not only did it bring together the new breed of thinkers about the African-American churches, but the students themselves were able to exchange ideas and develop a common strategy. In Boston, a new sense of purpose was forged, and a new willingness to fight the battle together emerged.[30]

Although Cone did not attend the Boston consultation, he was certainly one of "the new breed of thinkers" who would have a decisive impact on the content of American theological education. Several months after the meeting, Cone, still isolated in the quiet suburb of Adrian, Michigan, was invited by a former Garrett classmate to deliver a lecture at Elmhurst College in February 1968. He used the occasion to articulate his emerging thoughts on the relation between Christianity and Black Power, and to proclaim his "liberation from the bondage of white theology."[31]

"Christ's Central Message to Twentieth-Century America"

James Cone's 1968 essay "Christianity and Black Power" marked the beginning of his career as a provocative writer and militant theologian dedicated to the "full emancipation of black people from white oppression by whatever means black people deem necessary." Indeed, Cone's appropriation of Malcolm's "by any means necessary" position demonstrated his radical commitment to the spirit of Black Power. Yet, his conviction that

> the time has come for the Church to challenge the power-structure with the power of the *Gospel*, knowing that nothing less than *immediate* and *total* emancipation of all people is consistent with the message and style of Jesus Christ[32]

linked his views with the prophetic Christian stance of Martin L. King, Jr., and pre–Black Power theologians. Cone's essay also launched what would become an ongoing critique of the white church and its theology for ignoring the suffering of black people throughout history.

Like pre–Black Power religious thinkers, Cone criticized white Christians for failing to take a firm stance against racial injustice. As Benjamin Mays implored white denominations to do more than pass an occasional resolution and wait to be congratulated, Cone declared that if the church was to be faithful to the message of Jesus Christ, it must renounce its allegiance to the status quo and demand fundamental changes in the oppressive structures of American society. Like the Negro theologians of the 1940s and 1950s, he lamented that "the society is falling apart for want of moral leadership and moral example, but the Christian Church passes innocuously pious resolutions and waits to be congratulated."[33]

However, it is important to emphasize that Cone radicalized the critique of pre–Black Power thinkers and made bold theological assertions that Mays, Thurman, and King would not have made. First and foremost, integrationist thinkers who appealed to the moral conscience of white Christians would not have called the white church the contemporary manifestation of the Antichrist, as Cone did when he further developed his argument in *Black Theology and Black Power*.[34] They would have considered such inflammatory language a stumbling block to racial harmony and reconciliation. But Cone was not primarily concerned about reconciliation between the races; on the contrary, he was angered by white ministers who condemned the violence of riots but said nothing about the oppressive conditions that produced them. Accordingly, in his 1968 lecture Cone maintained that white clergymen who take this position forfeit the rights to their credentials as Christian ministers and become inhuman animals—"just like any other racist."[35]

Moreover, Cone called Black Power "Christ's central message to twentieth-century America" at a time when most Christian leaders were either skeptical or openly opposed to the concept.[36] Pre–Black Power theologians who objected to the connotations of violence and domination in the Black Power slogan must have cringed when Cone claimed that "the message of Black Power is the message of Christ Himself."[37] In fact, the thesis in Cone's 1968 essay was stated more sharply and provocatively than anything found in the NCBC statements of 1966 and 1967:

> If Jesus is not in the ghetto, if he is not where men are living at the edge of existence, if he is somehow ensconced in the split-level hypocrisy of suburbia, then the Gospel is a prevarication and Christianity is a mistake. Christianity cannot be alien to Black Power; it *is* Black Power![38]

To be sure, Cone knew that his close identification of Black Power with the Christian revelation was theologically dangerous. Having written his doctoral thesis on the theology of Karl Barth (who strongly criticized liberal theologians for ignoring the "infinite qualitative distinction between God and man"), he knew that some interpreters would think he was guilty of distorting the eternal gospel by linking it to a transient political movement.[39] But Cone was so convinced about the truth of his argument that he disregarded the traditional rules of European theology. As he saw it, the matter was quite simple: Both the gospel of Jesus and Black Power proclaim the liberation of the oppressed. If God is revealed in history liberating the oppressed from bondage, then God must be working through the secular activity of Black Power![40]

Cone's initial attempt to reinterpret Christianity in light of Black Power coincided with efforts made by African-American lay and clergy leaders in the United Methodist church. In many ways February 1968 proved to be an important turning point in Cone's career, for not only did he write his first essay on the relation between Christianity and Black Power, but he also attended the organizing meeting of the Black Methodists for Church Renewal in Cincinnati, Ohio. While there, Cone was introduced to the person who would become the most influential supporter of his work as a young theologian: C. Eric Lincoln, at the time professor of sociology and religion at Union Theological Seminary in New York. Lincoln read Cone's essay and assured him that he had the potential to make a significant contribution to African-American religious thought. From this point on, Cone's vocation as a black theologian with a distinctive perspective on the Christian faith became increasingly clear.[41]

The assassination of Martin Luther King, Jr., in April 1968 intensified Cone's commitment to reinterpret Christian faith in light of Black Power. The tragic irony that the great prophet of nonviolence was killed by white violence pushed many young African-Americans further in the direction of Black Power. As young inner-city blacks expressed their rage and grief in the form of riots, Cone expressed his anger by writing a book that would have a decisive impact on the American theological community. Indeed, when Cone sat down to write *Black Theology and Black Power* in the summer of 1968, he consciously intended to rock the theological community in the same way Karl Barth did when he repudiated liberal theology half a century earlier. The knowledge that his argument would cause "the theological hairs on the heads of white theologians and preachers to stand up straight" energized Cone and strengthened his resolve to expose the racist character of the white church and its theology.[42]

Whereas pre–Black Power theologians tended to write in a calm, objective style, Cone wrote with a passion and rage unprecedented in twentieth-century African-American Christian thought. If Jesus and the prophets got angry, Cone reasoned, "is it not time for theologians to get upset?" In light of his rearing in the segregated South; the racism he encountered at Garrett-Northwestern; the recent murder of Martin Luther King and the response of white preachers to the riots that followed, it was not possible for Cone to conceal his intolerance for traditional appeals to nonviolence and reconciliation. As he saw it, there was no time to engage in scholarly debates about the fine points of classical theology; the rise of Black Power demanded that African-American theologians demonstrate their uncompromising commitment to black liberation by reinterpreting Christian faith in the light of black oppression:

> This work, then, is written with a definite attitude, the attitude of
> an angry black man, disgusted with the oppression of black people
> in America and with the scholarly demand to be "objective" about
> it. Too many people have died, and too many are on the edge of
> death.[43]

Clearly, Cone believed that an interpretation of Christianity that emphasized universality and racial harmony would have been an inappropriate response to black oppression in a new age of Black Power and black consciousness. In fact, he proclaimed that the Black Power movement placed the African-American community "on the thresh-old of a new order" that was radically different from the old order of integration and assimilation.[44] "In a world that has taught blacks to hate themselves," Cone argued, "the new black man does not tran-scend blackness, but accepts it, loves it as a gift of the Creator."[45] Whereas integrationist thinkers downplayed the significance of color, the new order of black consciousness called on African-Americans to embrace blackness as "the primary datum of their humanity."[46] But what did Cone mean by this, and why did he take a theological posi-tion that would appear to distort the biblical notion of humanity?

To be sure, Cone's reading of the Bible confirmed that God did not intend for skin color to be the essence of humanity. Like Martin Luther King, he believed that human beings should be judged on the content of their character and not the color of their skin. But, for Cone, the historical reality of white racism forced black people to take a theologi-cal stand that would not be necessary in a perfect world free of racism. Since African-Americans are not living in the consummated Kingdom of God, they must come to understand "the meaning of their blackness in the context of whiteness" by affirming the very characteristic which white society denigrates.[47] Post–Black Power theologians, therefore, did not emphasize blackness simply because they thought it would be an interesting theological concept to discuss and write books about; rather, they believed the celebration of blackness was an essential part of black liberation. By rejecting white conceptions of their humanity and defin-ing themselves in light of blackness, African-Americans were asserting their determination to be free. Cone explains:

> The new black consciousness arises from the need of black people to defend themselves against those who seek to destroy them . . .
> Our defense is at the same time a definition, a way of moving in the world, and it is programmed according to our need for lib-eration.[48]

More than any other post–Black Power theologian, Cone took the themes of blackness and liberation and made them essential ingredi-ents of Christian theology. Indeed, his theological interpretation of these two concepts distinguished his thought from that of his predecessors, as well as some of his colleagues in the black theology movement. Re-garding black theology's doctrine of God, Cone's argument was per-suasive. Since black people are degraded *because* of their blackness, and the biblical record consistently demonstrates God's intention to liberate the oppressed, is it not theologically appropriate, even neces-sary, to speak of God's blackness when describing the essence of di-vine activity in America? For Cone, the answer was a resounding yes. As he saw it, "The blackness of God means that God has made the oppressed condition God's own condition. This is the essence of the biblical revelation."[49] No doubt, Cone was fully aware that he was departing radically from the integrationist stance of pre–Black Power theologians when he further asserted that:

> There is no place in black theology for a colorless God in a society where human beings suffer precisely because of their color. The black theologian must reject any conception of God which stifles black self-determination by picturing God as a God of all peoples. Either God is identified with the oppressed to the point that their experience becomes God's experience, or God is a God of racism.[50]

Likewise, christologically, Cone combined the themes of blackness and liberation in a style that was uniquely his own. In a society that despises dark skin, he argued, Christ "takes on blackness" as a sign of God's identification with the victims of society. Furthermore, since the historical Jesus was a poor Jew in active solidarity with the downtrodden of his day, the risen Christ is present in the ghetto where people are oppressed because of their blackness. Thus, for Cone, not only was Jesus of Nazareth literally non-white, but his earthly ministry in first century Palestine and present activity in contemporary America confirm the divine intention to liberate the black oppressed. Therefore, Christ cannot be white with blond hair and blue eyes; on the contrary, Christ meets oppressed blacks where they are and becomes one of them. Cone seems to have enjoyed driving home his point:

> The "raceless" American Christ has a light skin, wavy brown hair, and sometimes—wonder of wonders—blue eyes. For whites to find him with big lips and kinky hair is as offensive as it was for the Pharisees to find him partying with tax-collectors. But whether whites want to hear it or not, *Christ is black, baby*, with all of the features which are so detestable to white society.[51]

As Cone viewed it, to deny Christ's blackness in the twentieth century is equivalent to denying his Jewishness in the first century. Theological assertions about the blackness of God and Jesus Christ, therefore, were not merely attempts to rehabilitate the psyche of black people, as some pre–Black Power thinkers maintained. For Cone, they were affirmations of profound theological truth that revealed the very essence of the Christian faith.[52]

The publication of *Black Theology and Black Power* in March 1969—the same month student demonstrations began at Colgate Rochester Divinity School—catapulted Cone into the spotlight of the American theological community. Consequently, he left the isolated setting of

Adrian, Michigan, and joined the prestigious faculty of the Union Theological Seminary in New York City, where he relished the opportunity to articulate his scathing critique of Euro-American theology before "some of the most respected white theological minds in the country."[53] Yet, Cone also constructed his theology in dialogue with some of the best black theological minds in the nation, many of whom disagreed with his perspective. A brief discussion of their response will demonstrate the diversity of perspectives that characterized the black theology movement and provide more insight into the relationship between pre– and post–Black Power religious.

Cone's Black Theology on Trial

How Christian Is It?

By the time *A Black Theology of Liberation* appeared in 1970, Cone, still in his early thirties, had become the most prominent black theologian in the country. This was a source of great concern for older theologians such as J. Deotis Roberts and Major Jones, who believed Cone's militant perspective jeopardized the essence of the Christian faith. In opposition to what they regarded as Cone's exclusive concern for black people, they sought to develop what I call a black theology of race relations that was sensitive to the concerns of both pre– and post–Black Power theologians.

While Roberts and Jones embraced black consciousness, they were more inclined toward the integrationist, nonviolent perspective of Benjamin Mays, Howard Thurman, and Martin Luther King, Jr. Consequently, they raised the question, How Christian is Cone's black theology? Did not his unqualified support of the black revolution compromise his commitment to the ethical formulations of biblical Christianity? Both Roberts and Jones answered in the affirmative; they believed Cone's radical black theology jeopardized the universality of the Christian faith.

J. Deotis Roberts was the first black theologian to question the Christian identity of Cone's theology. Prior to the rise of Black Power, he studied Christian Platonism in the 1950s and wrote books on the relation between faith and reason in the thought of Pascal, and religion and philosophy in seventeenth-century England.[54] Roberts (an ordained Baptist minister deeply influenced by his contemporary, Martin Luther King, Jr.) was teaching at Howard University when the cry of Black Power shook the nation and inspired pastors and scholars to develop a *black* Christian theology. Like others, he responded to the challenge and shifted his intellectual interests from European philosophy to the development of black theology. Therefore, J. Deotis Roberts, by his own description, stood "somewhere between the generations—that is,

on the boundary between the black militants and the old fashioned
civil rights integrationists."⁵⁵

Though Roberts claimed to stand "somewhere between the generations," his theology was much closer to the pre–Black Power thought
of Benjamin Mays, Howard Thurman, and Martin Luther King, Jr. His
book *Liberation and Reconciliation: A Black Theology* (1971) expressed his
firm belief that Cone had overlooked the Christian doctrine of reconciliation and its implications for race relations in America. Roberts
maintained that the "inflammatory rhetoric" and "by any means necessary" approach of Cone's theology were a hindrance to racial reconciliation and an unbiblical foundation for Christian ethics.⁵⁶ Accordingly, Roberts wrote:

> While Cone confesses an indifference toward whites, I care. James
> Cone is on the fence between the Christian faith and Black Power.
> It will be necessary for Cone to decide presently where he will
> take his firm stand. The present writer takes his stand within the
> Christian theological circle.⁵⁷

Roberts was particularly distressed that Cone's status as "the diplo-
mat of black theology" caused some white theologians to ignore "all
other black theologians" and use "Cone's work as a 'straw man' to
reject the entire enterprise." Moreover, in Roberts's mind, black theologians uncritically accepted Cone's theology, making both white and
black scholars powerless to strike "a telling blow at the foundations of
the deficiencies in his program." Therefore, Roberts forcefully urged
the American Christian community to put Cone's theology on trial:

> His location as a professor in a prestigious theological school has
> given him a privileged status as a theologian at home and abroad
> . . . he has been approved by the theological establishment. And,
> therefore, he is endorsed by whites and anointed by blacks. This
> makes this critical task most urgent. He is the key spokesman for
> black theology at home and overseas. In addition, Cone assumes
> that he speaks authoritatively for the entire movement. *For the
> sake of this important movement in the life of the Christian Faith,* his
> credentials to make the claim to absolute truth for all black theo-
> logical reflection *must not go unchallenged* [emphasis mine].⁵⁸

Like Roberts, Major Jones evaluated Cone's theology in light of his
commitment to the pre–Black Power thought of Mays, Thurman, and
King. In fact, Jones and King were doctoral students at Boston University at the same time.⁵⁹ Trained in Christian ethics, Jones believed Cone's
unqualified commitment to black liberation caused him to overlook

the ethical formulations of biblical Christianity that are the foundation of the faith. Therefore, Jones sought to correct "the rather narrow and selective way" Cone applied scripture to the black liberation struggle, and to provide "broader ethical formulations for black theology and the politics of black liberation."[60]

According to Jones, Cone's pro–black theology compromised the Christian notion of a universal God who loves all people the same, the black oppressed and white oppressor. Accordingly, he emphasized that blacks cannot exempt themselves from biblical standards of ethical and moral conduct simply because they are the victims of oppression. Indeed, Jones restated the position of pre–Black Power theologians when he wrote, "Christian love would demand no less than that the ex-slave, oppressed black man must maintain a spirit of love which will dominate his attitude and his response toward both insult and injury from the oppressor." Moreover, an ethic of Christian love in race relations teaches the black oppressed to realize that their destiny is tied with that of white oppressors, and that "the slave cannot insist on being recognized as a human being unless he also extends recognition to the master as a human being."[61]

In opposition to Cone's ethic of "liberation by any means necessary," Jones contended that the Bible compels believers to use Christian (read: nonviolent) means to achieve the end of black liberation. For Jones, Cone's theology "seems to commit God to man's way, rather than to commit man to God's way."[62] Moreover, Jones believed Cone overstated God's identification with the black liberation struggle, thereby implying that "God is only on the black man's side." He was particularly concerned about Cone's provocative statement repudiating "any conception of God which stifles black self-determination by picturing God as a God of all people."[63] As Jones saw it, "If God is not the God of all people, then he is the God of no people." Jones rejected black theology that interpreted God on the side of blacks alone, "without compromise or willingness to recognize him as being the God of the enemy as well."[64]

Therefore, Jones raised questions about the Christian nature of Cone's theology, and basically re-presented Negro theology with a thin veneer of black consciousness. Like Martin Luther King, he raised questions about a brand of black consciousness that did not express itself in love for whites as well. Consequently, he asked, "Can human requirements be fully met by black people loving only black people," as implied in Cone's theology?[65] For J. Deotis Roberts and Major Jones, the answer was an emphatic no. They believed Cone's theology failed to emphasize the interrelated structure of human life, and so they articulated a black theology of race relations that sought to correct what they considered the excesses of his perspective.

How Black Is It?

On the other hand, there were some black theologians who argued that Cone's theology was too universal and lacked sufficient attention to non-Christian sources of black theological reflection. Scholars in the Society for the Study of Black Religion (organized in 1970 under the leadership of Shelby Rooks) launched a relentless critique of Cone's perspective, claiming that his dependence on European theological concepts severed black theology from its African roots and black folk culture.[66] For example, Gayraud Wilmore believed Cone's desire to legitimate black theology in the academic guild led to an inordinate "strain toward universality" and a serious neglect of non-Christian black religiosity. In *Black Religion and Black Radicalism,* first published in 1972, Wilmore expressed his concern poignantly:

> Is Black theology simply the Blackenization of the whole spectrum of traditional Christian theology, with particular emphasis on the liberation of the oppressed, or does it find in the experience of the oppression of Black people, as *black,* a singular religiosity, identified not only with Christianity, but with other religions as well?[67]

Wilmore called for a theological examination of the "ebb and flow of Black folk religion" that finds expression in the sects and cults of the ghetto, the black arts movement, and the philosophy of black nationalist organizations.

Likewise, Charles Long, a historian of religion trained at the University of Chicago, criticized Cone for failing to plumb the depths of the non-Christian black religious experience. In fact, Long maintained that non-church black religious orientations "have often touched deeper religious issues regarding the true situation of black communities than those of the church leaders of their time."[68]

Moreover, like Wilmore, Long claimed that Cone's allegiance to European theological categories kept him from grasping the true essence of black religion, which is not specifically Christian. Even more than Wilmore, however, Long believed that systematic theology is a Eurocentric discipline inherently incapable of penetrating the depths of black religion. Although Cone's theology focused on the black experience, its language and methodology were "still within the cultural arena of Western religious meanings," and therefore not consistent with the black reality he sought to describe.[69] For Long, black religion

> is more than a structure of thought; it includes experience, expression, motivations, intentions, behaviors, styles, and rhythms. Its first and fundamental expression is not on the level of thought.

It gives rise to thought, *but a form of thought that embodies the precision and nuances of its sources* [emphasis mine].[70]

Clearly, Long believed that the discipline of the history of religions, "though created from the Enlightenment understanding of the human venture,"[71] is considerably more open to the authentic expression of black religion and culture than the discipline of systematic theology.[72]

How Liberating Is It?

William R. Jones, a Unitarian-Universalist minister, philosopher of religion, and professor at Florida State University, shared the concerns of Wilmore and Long. But more than any other scholar during the period, Jones challenged Cone's central thesis that God is the Liberator of oppressed blacks. Given the ongoing legacy of intense black suffering, Jones challenged Cone to cite definitive black liberation events that validate his claim that God unequivocally delivers the *black* oppressed. In fact, Jones maintained that the historical reality of perpetual black suffering forced Cone and other black liberation theologians to respond to the provocative question, "Is God a white racist?"[73]

As Jones saw it, black theologians did not go far enough in their critique of white Christianity. He contended that "the entire tradition must be placed under a strict theological ban" until the question of divine racism is answered and Christianity is stripped of all oppressive images and symbols. For Jones, "not even God or Jesus Christ can a priori be regarded as sacrosanct" and "must be jettisoned if they flunk the test."[74] Jones succinctly captures the essence of his position in a 1980 essay on religious humanism:

> As a representative of black humanism I have often raised suspicions about Christian faith as a potent means for liberation. Though I am persuaded of its excellence as a survival religion, its quality as a religion of liberation is, for me, still unresolved.[75]

While these and other internal criticisms challenged Cone to think deeper about black theology's methodology, he understood his primary task as that of a prophet calling the church to be true to the liberating gospel of Jesus.

CONE'S CRITIQUE OF THE AMERICAN CHURCHES

Like his theological predecessors in the pre–Black Power era, James Cone placed the American churches under the careful scrutiny of the Christian gospel. Just as Benjamin Mays and others issued a prophetic critique of white and black Christians for tolerating segregation within the church, James Cone criticized the American religious community for failing to make the suffering and liberation of the black oppressed an integral part of its understanding of the gospel. How could white and black churches preach about God, Jesus Christ, and the Holy Spirit as if the demon of racism did not exist? Moreover, how could white and black Christians claim to follow Jesus if they did not commit their energies and resources to tearing down the structures of oppression and injustice? James Cone put these and other tough questions to the American churches in a manner that put Christianity on trial in a new and decisive way. In many respects, Cone's prophetic theology was at one and the same time a critique of the Western theological tradition; the white church and its theology; and the black church, especially his own denomination, the African Methodist Episcopal church.

Whereas Benjamin Mays affirmed the Western theological tradition, using it to emphasize his claim that neither the early church, Medieval theologians, nor the Protestant reformers sought theological justification for slavery, segregation, and racism,[76] James Cone indicted it for identifying the will of God with the status quo and failing to understand liberation as the basic content of the biblical message. For Cone, this distortion of the gospel began when Constantine made Christianity the religion of the Roman Empire, changing it from a religion for the oppressed to a religion of the state. Thereafter, Cone argued, "Christianity became the opposite of what Jesus intended."[77]

Indeed, for most Christians, the names Thomas Aquinas, Martin Luther, and John Calvin represent the theological foundation of Western Christianity. But for James Cone, all these persons supported the maintenance of a status quo that perpetuated the oppression of the poor and downtrodden. Specifically, Aquinas's claim that "between a master and his slave there is a special right of domination"; Martin Luther's identification with the state and condemnation of the Peasant's Revolt; the easy association of John Calvin's theology with capitalism; and the silence of them all concerning the horrors of the African slave trade,[78] led Cone to the conclusion that the giants of the Western theological tradition "did little to make Christianity a religion for the politically oppressed in society."[79]

Of course, Benjamin Mays and others from his generation exposed the moral hypocrisy of the "Christian" nations of the West, which preached the virtues of justice and equality but colonized and oppressed dark-skinned peoples around the world. The distinctive contribution James Cone makes to twentieth-century African-American religious thought, however, is his constant emphasis on the "theological blindness" that led to the ethical failure of Western Christianity. Cone was relentless in his efforts to expose the inadequacy of white theology because he believed that "the sickness of the church in America is intimately involved with the bankruptcy of American theology."[80] There-fore, it is important to underscore that Cone saw more clearly than his predecessors the connection between unethical behavior and heretical theology. For him, the ethical sins of Western Christendom in general and the American churches in particular were the byproduct of a "de-fective theology" that failed to proclaim liberation as the central theme of the Bible and Christianity.[81]

Having thus demonstrated the interdependent relationship between poor theology and poor ethics in the Western theological tradition, Cone proceeded to repudiate the "unexpressed assumption" on the part of white American Christians that "theology has nothing to do with the oppression of Black people, at least not directly."[82] In fulfilling this task, it is significant to note that he drew upon the work of pre–Black Power theologian George D. Kelsey.

The White Church as "The Contemporary Meaning of the Antichrist"

While much has been written about Cone's use of European neo-orthodox thinkers (especially Karl Barth and Paul Tillich) in his articu-lation of black theology,[83] few interpreters have emphasized his reli-ance on the work of African-American religious scholars of the post–World War II era. This is understandable, in part, because Cone himself consciously sought to distinguish his interpretation of black theology from the integrationist stance of Negro religious thinkers. In *Black Theology and Black Power* he lamented the fact that most pre–Black Power theologians failed to relate the gospel to the problem of racism:

Unfortunately, even black theologians have, more often than not, merely accepted the problems defined by white theologians. Their treatment of Christianity has been shaped by the dominant ethos of the culture. There have been very few, if any, radical, revolu-tionary approaches to the Christian gospel for oppressed blacks.[84]

Even a cursory reading of the essays appearing in the *Journal of Re-ligious Thought* from 1943 to 1969 shows that, barring few exceptions, the dominant theological concern revolved around issues defined by white theologians and not those emerging from the black church and community. As Shelby Rooks has shown, most African-American Ph.D.'s in religion prior to the rise of Black Power (including James Cone) wrote dissertations on topics unrelated to racism and the black experience.[85]

In an effort to correct this problem, Cone offered a bold reinterpre-tation of the gospel that spoke the language and expressed the passion of a new generation committed to Black Power. But it is important to note that while the militant style of Cone's work was a radical departure from the milder writings of pre–Black Power theologians, his critique of the white church as the contemporary manifestation of the Antichrist was based, in part, on his reading of George Kelsey's classic text *Racism and the Christian Understanding of Man* (1965).

James H. Evans, Jr., in his recent book *We Have Been Believers* (1992), rightly calls Kelsey's work "a foundational text for the development of Christian anthropology in black theology," and "a scathing critique of the marriage between European-American Christianity and racism."[86] Nonetheless, after summarizing the essence of Kelsey's argument, Evans neglects to demonstrate precisely the former's influence on Cone's theology.[87] I believe it is worth emphasizing, however, that Cone called Kelsey's book "an excellent theological analysis of the incompatibility" of racism and Christianity and used it to reinforce his critique of the white church and its theologians.[88]

As a professor and director of the Morehouse School of Religion from 1945 to 1948, Kelsey's analysis of the ideological, social, and political dimensions of racism had also influenced the thinking of his most famous student: the young Martin Luther King, Jr., who took several courses with him as an undergraduate. Like Benjamin Mays, Kelsey believed that "there is no area of American life in which the dynamic of the Christian religion is needed more than in that of Negro-White relations."[89] Indeed, as a regular participant of the Institute of Religion at the Howard University School of Religion and later as Professor of Christian Ethics at Drew University School of Theology, George Kelsey devoted much of his intellectual energy to the task of interpreting the Christian response to the problem of racism.

First, it is important to recognize that Cone relied on Kelsey's work in the presentation of his central thesis; namely, that Black Power and Christianity are compatible because both seek to liberate black victims and white oppressors from the demons of racism. In *Black Theology and Black Power*, Cone argued as follows:

> If the work of Christ is that of liberating men from alien loyalties, and if racism is, as George Kelsey says, an alien faith, then there must be some correlation between Black Power and Christianity.[90]

More than a passing reference, Cone's reading of Kelsey reinforced an important link between pre– and post–Black Power theology. The conviction that racism was an "alien power" that oppressed whites as well as blacks was central to the thinking of Mays, Kelsey, and King, and was reiterated by Cone when he argued that "the man who enslaves another enslaves himself":

> Unrestricted freedom is a form of slavery . . . Racism is that bondage in which whites are free to beat, rape, or kill blacks . . . Whites

are thus enslaved to their own egos. Therefore, when blacks assert their freedom in self-determination, whites too are liberated.[91]

Cone continued his argument:

> Christ in liberating the wretched of the earth also liberates those responsible for the wretchedness. The oppressor is also freed of his peculiar demons. Black Power in shouting Yes to black humanness and No to white oppression is exorcising demons on both sides of the conflict.[92]

Second, Cone's critique of the white church as the "contemporary meaning of the Antichrist" was also informed by his reading of Kelsey's classic text. Kelsey interpreted racism as an idolatrous belief system which represented a "Trojan horse" within organized Christianity.[93] In fact, he used the term "Christian racist" (although he knew that the phrase was a contradiction in terms) to refer to the many adherents of the racist faith who also claimed allegiance to Christianity. Significantly, the distinction Kelsey made between racism as an idolatrous faith and genuine Christianity was an essential ingredient in Cone's critique of the white church and its theology.

Drawing on Kelsey's interpretation, Cone called racism a "complete denial of the Incarnation and thus of Christianity." Furthermore, Cone's analysis of the perpetual racism exhibited throughout the history of the white church—from its active support of slavery and segregation to its conspicuous silence in the face of institutional racism—led him to conclude emphatically that "the white denominational churches are unchristian." Based on this argument, which found clear support in Kelsey's work, Cone reasoned that "if there is any contemporary meaning of the Antichrist (or 'the principalities and powers'), the white church seems to be a manifestation of it. It is the enemy of Christ."[94]

Finally, Cone's reading of Kelsey informed his understanding of the relation between racism and genocide. Kelsey stated his argument succinctly:

> The logic of racism is genocide. Since in-races consider out-races defective in their humanity, there is no solution to the problem created by their presence in the world short of genocide.[95]

Why then, with the notable exception of the Hitler regime in Nazi Germany, has genocide as a political plan been so infrequent? As Kelsey viewed it, sinful humanity's "insatiable need" to dominate others and "the domestication of racism in Christian civilization" explain why segregation evolved as the milder political plan of racist action instead of wholesale elimination.[96]

James Cone read carefully Kelsey's analysis of racism and genocide. But whereas Kelsey believed that Christianity, while allowing racism to grow and develop, "nevertheless softened the brutalities of racial relationships," Cone was far more cynical. If the white church could
pronounce God's blessings on slavery and racism, it could also conceivably sanction genocide against black people:

> As long as whites can be sure that God is on their side, there is
> potentially no limit to their violence against anyone who threat-
> ens the American racist way of life. *Genocide is the logical conclu-
> sion of racism.* It happened to the American Indian, and *there is
> ample reason to believe that America is prepared to do the same to
> blacks.*[97]

Cone's Challenge to White Theologians

As Cone read and learned from pre–Black Power thinkers like
George Kelsey, he radicalized their critique by appropriating the militant style of Malcolm X in his dialogue with white theologians. Because Cone believed God had prepared him for the special task of
"leveling the most devastating black critique possible against the white
church and its theology,"[98] he displayed a righteous indignation and
zeal similar to that of the ancient Hebrew prophets.

Throughout the early 1970s, Cone was particularly enraged by the
"intellectual arrogance" of white theologians, who condescendingly
dismissed black theology as if it had nothing to contribute to their understanding of the gospel. In these discussions, which sometimes "de-
generated into shouting matches," Cone refused to be intimidated; he
responded by attacking the *Christian* identity of white theologians who
ignored the suffering of the black poor, and the *American* identity of
scholars who knew nothing about the African-*American* religious tradition. Reflecting back on these exchanges in the 1986 edition of *A Black
Theology of Liberation,* Cone admitted that:

> I was often as arrogant toward white theologians as they were
> toward me. My style of doing theology was influenced more by
> Malcolm X than by Martin Luther King, Jr. And I am sure that
> my intemperate behavior prevented some whites, whose inten-
> tions were more honorable than my responses suggested, from
> dialoguing with me.[99]

While the James Cone of the 1980s and 1990s abandoned the combative, "intemperate" style of earlier years, the substance of his challenge to white theologians remains unchanged. Beginning in 1970, Cone
sought to expose the limitations of white theology by persistently argu-

ing that "no white theologian has taken the oppression of black people as a point of departure for analyzing the meaning of the Gospel to-day."[100] For Cone, the more grim fact that the overwhelming majority of white theologians "see no correlation between Jesus Christ and the slaveships, the insurrections, the auction block, and the Black ghetto" explains why black theologians question "whether White theology is Christian in any sense."[101]

Just as Benjamin Mays told post–World War II America that its statements about worldwide democracy would be evaluated in light of its treatment of racial minorities at home, Cone, quoting the French philosopher Jean-Paul Sartre, told the white theological community that "the only way of helping the enslaved out there is to take sides with those who are here." Therefore, Cone urged radical white theologians who supported revolutionary movements in Latin America and Asia, but ignored the black freedom movement in the United States, to consider the struggles of their African-American neighbors.[102] But unlike Mays, who focused on the *ethical* failure of white Christians in the area of race, Cone emphasized the failure of white American theologians to grasp the essential *meaning of the gospel* because of their tendency to overlook black suffering in the formulation of their theologies. For if the biblical God is only revealed in the historical struggles of an exploited people fighting for freedom, how can the white church be doing American Christian theology when it fails to consider the theological reflections of *oppressed* black *Americans*? As noted above, Cone's challenge to white theologians in more recent years has been less strident than his militant critique of the early 1970s. Cone softened his language, no doubt, because he appreciated the efforts of some white theologians to respond to black theology,[103] and he realized that his combative style often hindered meaningful dialogue. An example of this milder critique is seen in his 1983 address, "A Theological Challenge to the American Catholic Church."

While recognizing the significant contributions of the Catholic church to the struggles of the poor worldwide, Cone emphasized the "ambiguity" of the church's position in light of its failure to confront American racism.[104] Perplexed that radical and progressive Catholics appeared more concerned with injustice in Latin America than in the United States, Cone asked:

Why are liberation-oriented Catholics so silent about racism in American society and its churches and so supportive of the struggles of the poor for justice in Latin America? What does this contradiction tell us about the Catholic idea of justice? . . . Why are most Catholics, many of whom say that they are concerned about justice, so uninformed about the struggle for justice in black history and culture?[105]

Throughout his career, Cone has urged white Christians to confront honestly their own racism and to take seriously the religious and political history of African-Americans.

The Black Church and the Liberation Struggle

Although Cone's critique of the white church generated more discussion in American seminaries than his criticism of black churches, his challenge to the African-American Christian community was equally prophetic. Not since the ministry of Martin Luther King, Jr., has a Christian thinker so profoundly challenged the black church as has James Cone. Indeed, his scathing critique of the black church led many African-American clergy to the erroneous conclusion that the militant theologian had no appreciation whatsoever for the institutional black church. But the opposite is the case; Cone loved the black church, and that is why he devoted his intellectual energy to reinterpreting its liberating heritage for a generation that increasingly regarded it as an irrelevant "Uncle Tom" institution devoted to "the white man's Christianity." Therefore, those who question Cone's commitment to the black church would do well to acknowledge that he was, at one and the same time, an inspired critic *and* defender of Christianity and the black church.

In relation to the African-American *Christian* community, Cone understood his role as a prophet commissioned by God to call the church to radical obedience to the demands of the gospel. In this capacity he issued a scathing critique of the black church for failing to make the liberation of the oppressed its primary mission. However, in relation to *non-Christian* black nationalists who dismissed the black church, Cone acted as a defender of the faith who vehemently opposed sweeping, ahistorical indictments of Christianity and the black church. Here, as a defender and representative of the Christian gospel, Cone sought to "evoke a measure of respect for the faith of our mothers and fathers" in the minds of African-American college students who rejected Christianity and issued a destructive critique of the black church.[106]

In his role as one of the leaders of the religion workshop at the first annual convention of the Congress of African People (Atlanta, 1970), Cone realized anew the extent to which Christianity was on trial in the African-American community.[107] As the only one who publicly embraced Christianity and the black church of the nearly one hundred people who attended the workshop, Cone appropriated the wisdom of the writer of Ecclesiastes and operated from the conviction that there is "a time to be a critic of the black church, and a time to be its strongest advocate and supporter."[108] Certainly, the CAP meeting in Atlanta was a time to be an advocate.

Cone doubted the sincerity of militant youth who claimed African identity but mocked the religion that sustained their slave ancestors.

"The last thing a truly African people would do," Cone argued, "is to ridicule the religion of their ancestors." Cone reminded radical black nationalists that revolutionary movements cannot be sustained without respect for the elders, the majority of whom are Christians. "I must admit," he declared, "that I cannot support any revolution that excludes my mother, and she believes in Jesus."[109] Moreover, Cone told "ultra-Blacks who discard the Black Church" that "there can be no revolution without the masses, and the Black masses are in the churches."[110] But Cone's defense of the black church did not mean that he repressed his criticism of its leadership and ministry.

Like Benjamin Mays and other pre–Black Power religious thinkers, Cone's criticism of the black church was inspired by a profound love for the institution that shaped his spirituality. As Rufus Burrow, Jr., has rightly noted in his recent text, *James H. Cone and Black Liberation Theology*, Cone's decision not to preface his early critique of the black church with remarks about its positive impact on his life led many readers to the false conclusion that he had no love for the black church. After the publication of *Black Theology and Black Power*, however, Cone altered his approach and began to include explicit references to his love for the church—as seen in *God of the Oppressed* (1975).[111] Moreover, in a 1987 Founder's Day address at Turner Theological Seminary in Atlanta (the A.M.E. part of the Interdenominational Theological Center), Cone clarified his views for those who might have misunderstood the motivation behind his relentless critique of the black church:

> I am proud to be an AME! Any criticism, therefore, that I have made or will make about the church is motivated by my deep love and firm commitment to serve it the best way I know how.[112]

Having established Cone's personal commitment to the black church, we can now discuss the nature of his critique.

Using Black Power as his theological norm, the early Cone interpreted the pre–Civil War black church as a protest movement whose "stand on freedom and equality through word and action is true to the spirit of Christ."[113] Although some interpreters believe Cone overlooked the black church as an important source for black theology,[114] the analysis of black church history was an essential part of his early theology. In fact, Cone understood the formation of black denominations and the church's participation in the fight against slavery as visible manifestations of black theology in the pre–Civil War era.[115]

On the other hand, Cone interpreted the members of the post–Civil War black church as being "no more Christian than their white counterparts."[116] With the notable exception of Martin Luther King, Jr., and other activist ministers in the civil rights movement, Cone argued that the churches in the postbellum period failed to challenge the racist status quo and became "an instrument of escape instead of, as formerly, an instrument of protest."[117] While Cone acknowledged that the political retreat of the post–Civil War black church was a survival technique to protect blacks from the brutalities of white terrorist violence, he nevertheless held it accountable for failing to live up to the radical demands of the gospel. In light of the black church's enduring apostasy, Cone, like the NCBC clergy, advocated the acceptance of Black Power as the only hope for reviving its radical heritage.[118]

Cone's critics helped him to realize that his early interpretation of black church history made too sharp a distinction between radical (pre–Civil War) and conservative (post–Civil War) traditions in the black church. As Rufus Burrow has noted, Cone "was wrong to suggest that the black church was prophetic in one era and conservative in another. In every era of black Christianity there has been at least a remnant that has remained dedicated to identifying the Gospel with the black liberation struggle."[119] While Cone has changed his reading of black church history, throughout his writings he has consistently held it to the same standard he used to judge the white church. If African-American churches failed to participate in the black liberation struggle, then they were as un-Christian as white churches that ignored black suffering. Cone stated this uncompromising view in the provocative style that characterized his early theology:

> *Any* church that fails to focus on Black liberation as the sole reason for its existence has denied the Lord and Savior Jesus Christ and aligned itself with the anti-Christ.[120]

Clearly, pre–Black Power thinkers objected to Cone's exclusive focus on *black* liberation as opposed to human liberation as the churches' "sole reason for existence." In addition, many conservative black churches also rejected Cone's position that social and political liberation was more essential to the mission of the church than saving souls. But, for Cone, active participation in the black struggle for social and political liberation remained the criterion for evaluating the ministry of the black church. As we have seen, Cone's unswerving commitment to black liberation—which was informed by his reading of Benjamin Mays, Howard Thurman, Martin Luther King, Jr., Elijah Muhammad, and Malcolm X—was also the controlling norm that shaped his articulation of black theology. Since Jesus was committed to "the least of these," Cone maintained that the church and its theologians could only discover what it means to do Christian theology by "participating in the revolutionary practice of liberating the little ones from oppression."[121] Obviously, Cone directed his sharpest criticism toward his own denomination, the African Methodist Episcopal church. Having pastored two churches while still a teenager; studied and taught in A.M.E. schools;

and led bishop retreats and attended many General Conferences, Cone knew first-hand the corruption that permeated the hierarchy of the A.M.E. church. Concerned about the "unaccountable authority" that exists in positions of leadership within the denomination, Cone issued the following prophetic warning:

> When the church of Jesus Christ permits a few of its leaders to hold an inordinate amount of power over others in the community, it is sowing the seeds of its own destruction.[122]

More important, Cone reminded the church of Jesus' own words to his disciples that they were not to emulate the pattern of authority exercised by the Gentiles; instead, "whoever wants to be great must be your servant, and whoever wants to be first must be the willing slave of all (Mk 10:43-44)."

Cone also highlighted the gospel's emphasis on service to critique power-hungry bishops who were more concerned about their own personal status than fighting oppression. As was his custom, he referred to history to demonstrate to the contemporary A.M.E. church that it "ain't what it used to be." Noting that Bishop Daniel Payne, elected in 1852 by demand of his colleagues, turned down an invitation to the bishopric in 1848 because he felt unworthy, Cone asked, "Can you imagine some A.M.E. minister turning down the bishopric today because he felt unfit?"[123] To be sure, Cone frequently referred to the theology and ministry of Richard Allen, Daniel Payne, and Henry M. Turner to emphasize his claim that the twentieth-century A.M.E. church "has lost contact completely with its historical roots."[124]

Cone believed it was his duty as a theologian of the church to raise a prophetic voice of protest as long as the A.M.E. church and other black denominations emphasized building structures and playing denominational politics more than struggling for justice. Aware that "committed Christian theologians do not win popularity contests," he was therefore not surprised when the A.M.E. hierarchy criticized him for airing their "ecclesiastical laundry in public."[125] Cone has persistently argued that the black church needs prophetic theologians as much as it needs dynamic, responsible preachers. He continues to urge the black church to think *theologically* about its political struggle and to develop its own creeds, liturgies, and rituals so that its interpretation of the gospel is not derived from apolitical, white, evangelical Christianity.[126] For Cone, the black church has forgotten its distinctive historical and theological identity because it has promoted "the art of preaching to the exclusion of doing theology." However, without theologians charged with the task of evaluating church proclamation in light of the gospel, the church cannot be self-critical and overcome its weaknesses and limitations.[127]

Unfortunately, Cone did not realize that in his own commitment to proclaim the truth of the gospel, he had overlooked one of the most glaring sins of the black church: sexism. When Cone was made aware of his own sexism in the mid 1970s, he repented and began to incorporate a feminist critique into his theological perspective. But Cone's growth in this area is little consolation for African-American women, who remained invisible in his early work. What have black women had to say about black male theologians and their failure to address sexism as a theological problem? We turn to these questions now in the final chapter on Christianity, sexism, and the challenge of womanist theology.

CHAPTER 5

Christianity and Sexism

Delores Williams and the Challenge of Womanist Theology

Black Theology cannot continue to treat Black women as if they were invisible creatures who are outside looking into the Black experience, the Black Church, and the Black theological enterprise ... Black women represent more than 50 percent of the Black community and more than 70 percent of the Black Church. How can an authentic theology of liberation arise out of these communities without specifically addressing the liberation of women in both places?

—Jacquelyn Grant, 1979

If black liberation theology wants to include black women and speak in behalf of the most oppressed black people today—the poor homeless, jobless, economically "enslaved" women, men and children sleeping on American streets, in bus stations, parks and alleys—theologians must ask themselves some questions. Have they, in the use of the Bible, identified so thoroughly with the theme of Israel's election that they have not seen the oppressed of the oppressed in scripture? Have they identified so completely with Israel's liberation that they have been blind to the awful reality of victims making victims in the Bible? Does this kind of blindness with regard to non-Hebrew victims in the scripture also make it easy for black male theologians and biblical scholars to ignore the figures in the Bible whose experience is analogous to that of black women?

—Delores Williams, 1993

For pre– and post–Black Power male theologians, racism was the greatest evil corrupting the spiritual and political life of American society. The underlying premise that governed their work was the naive view that black liberation would be achieved once segregation and institutional racism were eradicated from the church and society. Although Benjamin Mays, Albert Cleage, and James Cone knew that racial oppression was compounded by economic injustice, their primary focus was on the issue of racism and its impact on the African-American community. However, the most glaring limitation of pre– and post–Black Power male theologians is their failure to identify sexism as a serious theological problem. Just as white theologians ignored slavery, segregation, and racism in their interpretation of the Christian gospel, Negro and black male theologians overlooked the gender oppression of black women in the formulation of their theological perspective.

Consequently, in the mid 1970s African-American women began to challenge black male theologians and church leaders on their interpretation and practice of the Christian faith. While pre– and post–Black Power male theologians put white Christianity on trial for supporting the racist status quo, womanist theologians put Christianity as represented by black men (and white women) on trial for ignoring the unique suffering of African-American women. Delores Williams, associate professor of theology and culture at Union Theological Seminary in New York, Jacquelyn Grant, an ordained minister in the A.M.E. church and associate professor of systematic theology at the Interdenominational Theological Center in Atlanta, and other emerging womanist scholars began to ask how black theology differs from white theology if it overlooks the sexist oppression of African-American women? How could pre– and post–Black Power male theologians level a prophetic critique against the racism of the white church and fail to criticize the black church for its oppressive sexism? Moreover, how can black theology claim to be liberation theology if it fails to make the liberation of black women an integral part of its message?[1] With the dramatic increase in the number of African-American women in seminaries and graduate theological programs in the 1980s and early 1990s, these and other questions are forcing the black church and its theologians to review the Christian gospel as they prepare for ministry in the twenty-first century.[2] Fortunately, there is now a significant number of womanist religious scholars in scripture, systematic theology, ethics, history, and sociology to assist the church in its efforts to be true to the gospel of Jesus.

More than any other scholar, Delores Williams has plumbed the depths of black women's history, culture, and literature as sources for a constructive womanist theology. In her efforts to bring black women's experience "into the hermeneutical circle of Christian theology," Williams discovered a female-centered tradition of African-American biblical appropriation that highlighted the similarities between the story of Hagar (Gn 16:1-16, 21:9-21) and the historic experience of black women and the black community. In Williams's mind, this heritage provides a more adequate framework for examining African-American women's experience than the male-centered liberation paradigm focused on the Exodus event, Moses, and other male personalities in the Bible. Williams named this female-centered heritage "the survival/quality-of-life tradition of African-American biblical appropriation," and she utilizes it as the theological foundation for her construction of womanist theology.[3]

This chapter examines the challenge of womanist theology in general and the writing of Delores Williams in particular. After discussing black women's response to the problem of sexism in the black church and the liberation movements of the 1950s and 1960s, I will examine Williams's contribution to African-American religious thought, paying special attention to her challenge to black male theologians and the African-American denominational churches.

CHRISTIANITY, SEXISM, AND THE BLACK COMMUNITY

Pre– and post–Black Power male theologians operated on the premise that Christianity functioned as both a source of liberation and oppression in the African-American community. Christian thinkers like Benjamin Mays, James Cone, and Albert Cleage emphasized the liberating character of Christianity and attributed its oppressive aspects to white racist corruptions of the gospel. Elijah Muhammad, on the other hand, emphasized the oppressive character of Christianity and rejected it altogether as a white religion specifically designed to oppress the so-called Negroes. However, both Christian and non-Christian male thinkers agreed that race was the controlling category that determined the liberating or oppressive nature of Christianity. Unfortunately, this exclusive focus on black-white relations blinded pre– and post–Black Power male theologians to the existence of oppression within their own community.

Although Negro and black male theologians rejected the myth of white supremacy, they had no problem accepting white men's views on male superiority and female inferiority. The critical reading of the Bible employed in their opposition to white racism was all but forgotten when interpreting texts that revealed the patriarchal bias of scripture. Did not racist *and* sexist distortions of the Bible make Christianity a unique source of oppression for black women? Moreover, did not black male preachers and theologians also corrupt the gospel when they accepted patriarchy as the divine plan for human relations?

Just as Negro and black male theologians intensified their critique of white Christianity in the post–World War II years, African-American women heightened their protest against sexism in the black church and community. Post–World War II black Christian women established organizations such as the Women's Political Council (1946), which called for a city-wide Montgomery bus boycott months before the male-led Montgomery Improvement Association was established.[4] In similar fashion, postwar black women finally succeeded in pressuring the A.M.E. church to ordain the first black woman in the denomination's history, Martha J. Keys, in 1948.[5] These events, and countless others, were indications that twentieth-century African-American Christian women were prepared to continue the long struggle against racism and sexism initiated by their nineteenth-century ancestors.

Black Women, Sexism, and the Black Church

The ongoing struggle of African-American women to serve God in the church and society on an equal basis with men demands more serious attention by historians and theologians alike. How is it that black women have been able to dedicate themselves so faithfully to a church that has historically demonstrated an unwillingness to view them as equal partners in the Lord's service? From the time Richard Allen told Jarena Lee that the A.M.E. discipline "did not call for women preachers"[6] to contemporary arguments against the ordination of women, the black church has oppressed its most committed members and generous supporters. Indeed, the subordination of women in African-American churches led Theressa Hoover, a former denominational executive of the United Methodist church, to argue that black women— by virtue of their gender, race, and inferior status in the church—labor under triple jeopardy.[7]

Although African-American men and women share a common heritage of immense suffering, black men have been slow to realize how sexism compounds the oppression of black women. Despite the fact that male and female slaves endured the lash of the whip *together,* "stole away to Jesus" to pray for strength *together,* ministered to the needs of the sick and dying *together,* and shared in spreading the good news about Jesus *together,* the postbellum institutional black church copied the patriarchal structure of the white church and organized itself around male leadership. As Jacquelyn Grant observed in "Black Theology and the Black Woman":

> It is often said that women are the "backbone of the church." On the surface this may appear to be a compliment, especially when one considers the function of the backbone in the human anatomy . . . In any case, the telling portion of the word backbone is "back." It has become apparent to me that most ministers who use this term have reference to location rather than function. What they really mean is that women are in the "background" and should be kept there.[8]

Sadly, the prevailing assumption undergirding gender stereotypes in many black churches is that women belong in support roles but not in leadership, policy-making roles. Even in churches where women do occupy key leadership roles such as trustees and deacons, there often remains a deep-seated reluctance to accept the viability of female *pastoral* leadership. Arguments against women pastors range from the maleness of Jesus and the twelve apostles to claims that women lack the necessary skills required for dynamic preaching and effective leadership. Often, these heretical claims are reinforced by authoritarian leadership styles and sexist biblical hermeneutics that justify the subordination of women in the church and society.

Perhaps the most dangerous effect of this patriarchal theology is seen in black women's internalization of sexist attitudes. Like other oppressed groups throughout history, black women have often embraced the values of their oppressors. In fact, many black churchwomen have been socially and theologically conditioned to prefer male ministers and to be suspicious of female religious leadership. The reality that some African-American women themselves express opposition to the idea of female pastors only indicates the extent to which they have internalized the sexist values of their oppressors.

Yet despite the biblically sanctioned male chauvinism that pervades much of the black church, African-American women have exercised their spiritual gifts as ordained clergy, trustees, deacons, teachers, and evangelists. For example, womanist scholar Cheryl Townsend Gilkes, associate professor of sociology and African-American studies at Colby College in Waterville, Maine, and an ordained Baptist minister, has noted that black women in Holiness and Pentecostal churches "carved out prominent and important roles for themselves" despite the patriarchal structure of their denominations. Moreover, militant women in the Sanctified Church established churches, served as community leaders, and developed a political consciousness "fueled by spiritual zeal."[9]

The political consciousness and spiritual zeal of black Christian women were embodied in the distinguished careers of leaders such as Anna Arnold Hedgeman and Pauli Murray. Hedgeman, a national civil rights leader and administrative staff member of the National Council of Churches in the 1960s, worked closely with ministers before and after Black Power; she knew firsthand the strengths and weaknesses of the black church (more will be said about her political career later). While most interpreters of twentieth-century African-American religious thought are familiar with criticisms of the black church made by male theologians, the prophetic critique of black Christian women like Anna Hedgeman is often overlooked.

Like pre–Black Power male theologians, Hedgeman criticized the black church for its lack of social relevancy. As an executive of the Harlem YWCA in the 1930s, she became disillusioned when Negro

ministers gave a lackluster response to her efforts to organize a com-
munity-wide protest against the exploitation of laundry and domestic
workers. Hedgeman later offered this description of what she regarded
as the typical Harlem pastor:

> The Negro minister exhorted his parishioners to love God and
> be faithful, but he brought no broad social message except at
> moments of special crisis in the Negro community. The people
> flocked to church and seemed to love it. The church was usually
> thought of as responsible for the "spirit" of man with no basic
> realization of the social message of Jesus Christ.[10]

Determined to challenge the theology of these pastors, Hedgeman cited
New Testament passages that depicted Jesus' concern for the social predicament of the oppressed.[11] Thirty years later, in the early 1960s,
Hedgeman's efforts to mobilize Harlem churches to support city-wide
political reform under a Negro mayoral candidate evoked a similar
apathetic response from many Harlem ministers:

> Some of them offered to be allies, but many of them were caught
> in the structure, too, for they had large church budgets to be raised
> and large congregations to organize for the so-called ends of the
> church. I listened to magnificently constructed sermons but found
> little in them which met the needs of the spiritually and physi-
> cally hungry.[12]

While there are similarities in the critiques articulated by Anna
Hedgeman and Negro male theologians, the differences are more important for understanding the diversity of pre–Black Power religious
thought. First, Hedgeman did not emphasize a theology of race relations as did Mays, Thurman, and King. Although she affirmed the ideal
goal of an integrated Protestant church, she saw "little point in wor-
shipping with white people who had yet to evidence in their behavior
toward others the elemental meaning of the Christian faith."[13] Moreover, although Hedgeman's encounter with racial segregation created
in her "a deep hate for all southern whites," especially those who "dared
call themselves Christians,"[14] she was not apologetic, nor did she emphasize to Negro Christians the moral and ethical danger of hatred as
did pre–Black Power male theologians.

Lastly, Hedgeman's critique of the speeches by Benjamin Mays and
Martin Luther King, Jr., at the National Conference on Religion and
Race (January 1963) is significant because it indicates that even before
the rise of Black Power there were Negro Christians who objected to
the integrationist tendency to minimize fundamental differences between Negro and white Christianity. Hedgeman was dismayed that

neither Mays nor King addressed the distinctive history and theology of the Negro church or the role it could play "in the potential reunification of the Protestant church in America." As she saw it, their commitment to racial integration caused them to overlook "the structure which the Negro church had built"; "its lack of communication with the total church"; and "its distrust of the Christianity of the white communions." Hedgeman stated her criticism sharply:

> Dr. Mays, who is an authority on the Negro church and who has theological training, might well have told the dramatic story of the meaning of the Negro church to the total church and to the nation. He might have presented the way in which the Negro church too has developed structure and power. Dr. Mays could easily have indicated that there would be need for much conversation between Negro and white church leaders . . . Would the Negro be willing to play a secondary role if churches merge? Could he have confidence in the leadership of the white churches? These questions were not discussed at Chicago. Negroes at this Conference on Religion and Race were talked to and about, but we ourselves did not speak of our faith which "passeth all understanding."[15]

These words reveal a deep commitment to the unique racial heritage of the black church. Although Hedgeman's contribution as a religious thinker and activist is not celebrated by the black church and its theologians, her work must be recognized by all who seek to write a balanced interpretation of twentieth century African-American religious thought and history.

Like Anna Hedgeman, Pauli Murray, an attorney who staged sit-ins in Washington, D.C., in the 1940s and one of the first women ordained in the Episcopal church in 1977, was a committed civil rights leader and dedicated churchwoman. Murray protested sexism in the church long before the Episcopal church finally decided to ordain women to the priesthood just eight years before her death in 1985. On a Sunday morning in March 1966, during the celebration of the Holy Eucharist, "an uncontrollable anger exploded" inside Murray over gender discrimination in the Episcopal church. Convinced that sexism was "a stumbling block to faith," she stormed out of the church and later sent a poignant letter to parish leaders that captured the feelings of churchwomen across the nation:

> Why cannot women and men, boys and girls, participate equally in every phase of Church activity? If, as I believe, it is a privilege to assist the priest in the solemn Eucharist . . . why is this privilege not accorded to all members without regard to sex? Suppose

only white people did these things? Or only Negroes? Or only Puerto Ricans? We would see immediately that the Church is guilty of grave discrimination. There is no difference between discrimination because of race and discrimination because of sex. I believe . . . that if one is wrong, the other is wrong.[16]

Black Women, Sexism, and the Liberation Struggle

Male civil rights and Black Power leaders embraced the sexist ideology of the black church. In fact, because black preachers were often the visible leaders of local civil rights organizations, it is not surprising that the patriarchal orientation of the black church was also manifested in the freedom movement of the 1950s and 1960s. However, it must be emphasized that no civil rights victory—from the 1955 Montgomery bus boycott to the 1965 Selma March—would have been successful without the leadership and organizational skills of black women. Although the familiar expression, "If Rosa Parks had not sat down, Martin King would not have stood up," seeks to correct the false notion that black women made no significant contribution to the civil rights movement, it also appears unintentionally to reinforce the sexist view that women played minor roles compared to the dynamic leadership of black men.

In recent years scholars have begun to uncover the crucial role African-American women played in the black freedom struggle of the 1950s and 1960s.[17] As Ella Baker—former national director of NAACP branches, coordinator of SCLC, and advisor to SNCC—and others have noted, black churchwomen were the major force behind this movement for social equality. Indeed, it is because of the spiritual courage and political commitment of African-American Christian women—from Sojourner Truth and Harriet Tubman to Rosa Parks and Fannie Lou Hamer—that the black community has survived the harsh realities of white racism to the extent that it has.[18]

However, despite the contributions of African-American women to the civil rights and Black Power movements, most male leaders either downplayed or completely overlooked the significant role they played in the liberation struggle. For example, although Ella Baker, a veteran activist long before Martin Luther King, Jr., emerged as a national leader and was instrumental in the founding of SCLC and SNCC, she was not given the same measure of credit and respect as male civil rights leaders. Of course, Baker realized that being an outspoken woman in a movement dominated by black clergymen meant that her contributions would be disregarded:

There would never be any role for me in a leadership capacity with SCLC. Why? First, I'm a woman. Also, I'm not a minister. And second . . . I knew that my penchant for speaking honestly

. . . would not be tolerated. The combination of the basic attitude of men, and especially ministers, as to what the role of women in their church setups [should be] . . . would never have lent itself to my being a leader in the movement there.[19]

As with Ella Baker, most male activists did not acknowledge the important contribution Anna Hedgeman made to the civil rights movement. Like Benjamin Mays, Adam Clayton Powell, Jr., and other influential leaders, Hedgeman played a pivotal role in the emergence of the black freedom movement of the 1940s. In 1934 she was appointed the first Consultant on Racial Problems for New York City's Department of Welfare, addressing issues ranging from discrimination in policy-making to the exploitation of black women domestic workers.[20] Twenty years later, in 1954, Hedgeman returned to New York City politics as a member of Mayor Robert F. Wagner's cabinet.

On the national level Hedgeman worked as a race relations official for the federal government's Civil Defense Program during World War II. In this capacity she, like Benjamin Mays and other religious thinkers in the early 1940s, dramatized the need for racial integration in the armed services and American society as a whole. Several years earlier Hedgeman had worked with A. Phillip Randolph, founder of the Brotherhood of Sleeping Car Porters (1925), in the proposed 1941 March on Washington for job equality in the defense industries; she was among the group of leaders who eventually forced Franklin D. Roosevelt to establish the Federal Commission on Fair Employment Practices as a temporary wartime agency.[21] Consequently, in 1944 Randolph selected Hedgeman as the first executive director of the newly formed National Council for a Permanent Fair Employment Practices Commission. It is also significant to note that after Vice President Harry Truman, who actively supported the FEPC bill, completed FDR's term and ran for re-election in 1948, Hedgeman worked on the successful campaign. As president, Truman appointed her an executive assistant in the Department of Health, Education, and Welfare, making Hedgeman the first African-American woman to hold a top administrative position in the nation's history.[22] Finally, in 1963 Hedgeman served as the only female civil rights leader on the administrative committee which organized the second national March on Washington for Jobs and Freedom.

The strength of Anna Hedgeman's political commitment forced male civil rights leaders to accept her as a dedicated co-worker in the struggle against segregation and racial discrimination. However, when Hedgeman raised the issue of sex discrimination in the planning of the 1963 March on Washington, she encountered male insensitivity and indifference. First, the male civil rights leaders disregarded Hedgeman's objections about being the only woman on the organizing committee and ignored her suggestion that the leaders of women's organizations such as the National Council of Negro Women be included. Not surprised by this response (or lack thereof), Hedgeman lamented:

> As usual, the men must have discussed the matter in my absence and when the first leaflet was printed, I was embarrassed to find that I was still the only woman listed.[23]

Likewise, Hedgeman's protest against the committee's refusal to select a woman as a featured speaker was largely ignored. Two weeks before the historic March, Hedgeman wrote a letter to A. Phillip Randolph and sent copies to the other five leaders on the administrative committee (Whitney Young, James Farmer, Martin Luther King, Jr., Roy Wilkins, and John Lewis). "In light of the role of Negro women in the struggle for freedom," Hedgeman wrote, "it is incredible that no woman should appear as a speaker at the historic March on Washington Meeting at the Lincoln Memorial." Noting that "the 'Big Six' have not given women the quality of participation which they have earned through the years," Hedgeman suggested that either Mrs. Medgar Evers or Diane Nash Bevel represent the contributions of Negro women.[24] It came as no surprise that on August 28, 1963, black women were assigned minor speaking roles while male leaders were featured as the main attraction.[25]

The younger generation of civil rights leaders also failed to respect black women as equal partners in the struggle. In an effort to confront the male dominated SNCC leadership, a 1964 Position Paper denounced the sexist practice of denying competent female activists jobs commensurate with their abilities. After citing specific examples of sex discrimination within SNCC, the anonymous authors (white women in SNCC who believed they also represented black women) concluded that "assumptions of male superiority are deep rooted and every much as crippling to the woman as the assumptions of white supremacy are to the Negro":

> Consider why it is in SNCC that women who are competent, qualified, and experienced, are automatically assigned to the "female" kinds of jobs such as typing, desk work, telephone work, filing, library work, cooking, and the assistant kind of administrative work but rarely the "executive" kind.[26]

Although black women were angry about the male chauvinism that pervaded the civil rights movement, they did not organize a mass protest against it. Like their male counterparts, African-American women operated on the assumption that racism and not sexism was the primary source of black oppression. Accordingly, they believed that raising the matter of gender discrimination in a determined manner would only detract from the community's struggle against the greater evil of racism. No doubt, this relative silence of black women themselves regarding sexism in the freedom movement and wider black community contributed to black men's perception that feminism was a white woman's issue unrelated to black liberation. Finally, many African-American women concluded that sexism was not a major problem in the civil rights movement because women like Jo Ann Robinson, Ella Baker, Dorothy Cotton, Diane Nash, and Ruby Doris Smith Robinson were widely recognized as veteran leaders of the freedom struggle.[27] Not surprisingly, the presence of a few persons in official leadership roles obscured the reality that the majority of black women were not regarded as equal partners in the struggle for racial justice.[28]

According to Sara Evans and Paula Giddings, black women in SNCC were, in fact, more disturbed about black men's sexual attraction to white women than their unequal status within the organization. Widespread sexual activity between black men and white women in the summer of 1964 not only created a barrier between black and white women "that shared womanhood could not transcend," it also put an extra strain on relationships between black men and black women.[29] For many African-American women, black men's sexual preference for white women perpetuated the racist stereotype that white women were the embodiment of beauty and femininity, while black women were "uppity," "domineering," and "emasculating." Devalued by black men, white men, and white women, African-American women became increasingly aware of the need to cultivate a positive self-concept in opposition to the racism of white society and the sexism of black men. Significantly, it was the realization that neither white women nor black men respected the unique experience of black women that formed the existential background for a distinctive womanist theological perspective.

Black Women, Sexism, and Nascent Black Theology

The sexism black women encountered in the civil rights movement was mild compared to the blatant misogyny that permeated the Black Power movement of the late 1960s and early 1970s. The oft-repeated claim that aggressive black women aided in the "castration" of black men became a dogmatic faith claim of black nationalism. Similarly, the militant call for the realization of black manhood was a hallmark feature of the Black Power movement. Indeed, as Paula Giddings observed, "a male-conscious motif," symbolized in the clenched fist of the Black Power salute, permeated the 1960s making it "the masculine decade."[30] For many African-American women, Black Power meant Black Patriarchy. In her controversial text, *Black Macho and the Myth of the Superwoman,* Michele Wallace captured the misgivings many black women had regarding Black Power:

> Come 1966, the black man had two pressing tasks before him: a white woman in every bed and a black woman under every heel. Out of his sense of urgency came a struggle called the Black Movement, which was nothing more nor less than the black man's struggle to attain his presumably lost "manhood."[31]

Regrettably, black male theologians accepted the sexist orientation of black nationalist leaders. As James Cone confessed, "Black theology learned the patriarchal bad habits of its progenitors."[32] Thus, while the African-American Christian community ultimately benefitted from the nationalist critique of Elijah Muhammad, Malcolm X, and secular Black Power advocates, it suffered a major setback when black male preachers and theologians adopted the male exclusivism and sexist rhetoric of black nationalism. Like male civil rights and Black Power leaders, black preachers and theologians dismissed sexism as "a white woman's issue" because they believed racism to be the major cause of black oppression. Having inherited a one-dimensional analysis of oppression from pre–Black Power integrationists and the patriarchal views of post–Black Power nationalists, black male preachers and theologians developed an interpretation of the gospel that ignored the unique plight and religious experience of African-American women.

Consequently, when radical black clergymen responded to the cry of Black Power by forming the National Committee of Negro Churchmen and black caucuses in white denominations, it was inevitable that notions of male superiority appear in their published statements. Considering that Anna Arnold Hedgeman was the only woman invited to sign the NCNC 1966 "Black Power Statement," it is not surprising that the male organization ignored the theological insights of black women.

By the time the organization changed its name to the National Committee of *Black* Churchmen in 1968, it became more deliberate in its usage of black nationalist rhetoric. The group's 1969 "Black Theology" statement declares its affirmation of the "dignity of black personhood," but then borrows words that reflect the sexism of male black nationalists:

> We do this as men and as black Christians. This is the message of Black Theology. In the words of Eldridge Cleaver: We shall have our manhood. We shall have it or the earth will be levelled by our efforts to gain it.[33]

Moreover, when NCBC statements invoked "the faith of our fathers" and celebrated "our own Black Heroes," only men's names appeared on the list: Nat Turner, Denmark Vesey, Richard Allen, James Varick, Absalom Jones, Frederick Douglass, Marcus Garvey, W.E.B. Du Bois, Malcolm X, and Martin Luther King, Jr. In fact, readers of NCBC documents are left to assume that women were at least included in the organization's salutary reference to "all Black People past and present, great and small."[34]

The sexism of the NCBC was also seen in their lack of public support for the ordination of women and stubborn refusal to change the name of the organization to the more inclusive title the National Conference of Black *Christians*. The fact that the NCBC, despite the persistent objections of African-American women, did not modify its name until 1982 indicates how deeply sexism was entrenched in nascent black theology.[35]

Black caucuses in white denominations also borrowed the sexist rhetoric of the Black Power movement. For example, the Black Methodists for Church Renewal, though comprised of male and female Christians, published a 1968 statement that reflects the black nationalist emphasis on manhood:

> We are new men—the old man, "nigger," is dead. The "boy" is now a man! We now stand as proud black men prepared to embrace our blackness.[36]

Similarly, the early writings of black male theologians reveal an uncritical acceptance of Black Power's patriarchal worldview. The notion that the attainment of black manhood was more important than the liberation of black women is seen in the position of J. Deotis Roberts:

> Black Theology speaks about overcoming a childhood imposed by a paternalistic society. Black women joining the Women's Liberation Movement should bear in mind that Black men have been "boys" all these years and perhaps they should be allowed to be men before being robbed of their manhood. The passion of Black men to be men in society must not be denied them by their wives . . . At a time when we are trying to unite the Black family, Black church and Black community, Black men need the full understanding and support of their women and children.[37]

Roberts said plainly what countless other men accepted as gospel; namely, that women's liberation was "a white thing" unrelated to the cause of black liberation. Although the expression of sexism in James Cone's early writings was not as blatant as Roberts's, he later confessed what must have already been clear to many African-American women: sexism was "not a part of [Cone's] theological consciousness" when he began writing black theology, and that he rejected women's liberation as "a joke," "an intrusion," and "a white trick to distract from the injustice being committed by whites against blacks."[38] Significantly, when Cone did become fully aware of the evil of sexism in 1975, it was not the result of his sensitivity to the plight of African-American women, but rather in the context of responding to Korean Christian women who objected to their subordination within the church.[39]

CHRISTIANITY, WOMANIST THEOLOGY, AND THE EMERGENCE OF DELORES WILLIAMS

The silence of black male theologians regarding the oppression of black women served as a major catalyst for the rise of womanist theology. As African-American women in seminaries became increasingly aware that neither white feminist nor black male theologians represented the uniqueness of their religious experience, they began to develop their own distinctive theological voice. They formed black women's caucuses to provide support and encouragement for one another and to plan strategies in their fight against the racism of white women and the sexism of black male religious leadership. African-American women at Union Theological Seminary in New York took the lead in this development and issued a prophetic challenge to white female and black male students, as well as to their esteemed professors Beverly Harrison and James Cone, pioneers in feminist and black liberation theologies respectively. Deeply influenced by the writings of Alice Walker, especially *The Color Purple* (1982) and *In Search of Our Mother's Garden* (1983), black female religious scholars such as Jacquelyn Grant, Katie Cannon, Kelly Brown Douglas, and Delores Williams, themselves recent graduates from Union Seminary, began to use the term *womanist* to distinguish themselves from white feminists and black male theologians.[40]

Yet, it is important to note that womanist theology is not simply a critique of white feminist and black male theologies. While this is a crucial part of its work, its more significant constructive task is to dialogue with African-American churchwomen and make their faith, thought, and experience the primary source for theological reflection. Although many progressive white and black male scholars have supported and read their work closely, womanist theologians realize that their primary aim, as Delores Williams has repeatedly emphasized, must be "discourse and work with black women in the churches."[41] Similarly, Kelly Brown Douglas, in her recent book, *The Black Christ* (1994), admonishes womanist theologians to "resist the urge to retreat behind the walls of seminaries and universities" and be accountable to "ordinary" black women in churches and community groups. Aware that "womanist theology can impact the church only as much as it impacts the women in the pews," Brown Douglas, an Episcopal priest and associate professor of systematic theology at the Howard University School of Divinity, calls for appropriate pedagogies that will foster dialogue and assist African-American women to claim their voice and power in the church.[42] One of the most important issues womanists have emphasized in this regard is the analysis of black women's oppression and the strategies they have employed to survive and be whole.

Beyond Race Relations:
The Multidimensionality of Black Women's Oppression

While white feminist and black male theologians focused on sexism and racism respectively, womanist theologians highlight the interrelatedness of race, sex, and class as multidimensional factors in the reality of black women's oppression. Victimized by race and sex oppression, black women also make up a disproportionately high percentage of the working poor and underclass. Accordingly, womanist thinkers argue that a holistic theology of survival and wholeness must address all aspects of black women's oppression. As Jacquelyn Grant stated, a womanist theology that only addresses the concerns of middle-class women "would be meaningless to the majority of black women, who are themselves poor." Therefore, Grant rightly argued that "the daily struggles of poor black women must serve as the gauge for the verification of the claims of womanist theology."[43]

Moreover, for Grant, the tri-dimensionality of black women's oppression has profound implications for womanist christology. As the "poorest of the poor," African-American women embody Jesus' concern and solidarity with the "least of these." However, because their experience encompasses the reality of black men (racism), white and third-world women (sexism), and the poor of every race and culture (classism), "there is an implied universality" that connects black women's reality with the experience of others. Therefore, for Grant, "Christ among the least" means that Christ is present in the community of black women and is found in their experience as black women.[44]

More recently, some womanist theologians have begun to address—in addition to racism, sexism, and classism—the problem of homophobia in the African-American community. Kelly Brown Douglas has called for a "social-political analysis of wholeness" that confronts racism, sexism, classism, *and* heterosexism as they affect and are manifested in the African-American community.[45] Urging her womanist colleagues to be self-critical, Brown Douglas states her point forthrightly:

If womanist theologians continue to maintain silence concerning the oppression of our lesbian sisters, not only do we perpetuate their oppression, but we fall short of our own vision for whole-ness.[46]

For Brown Douglas, a social-political analysis of wholeness seeks "to eliminate anything that prevents Black people from being whole, liberated people, and from living as a whole, unified community." This analysis will confront oppressive forces from outside and within the African-American community, and will "help womanist theology to make clear that the Black community is not free if any of its members are 'unfree' because of their color, gender, sexual preference or economic condition."[47]

In similar fashion, Renee L. Hill, a graduate of Union Seminary and a self-identified lesbian, criticizes womanist theologians for failing to "recognize heterosexism and homophobia as points of oppression that need to be resisted if *all* Black women (straight, lesbian, and bisexual) are to have liberation and a sense of their own power."[48] By listening to "the lesbian voice of womanism," Hill believes womanist theologians will be in a better position to address the problem of oppression *within* the African-American community and work toward more liberating images for all black women.[49]

Whereas Jacquelyn Grant and Kelly Brown Douglas interpret the multidimensionality of black women's oppression in light of their understanding of Jesus Christ, Delores Williams examines it in relation to black women's literature.[50] In fact, no womanist scholar has done more to describe the religious experience of African-American women via literature than Delores Williams. A poet and writer herself, Williams analyzes black women's literature to plumb the depths of African-American women's experience of God as they struggle to survive in a hostile world. Moreover, Williams's biblical interpretation and doctrinal critique of classical Christianity present an ongoing challenge to black theology and the black church in particular and the Christian church in general. Certainly, one cannot begin to appreciate the unique contribution womanist theology makes to twentieth-century African-American religious thought without being acquainted with the life and work of Delores Williams.

Biographical Sketch

Like Benjamin Mays, Elijah Muhammad, and James Cone, Delores Williams was born and raised in the South. Born in Louisville, Kentucky, on November 17, 1943, the reality of racial segregation and discrimination shaped Williams's formative years as it did her male counterparts. In fact, as a young girl, Williams remembers the experience of hearing Benjamin Mays describe a trip to India where he was introduced as an "American untouchable"—an event that, no doubt, influ-

enced her emerging racial consciousness.[51] In addition, childhood
memories of the lynching of a black man and the brutal rape of a black
woman by a white man are prominent examples of the racist violence
that left an indelible imprint on Williams's developmental years.[52] Like
pre– and post–Black Power male theologians from the South, Williams
faced the existential contradictions between the faith claims of the gospel on the one hand, and the practice of racial segregation by white
Christians on the other. Needless to say, her emphasis on the survival
and liberation of the African-American community is derived from
the same political and religious tradition that shaped the views of Benjamin Mays, Martin L. King, Jr., and James Cone.

But unlike male religious thinkers, the reality of black women's oppression at the hands of black men also affected Williams's early consciousness. In *Sisters in the Wilderness* she poignantly describes these
memories:

> I remember hearing the bloodcurdling screams of the woman in
> the house next to ours when her husband beat her for acting uppity–
> showing off her education, he said. She had been a schoolteacher.
> She packed her clothes, took her child and went to her mamma's
> house. She never returned to her husband. I remember the man
> living in an alley house at the rear of my grandmother's property.
> One night, when I was ten years old, I saw him beat his wife un-
> mercifully. She had hidden her day-work money and would not
> give it to him. She left the next day and never came back.[53]

In addition to physical violence, Williams recalls the "emotional and
psychological pressure" put upon African-American women by many
black men in leadership positions (school principals, social service administrators, and preachers) who would often threaten to withhold assistance if black women did not consent to their sexual propositions.
Indeed, the fact that African-American women resisted exploitation
and clung to faith in God–despite the awareness that "nobody in the
community did anything to stop this oppression"–led Williams to a
profound respect for the life-struggles and religious experience of African-American women. Concomitantly, Williams learned from observ-
ing the women in her hometown that sexism within the community
must be confronted with the same vigilance as the racist oppression
from the outside.[54]

Clearly, the reality of sexism in the African-American community
and freedom struggle forced Williams to develop a perspective on the
Christian faith that was distinct from the male theologians we have
examined. Therefore, although there is an important stream of continuity between the womanist theology of Delores Williams and the thinking of Benjamin Mays and James Cone, the discontinuity between them

is far more significant for an understanding of African-American religious thought.

Unlike James Cone, her post–Black Power male counterpart, Williams was raised in an extended family with an "eclectic religious background"; her mother's relatives were Seventh Day Adventist and Presbyterian, while her father and stepfather were Catholic and Baptist, respectively. No doubt the absence of strong denominational ties contributed to shaping Williams's nontraditional perspective on Christianity and the black church, and may help to explain why in her recent work she makes a clear distinction between African-American denominational churches and "the black church invisible." For Williams, the latter "does not exist as an institution," but rather as "the heart of hope" in the African-American community's struggle for survival, liberation, and a productive quality of life.[55]

Moreover, Williams's interpretation of the invisible black church was formed, in part, by her "tendency to be very open to other faith traditions." Like Howard Thurman, Williams maintains that religious truth is not confined to Christianity but is also revealed in Islam, Buddhism, Judaism, African traditional religions, and other faith traditions; as she remarks forthrightly, "The question of whether one is more valid than the other doesn't make much sense to me."[56] Therefore, it appears that Williams's ecumenical background influenced her interpretation of the black church invisible:

> It has neither hands nor feet nor form, but we know when we feel it in our communities as neither Christianity, nor Islam, nor Judaism, nor Buddhism, nor Confucianism, nor any human-made religion. Rather, it comes as God-full presence to our struggles quickening the heart, measuring the soul and bathing life with the spirit from head to toe.[57]

Clearly, the different religious environments of James Cone and Delores Williams were bound to produce two very different approaches to Christianity. While Cone's early Christian identity was formed exclusively in the context of the African Methodist Episcopal church, Williams's formative spirituality was shaped by an openness to interdenominational and interfaith dialogue.

As a student at the University of Louisville, Williams became involved in the civil rights movement through the NAACP Youth Council. Like many other young activists, her commitment to the freedom struggle overshadowed her participation in the black denominational churches—institutions she considered to be increasingly out of touch with the social and political needs of black people. Despite her marriage to a young minister, Robert Williams, Delores was more interested "in the black religious ethos" and powerful gospel music that inspired young activists than the black church as an institution.[58] No doubt, Williams's dissatisfaction with the black denominational churches was heightened by Black Power's radical critique of Christianity. Along with her "eclectic religious background," Williams's growing racial and political consciousness pushed her further to the periphery of the institutional black church. Thus, it was Williams's participation in the black freedom movement, and not the mainline black church, that formed the context for her new self-awareness as a black woman:

> I moved inside and outside the liberation movements of my time, looking for a new way of saying: I am a black woman. Up the dirt roads of rural Alabama. Through hot, southern boulevards marching with the youth of my time . . . They spat on us. I spat back, showing them the new meaning of black. Yet there was more of me that needed telling: the woman part.[59]

Williams found her voice as a black woman when she moved to New York City with her husband, a doctoral candidate at Union Seminary, and children in 1968. As the mother of three (she now has four children), Williams still found time to pursue the M.A. degree in comparative religion and literature at Columbia University; write and recite poetry with the "Bud Jones Poets"; type her husband's theology papers; and take classes at Union with Beverly Harrison, Tom Driver, and James Cone. Indeed, Cone's *Black Theology and Black Power* had a profound impact on Williams as she studied theology, literature, and black religious history for more liberating possibilities for African-American churchwomen. Yet, while Williams learned from white feminist and black male theologians, she also realized the urgent need for theological reflection on black women's religious experience. Williams's research took her from doctoral studies at Union to teaching positions at Harvard Divinity School and later Drew University School of Theology, where she taught for four years before returning to Union in 1991 as associate professor of theology and culture. Articles published during these years, as well as her addresses at national academic conferences, established her as a prominent voice in the emerging discipline of womanist theology in particular and North American theology in general.

Black Women's Literature and the Task of Womanist Theology

One of Williams's greatest contributions to womanist thought is her use of black women's literature as a source for doing theology. Unlike pre– and post–Black Power male theologians, Williams examined the writings of black women like Alice Walker, Margaret Walker, and Zora Neale Hurston in order to portray black women's religious experience.

For her, these literary giants yield significant insights for the development of womanist theology by helping to define the nature of black women's oppression and provide effective strategies of resistance.

Alice Walker's *The Color Purple* is an important source for Williams. She is especially drawn to Walker's depiction of Celie's transformation from "debilitating impotence" to empowerment and self-confidence. For Williams, Shug Avery, the liberated bisexual woman who befriends Celie, is the important catalyst who initiates the radical changes of consciousness—new notions about female sexuality, God, men, church, female bonding, and women's economic independence—that lead to Celie's deliverance from self-hatred and shame.[60] Accordingly, Williams interprets Shug's relationship with Celie as an example of what she calls "the catalyst and moral agent model" for resisting oppression, wherein liberated black women help oppressed black women "take the moral action necessary for gaining control of their lives."[61]

Williams also examines Celie's religious experience in order to show that "black Christian women often support their own victimization when they cling to traditional ideas about God." Instead of viewing God as a big white man in heaven, as Celie initially did, Williams urges African-American women to understand God in ways that support "their struggle for liberation as women." However, it is important to note that Williams, like Kelly Brown Douglas, cautions that "a female god, black or white" is not an improvement on the concept of a male god because "exclusive gender designations for God destroy human ability to recognize and appreciate" that God as divine spirit is connected to all of life. Again, it is Shug who helps to expand Celie's concept of God by persuading her that God is neither male nor female, black nor white, but rather a Spirit which lives inside of her and in all of nature.[62]

Regarding Margaret Walker's *Jubilee*, Williams analyzes the experience of the protagonist Vyry, a slave-mother whose deep spirituality enabled her to survive the physical, psychological, and emotional horrors of slavery. Having learned political and spiritual "survival intelligence" from two older black women (Mamma Sukey and Aunt Sally), Vyry worked and prayed for the survival of her children and community.[63] Thus, for Williams, Walker's *Jubilee* confirms an important womanist principle: black female survival/liberation is inseparable from the context of the entire African-American community. Contrary to the misgivings of male activists and theologians during the 1960s, black women's historic struggle for wholeness did not detract from the community's broader political struggle, rather, it enhanced it. In fact, Williams finds in Walker's description of Vyry an example of what she calls "the communal life support model" for fighting oppression:

Everything transformative that happens to this black woman oc-
curs within the context of her commitment to support black community, group, and family goals and aspirations.[64]

Unlike the positive transformations of black women in the works of
Alice Walker and Margaret Walker, the protagonist in Zora Neale
Hurston's *Jonah's Gourd Vine* depicts what Williams calls "the tragic
victim." For Williams, Lucy's experience ("an intelligent black mother
emotionally bedazzled by her philandering preacher husband") resembles that of many African-American women who love men before
loving themselves. As she see it, this creates an overdependence on
men economically and emotionally, and leads to an oppressive, self-
denying love. Therefore, Williams emphasizes Hurston's advice to black
women through Lucy's dying words: "Don't love nobody bettern' yo'
self, do you'll be dying before your time is out."[65] For Williams,
Hurston's tragic victim teaches African-American women that "woman's
greatest gift to herself is self-love. From this love proceeds all positive
action and neighborly care."[66] Just as male Black Power advocates
claimed that black self-love was a prerequisite for universal love, Delores
Williams contended that black women must love themselves in order
to properly love their family and community.

Finally, Williams refers to the work of Alice Walker, Margaret Walker,
and Zora Neale Hurston to demonstrate the fact that black women's
oppression is the result of a multidimensional assault. During slavery,
African-American women were not only the targets of physical and
sexual assault, but their spirits were harassed constantly by white men
who exercised control over their bodies. In the postbellum years, black
men adopted the patriarchal attitudes of white men, thus creating the
second dimension of black women's oppression. Lastly, white women
joined the assault by perpetuating and benefitting from the subjuga-
tion of black women. Although each writer portrayed different aspects
of this oppression, Williams uses their work to emphasize her point
that there is a big difference between the oppression of black and white
women:

> The Afro-American woman's oppression is distinct from that of
> the Anglo-American woman. The Afro-American woman's sexu-
> ality, procreative powers, even her capacity to nurture, are ap-
> propriated by the white ruling class, providing economic ben-
> efits and personal comforts for white men and women.[67]

Because white women have historically compounded the oppression of African-American women, Williams argues that patriarchy is
not the only force determining black women's reality. Therefore, to

define more accurately the nature of black women's oppression, she coined the term *demonarchy*, which means "the demonic governance of black women's lives by white male and female ruled systems using racism, violence, violation, retardation, and death as instruments of social control."[68] Biblically, Williams interprets the story of Hagar as representative of black women's oppression, while Sarai, born in privilege, embodies the experience of white feminists.

CHRISTIANITY, THE BIBLE, AND BLACK WOMEN

Delores Williams's greatest contribution to womanist theology is her work relating the wilderness experience of Hagar (Gn 16:1-16, 21:9-21) to the contemporary social, political, and economic realities facing African-American women. Williams utilizes her skills as a biblical interpreter, historian, and theologian to illuminate the experience of the "oppressed of the oppressed" in scripture and in the African-American community. The implications of her groundbreaking investigation present awesome challenges to black liberation theologians, preachers, and the entire black church and community. More forcefully than any other contemporary theologian, Williams challenges black churches to be critical of the Bible itself "in those instances where the text supports oppression, exclusion, and even death of innocent people." Indeed, she prophetically urges the black community and its theologians to "explore the moral status of violence in *scripture* when the violence is mandated and/or supported by God."[69]

Williams joins Palestinian and Native American theologians, who identify with the Canaanites in the Old Testament rather than the Israelites, in calling for a critical reading of scripture from the perspective of the non-Hebrew victims in the Bible. How can black liberation theologians ignore the fact that the Bible depicts a God who liberates the Israelite slaves from Egypt and then sanctions the perpetual enslavement of non-Hebrews in their midst (Lv 25:46)? How can black liberation theologians identify exclusively with the former Hebrew slaves and overlook the divinely authorized genocide of the Canaanites and the taking of their land? Does the inability to see the "oppressed of the oppressed" in scripture "make it easy for black male theologians and biblical scholars to ignore the figures in the Bible whose experience is analogous to that of black women?"[70] These are challenging questions that cannot be dismissed. Whereas contemporary male religious thinkers have tended to ignore such issues and overlook the experience of biblical women like Hagar, Williams uncovered a vital black cultural tradition which emphasized Hagar's story and its relation to the African-American experience.

Hagar and the Wilderness Experience

Williams researched African-American history and culture and discovered that for over a century the story of Hagar was a recurring theme for male and female sculptors, writers, poets, preachers, scholars, and "just plain folks."[71] This female-centered tradition of African-American biblical appropriation is a valuable source for womanist scholars as they seek to correct black male theologians' exclusive emphasis on the exodus/liberation paradigm. According to Williams, there are "striking similarities" between Hagar's story and that of African-American women, including African heritage; experience of slavery; single motherhood; poverty; forced surrogacy; and salvific wilderness encounters with God.[72]

This common legacy of survival in the midst of oppression indicated to Williams that there are "non-liberative strands" in the Bible and black women's experience that raise serious doubts about black theology's unequivocal claim that God is a liberator of the oppressed. Since God did not liberate Hagar, and since African-American women continue to be invisible victims, how can black liberation theologians make absolute theological claims about God's liberating activity on behalf of *all* oppressed peoples? While Williams acknowledges that God gives survival resources to victims, she insists that she "can't make a once and for all time valid theological claim that God is on the side of the oppressed." As she views it, black theologians who highlight the exodus/liberation tradition have not adequately responded to William Jones's query, Is God a white racist? Williams put it like this:

> If God is on the side of the oppressed, tell me for God's sake—and I do mean for God's sake—why everybody black has been oppressed for all these years. Come on, you either got a weak God or the Devil is more powerful.[73]

Hence, Williams maintains that the experience of Hagar and other non-Hebrew victims in scripture points to a survival/quality of life biblical hermeneutic that is more consistent with the complexities of the African-American experience. This "biblical wilderness tradition" is a more appropriate paradigm because it is female inclusive and emphasizes the vital role of human initiative and responsibility (along with divine intervention) in the community's struggle for survival and liberation. Williams reminds black theologians who accentuate the exodus/liberation tradition that there is a significant wilderness experience in the exodus story, in which the ex-slaves complained to God about the burdens associated with the work of building community and maintaining freedom.[74] Along with Hagar's story, this wilderness experience within the exodus tradition poses a new question for womanist and black liberation theologians: "What is God's word about survival and quality-of-life formation for oppressed and quasi-free people struggling to build community in the wilderness?"[75]

For Williams, God's word to black people in the wilderness of North America is heard in the command given to exiled Jews in Babylonian captivity. The exiles were told:

> Build houses and live in them; plant gardens and eat their pro-
> duce. Take wives and have sons and daughters . . . multiply there,
> and do not decrease. But seek the welfare of the city where I have
> sent you into exile, and pray to the Lord on its behalf, for in its
> welfare you will find your welfare (Jer 29:4-7).

Williams believes that African-Americans will hear in this text God's advice about how to resist "economic captivity" (producing homes and food for themselves) and genocide (producing children to carry on their culture). Furthermore, God's command to the exiles to seek the welfare of the city is a cogent reminder to blacks that their active political involvement and prayers on behalf of American society are the means by which they will secure their own welfare.[76] Like the Hagar and exodus/wilderness experiences, the Babylonian captivity illustrates that both human initiative and divine guidance are required for the survival and well-being of the oppressed. Therefore, Williams concludes that the womanist survival/quality-of-life hermeneutic teaches African-American Christians that

> liberation is an ultimate, but in the meantime survival and pros-
> perity must be the experience of our people. And God has had
> and continues to have a word to say about the survival and qual-
> ity of life of the descendants of African female slaves.[77]

It is important to note that Williams's emphasis on the survival/ quality-of-life paradigm is not a denial of the significance of the exodus/liberation tradition of black biblical interpretation. Williams does not propose that black preachers and theologians cease using the language and ideas of liberation as found in the Bible and black people's historic experience. However, she underscores the point that while the exodus paradigm was the most meaningful to blacks during the period of American slavery, it is not the *only* way subsequent generations have interpreted scripture. Equally important is the manner in which blacks in the post–Civil War era appropriated the biblical wilderness tradition with its emphasis on survival, the building of community, and securing a productive quality of life. Therefore, Williams rightly asserts that any contemporary African-American systematic theology built on the exodus paradigm *alone* ignores "generations of black history subsequent to slavery" and relegates "the community and the black theological imagination to a kind of historical stalemate that denies the possibility of change with regard to the people's experience of God and with regard to the possibility of God changing in relation to the community."[78]

Jesus Saves: Through His Life or His Death?

No aspect of Williams's theology has generated more controversy and debate that her rejection of the classical Christian doctrine of the atonement. In a bold and straightforward fashion, Williams repudiates the orthodox notion that the redemption of sinful humanity is accomplished by Jesus' sacrificial death on the cross.

It is important to stress that Williams's objection to the substitution theory of atonement is based on her strong belief that it reinforces the oppression of black women in particular and the black community in general. Indeed, one cannot understand Williams's position without seeing how black people's experience as surrogates and scapegoats informs her interpretation of the Christian doctrine of salvation.

Like James Cone, Williams insists that African-American Christians cannot accept any interpretation of Christian doctrine that does not enhance the black struggle for survival and liberation.[79] Thus, she contends that black women's historic experience with surrogacy raises serious questions about the way Christians understand redemption. Whether one considers the coerced (antebellum) or voluntary (postbellum) surrogacy roles filled by African-American women, Williams maintains that it is an exploitative function that reinforces negative stereotypes of black women; robs them of "self-consciousness, self-care, and self-esteem"; and puts them "in the service of other people's desires, tasks, and goals."[80] For Williams, the notion that Jesus died on the cross as the ultimate surrogate endows surrogacy with "an aura of the sacred" and is, therefore, an oppressive image for black women, who have been the victims of surrogacy. Williams asks, "Can there be salvific power for black women in Christian images of oppression (for example, Jesus on the cross) meant to teach something about redemption?"[81] Williams answers with a resounding "No!"

Similarly, Williams argues that the scapegoating of black people throughout American history forces African-American Christians to re-evaluate what they teach about redemption and salvation. The Old Testament image of the goat who symbolically carries the sins of the people into the wilderness on the day of atonement was appropriated in the New Testament, where Jesus is depicted as the sacrificial lamb who bears the sins of the world. However, for Williams, the notion of the innocent dying for the sins of the guilty reinforces and legitimates white people's tendency to scapegoat African-Americans and must be discarded post haste.[82] In her opinion, scapegoated black Christians who embrace the classical doctrine of the atonement cannot struggle effectively against white oppressors who have been programmed to adopt racial scapegoating as a means of their economic and political salvation. Contrary to Benjamin Mays and other pre–Black Power male theologians, Williams argues that "it is of no avail for scapegoated people to appeal to the conscience of Christian oppressors." In fact, she suggests that African-American Christians who interpret Jesus as the divine scapegoat may be "participating in our own victimization" and "inadvertently teaching Black people to accept their own status as scapegoats."[83]

For Williams, the best way to avoid this theological error is to emphasize that Jesus redeemed humanity through his "*ministerial* vision of life and not his death." Like pre– and post–Black Power male theologians, Delores Williams believes that the chief significance of Jesus is found in his compassionate, ethical, and militant ministry on behalf of suffering humanity. For Williams, "Jesus did not come to be a surrogate"; rather, he came to heal broken bodies, minds, and spirits through a "ministry of righting relationships" that showed human beings how to live abundant, productive, and compassionate lives. Thus, the cross is not an image of redemption, but rather "a gross manifestation of collective human sin," and "a reminder of how humans have tried throughout history to destroy visions of righting relationships" that fundamentally challenge the status quo. For Williams, the continuing presence of radical human evil demonstrates that Jesus did not conquer sin on the cross; instead, Jesus defeated sin in life by resisting the evil forces that tempted him to compromise the integrity of his ministerial vision (Mt 4:1-11).[84]

Williams's emphasis on the earthly ministry of Jesus as recorded in the synoptic gospels is consistent with the views of male Christian thinkers in the periods before and after Black Power. As we have seen, both Benjamin Mays and James Cone stress Jesus' profound love for humanity, and interpret his death *primarily* as a political consequence of his commitment to the oppressed. In this regard, there is a thread of continuity that ties Williams's theology to that of her male counterparts. However, Williams's total *rejection* of the classical doctrine of the atonement shows the discontinuity between her theology and that of Mays and Cone. More than pre– and post–Black Power male theologians, Williams wants to *ensure* that Jesus' death is not interpreted in a manner that supports the oppression of black women in particular and African-Americans in general. First, Williams reminds black women that genuine Christianity does not endorse their surrogacy experience, but rather denounces it as sin. Moreover, she urges black Christian women to realize that "There is nothing divine in the blood of the cross":

As Christians, black women cannot forget the cross, but neither can they glorify it. To do so is to glorify suffering and to render their exploitation sacred. To do so is to glorify the sin of defilement.[85]

Similarly, Williams calls on the entire African-American Christian community (male and female) to "throw out all images, beliefs, and practices that support scapegoating of any person or group." In her mind, blacks "do not need images of bloodthirsty gods," and therefore "cannot affirm any salvific power in a poor, innocent man dying on the cross for our sins or anybody's else's."[86]

Lastly, it is important to emphasize that Williams, like the male thinkers we have discussed, develops her theology in light of her awareness that Christianity is on trial in the African-American community. For her, a major aspect of this ongoing critique hinges on the classical doctrine of the atonement and the way it functions in the oppression of African-Americans. How can the black church correct many youths' perception of Christianity as a weak religion when its doctrine of salvation is based on a crucified Jesus, sacrificed for the sins of the world—including those of his executioners? Just as black preachers and theologians of the late 1960s believed that a reinterpretation of the faith was necessary if the black church was to reach young people, Williams suggests that current religious leadership should "call together councils of African-American Christendom to examine what we teach and believe":

Perhaps when we rid our religion of debilitating images, more of our young Black children will be able to affirm the value of the Christian religion. Perhaps more of them will turn away from the streets and come into the churches. Perhaps African Americans will then see and identify with Jesus whose activity is not salvation in death, but liberation into an abundant life.[87]

The "Re-Imagining 1993" Controversy

Williams sparked a wave of controversy when she presented her nontraditional ideas on the atonement at the "Re-Imagining 1993" Conference in Minneapolis (November 4-7, 1993). More than two thousand women attended the international gathering as part of the World Council of Churches' Ecumenical Decade in Solidarity with Women. The workshops, liturgies, and addresses examined new feminist/womanist images of God, Jesus Christ, the Holy Spirit, and the church. Creative liturgies invoking Sophia (Greek for "Wisdom") as a biblical feminine metaphor for God, and theological discussions on the relationship between sexuality and spirituality caused an uproar among conservative groups in some mainline denominations and brought widespread charges of goddess worship, heresy, and apostasy. Conservatives in the United Methodist and Presbyterian (U.S.A.) churches used their magazines to express their opposition and demand the resignation of female denominational officials who supported and participated in the conference. Moreover, conservatives highlighted Delores Williams's widely publicized remark, "I don't think we need folks hanging on crosses and blood dripping and weird stuff," as an example of the "heretical" ideas that characterized the conference.[88]

Somewhat surprised at the "storm of vengeful criticism" that followed, Williams responded with a prophetic critique of the "conservative, patriarchal forces" in the white denominations reminiscent of James Cone's early writing. Reflecting upon the history of black people's encounter with racist, white Christianity, Williams realized that "black Christians have always been forced to re-image the Christian religion." This tradition of re-imaging was necessary to redeem the gospel from "the desecrated imagery of White Christians," and ultimately gave rise to a "beautiful, redemptive Black liberation theology." However, Williams observed that the same conservative forces that criticized James Cone's black theology in the early 1970s are now attacking contemporary women's re-imaging of patriarchal Christianity.[89]

Just as James Cone revealed the insincerity of white theologians who questioned the Christian identity of black theology while remaining silent about the racial sins of the white church, Williams exposes the *hypocrisy* of conservative, white male Christians who criticize feminist/womanist re-imaging and ignore their own re-imaging of Jesus as a white-skinned, blue-eyed, middle-class, Euro-American male with long, straight hair. "If this Jesus is not the product of reimaging," Williams argued, "nothing is." But more important, Williams criticizes the opponents of the conference for attacking women's voices while neglecting the massive social problems that confront poor, suffering people. Instead of developing a prophetic social ministry that seeks to raise consciousness about the plight of the poor by confronting the "powers and principalities," Williams contended that "the church is being manipulated to engage in a foolish battle to control women and to silence God's voice within and among us." But boldly and defiantly, Williams assured the white conservative critics of "Re-Imagining 1993" that "the unfolding of God in our midst will not be controlled—by anyone."[90] As we shall see below, Williams's critique of African-American male Christian leadership is equally prophetic.

WOMANIST CRITIQUE OF THE AFRICAN-AMERICAN DENOMINATIONAL CHURCHES

Like the male Christian thinkers examined in this study, Delores Williams issues a challenging critique of the African-American denominational churches. Like James Cone, Williams is a keen observer of the strengths and weaknesses of the institutional black church; indeed, her penetrating critique demonstrates her deep commitment to serve her people as a prophetic and creative theologian. Hence, I contend that a faithful response to her challenge to the black church is essential if the church is to regain its credibility as an effective vehicle of black liberation in the twenty-first century.

Strengths of the African-American Denominational Churches

As I see it, Williams's trenchant critique of the black church is best interpreted in light of her acknowledgment that despite its sins against black women, "there have been moments in African-American history when some of the denominational churches have been effective instruments of freedom, survival and positive quality of life formation for all black people."[91] For Williams, these "moments" constitute historical periods when the African-American denominational churches embodied the invisible black church as the "holy Godforce" empowering the community in its fight for justice. Inspired by the faith of their slave foreparents, the black denominations founded schools, built housing for the poor, and produced "black salvation-bearers" like Harriet Tubman, Sojourner Truth, Ida Wells Barnett, Frederick Douglass, Martin Luther King, Jr., and many others whose names are not remembered. Thus, for Williams, "The black church has been the holy Godforce holding black people together body, soul and spirit as the perpetrators of genocide tried to exterminate the community."[92]

Like James Cone, Williams evaluates the contemporary black denominational churches in light of this legacy of social and political action. Both thinkers emphasize the crucial role the church must play in the community's fight against genocide, which Williams defines as *all* attempts to weaken the viability of the African-American community— from attacking its leaders to undermining the political and economic independence of the community.[93] Moreover, just as Cone proclaimed that the church's Christian identity hinged on its active participation in the liberation struggle, Williams argues that solidarity with suffering humanity is the distinguishing mark of the authentic Christian:

> To be Christian is to share one's skills and economic resources with victims. To be a Christian is to affirm the life of black Americans and other threatened groups by joining their survival struggle against genocide . . . To be a Christian in North America is to wage war against the white cultural, social and religious values that make the genocide of black people possible. To be a Christian is to wage this war in the name of Jesus and his ministerial vision of relationship.[94]

According to Williams, the African-American denominational churches (despite patriarchal liturgy and leadership) have been "psychosocial places" that affirm black women's humanity and offer relief from the everyday domestic, social, and economic burdens of life.[95] In an earlier essay she described this healing function of black worship as "casting out the intolerable pain demonic rule instills in its victims." The "joyful noise" and deep spirituality that often characterize the worship of African-American denominational churches "represent the black woman's thanks to God for the revitalization of her spirit which demonarchy has tried to destroy."[96]

Nevertheless, Williams concludes that institutional black churches function like "two-edged" swords with respect to black women: they sustain black women emotionally, but they also "suppress and help to make invisible black women's thought and culture," which is rarely reflected in the sermons, liturgies, and educational materials of the black denominational churches.[97] Hence, along with the strengths that characterize periods of the churches' valiant struggle for survival and liberation, there are serious limitations that must be addressed if the contemporary black church is to be true to the gospel of Jesus Christ.

Weaknesses of the African-American Denominational Churches

While Williams acknowledges the "outstanding work" some black ministers and congregations are doing to address the enormous social problems facing the African-American community (gang violence, drug addiction, homelessness, AIDS, poverty, and joblessness),[98] she also levels a prophetic critique of black denominational churches that essentially falls into two basic categories: the *general* failure to live up to the social and political legacy of the invisible black church, and the *specific* "multitude of sins against black women prevalent in the African-American denominational churches on a daily basis."[99] Let us first examine Williams's critique as it pertains to the churches' social and political witness.

Like pre- and post–Black Power male theologians, Delores Williams reiterates the otherworldly critique of African-American churches. She argues that the teaching and proclamation of the churches is often too "heaven directed" and insufficiently grounded in the social, political, and economic realities that hinder the productive quality of life of black people. Closely related to this limitation is the misplaced priorities of some churches, which frequently lead to an overemphasis on building costly new edifices "while thousands of black people live in dire poverty." Of what value is a new, million dollar building if there are no viable social programs there *during* the week to meet the needs of the black community? Instead, Williams believes that the African-American denominational churches should focus on consistently pooling their resources (across denominational and class lines) in order to develop effective ministries that address the needs of people who are drug-addicted, homeless, poor, unemployed, incarcerated, and suffering with health problems such as AIDS.[100]

Second, Williams addresses the lack of political commitment and moral integrity on the part of black male ministers who abuse their office for selfish, personal gain. This popular critique of black religious leadership has been widely discussed by scholars and lay observers alike since the 1940s; it continues to shape the image of ministry in the minds of many African-Americans.[101] In *Revolution in Zion* Charles Shelby Rooks reveals his own negative perceptions of black ministers, far too many of whom "seemed to live in large houses and drive big cars while their members lived in poverty." Indeed, when Rooks became the executive director of the Fund for Theological Education in 1960, he was "convinced of the need to develop new images of ministerial behavior in the African-American community."[102]

Like pre– and post–Black Power male thinkers, Williams is critical of the unethical alliances that are often formed between some black ministers and the white power structures that reward them in exchange for their political endorsement. For her, the stereotypical notion ("fostered by white politicians, media, and power structures") that black preachers head the *only* viable black institution leads to the false perception of them as *the* "power brokers" between the black community and the white establishment, and invites corruption and the misuse of pastoral authority. Moreover, Williams contends that this alliance is especially dangerous because "the liberation interests of the black community become highly compromised as the preacher's personal ambitions are rewarded by the collusive white power structures." Williams goes on to contrast the conservative black religious leadership of the denominational churches with the courageous political challenge posed by ministers such as Martin L. King, Jr., and Malcolm X–leaders who founded religio-political organizations that operated "beyond the power range of either the denominational churches or the black Muslim movement."[103]

While there are similarities between the criticisms levelled by African-American male theologians and those of Delores Williams, the differences are more important for understanding the unique contribution womanist theology makes to the tradition of African-American prophetic Christianity. Unlike male thinkers, who failed to criticize the oppressive sexism of the black church until the error was forcefully pointed out by womanist theologians, Williams issues a scathing indictment that pronounces God's judgment on the African-American denominational churches. Just as some black male theologians argued that God will judge the white church for practicing racism, Williams proclaimed that "God will surely judge the African-American denominational churches for oppressing women."[104]

Like her nineteenth-century womanist foremothers, Williams criticizes black denominational structures for rejecting black women's equal right to ordination and positions of pastoral leadership. This specific sin not only insults black women, it actually "opposes God by denying God's call to black women to preach." Although more male pastors have been forced to recognize black women's profound gifts for preaching and ministry, there remains a stubborn resistance to view them as *equal* partners in the Lord's service. Thus, while the most blatant manifestations of sexist discrimination in some denominations may have diminished in recent years, the subtle and covert forms of resisting female pastoral leadership continue to put formidable obstacles in the path of black women ministers. To be a female seeking ordination and respect in the National Baptist Convention is still a lonely and difficult task. Even some churches with a more inclusive policy on female pastors are shamefully reluctant to criticize the oppressive habits that discourage rather than embrace women as pastoral leaders. "Time and time again," Williams reports, "black women have told me some of their male colleagues try to 'set them up' to fail in their ministries."[105]

In addition to the sin against black female ministers, Williams criticizes the black church for tolerating the sexual exploitation of black women. As she views it, the countless reported and unreported cases of male ministers' immoral sexual behavior with female parishioners weakens the churches' credibility and "sets a terrible example" for black youth in need of moral models of responsible and honest leadership. Convinced that "this kind of activity in the denominational churches will only stop when black women open their mouths and tell their stories," Williams urges African-American women to tell the truth about their sexual, financial, and emotional exploitation in the denominational churches "for the benefit of black people, so that the churches can be cleaned up within, so that the salvation and liberation of black women in the churches can occur."[106]

While there are endless examples of overt, blatant sexism in the African-American denominational churches, Williams focuses her critique on what she calls the "colonization of female mind and culture."[107] This refers to the manner in which black women have been encouraged to read the Bible uncritically and accept the patriarchal liturgy and leadership of the black church as sacred. Indeed, it is black women's internalization of sexist oppression that presents the most fundamental challenge for womanist theology. As Williams notes, the black denominational church (composed of nearly 85 percent women) "is basically a women's community" that can be "transformed from within if the sisters decide to do so, since they control the purse strings in the church."[108] Thus, Williams calls for a movement within the denominational churches "to free women's minds and lives of the androcentric indoctrination and exploitative emotional commitments that cause many women to be tools of their own oppression and that of other women."[109]

In addition, Williams calls for the development of "resistance doctrines" and "rituals of resistance" to preserve the memory of black women's and the black community's unique faith experience. For Williams, African-American denominational churches have failed to write their own faith story into black scripture that records for future generations "God's wondrous way of dealing with them during bondage and in liberation."[110] Moreover, in her essay "Rituals of Resistance in Womanist Worship," Williams maintains that womanist worship (inclusive black church worship where women's thought and experience are reflected in every aspect of the service) calls for "resistance rituals" using items such as overturned pots to remind black congregations of their origins in slavery, as well as other rituals that celebrate important male- and female-led events in the civil rights movement.[111]

For Williams, the black church and people will remain in bondage until the community writes its own "African-American scripture" (which includes the visions and testimonies of nineteenth-century preaching women such as Jarena Lee, Zilpha Elaw, and Julia Foot) and develops female inclusive "resistance rituals" to commemorate its rich history of faith and struggle. In a manner that reflects the biblical emphasis on teaching faith to succeeding generations (e.g., Psalm 78:1-8), Williams contends that until the black church develops liberating womanist liturgy, "African-American children, female and male, will continue to be ignorant of the historical foundations of the great spiritual heritage of which they are the recipients."[112]

Thankfully, there are some churches that have responded to the challenging critique of Delores Williams and other womanist theologians. These churches embrace women's language, thought, and experience as an integral part of ministry and understand the importance of resistance doctrines and rituals. But, unfortunately, many more black churches continue "business as usual" and cling to sexist language, biblical interpretation, practices, and traditions that oppress women and rob the church and community of the spiritual and intellectual gifts God gave to women. The black church will continue to have a credibility problem as long as it persists in denying and failing to respect its most faithful members.

Conclusion

Reclaiming a Self-Critical Black Faith

Examine yourselves, to see whether you are holding to your faith. Test yourselves. Do you not realize that Jesus Christ is in you?—unless indeed you fail to meet the test! I hope you will find out that we have not failed.
  —2 Corinthians 13:5-6

If Christian theology is the critical self-testing of church proclamation in light of the gospel, then black slaves who reshaped oppressive white missionary Christianity into a liberating black faith were theologians par excellence. Contrary to Joseph Washington's claim that the black church was not Christian because of its failure to develop a creedal tradition,[1] black slaves and their descendants have produced a rich theological legacy that issues a prophetic challenge to both black and white churches. In the pre– and post–Black Power eras, Christian thinkers from Benjamin Mays and Anna Arnold Hedgeman to James Cone and Delores Williams have critically examined the theology, preaching, and ministry of American churches in light of the liberating gospel of Jesus Christ.

Critics and Defenders of the Faith: A Summary

Themselves the victims of oppression sanctioned by Christian churches (slavery, segregation, and sexism), African-American religious thinkers have sought to reveal the distinction between liberating Christianity and oppressive Christianity. In the post–World War II years, Negro, black, and womanist theologians became increasingly aware of how Christianity had been used to reinforce their oppression. In their effort to cling to faith, these Christian thinkers articulated a theological perspective that called for the ongoing testing of the church's ministry in light of Jesus' message of freedom and justice for the oppressed.

Although African-American Christian theologians subjected their faith to deep internal critique, they were also criticized from the outside by non-Christian black nationalists, who charged that "Christianity is the white man's religion." Elijah Muhammad and members of the Nation of Islam represented thousands of ex-Christians who were no longer able to embrace the faith of their integrationist brothers and sisters in the churches. As they saw it, Christianity was an oppressive, slave-making religion that would never produce freedom for African-Americans.

The widespread appeal of the nationalist critique put Negro Christians in an awkward position. On the one hand, they knew that racism and segregation in the church made it an oppressive institution; consequently, they could not dismiss as ill-founded the Negroes' rising loss of faith in Christianity. Members of the Institute of Religion at Howard University discussed this issue in deliberations on "The Christian Imperative in Race Relations" in the mid 1940s. William Stuart Nelson, the founding editor of the *Journal of Religious Thought* (1943), accepted as legitimate the complaints many African-Americans had against Christianity:

> Of all the offenses from which Negroes have suffered, none is so tragic as that which has affected their spirit. Many things have happened to the Negroes' spirit since they became slaves. They have learned to hate, to accommodate, to dissemble. But the affliction that concerns us most . . . is their loss of faith—faith in their religion and in their country. It is not a complete loss of faith but it is a mounting one and a dangerous one.[2]

While Negro theologians shared the frustrations of those who were abandoning the faith, they insisted that Christianity was essentially a religion of liberation that offered practical solutions to the problem of race relations in America. Therefore, they found themselves in the position of having to criticize the church for preserving the racist status quo, and defending it on the basis of its noble ideals and principles. As critics and defenders of the faith, Negro theologians were the prime targets of the Nation of Islam and other black nationalist groups who wondered why Negro Christians would embrace a faith they themselves criticized, and then turn around and defend it in the presence of those who would discard it.

Negro theologians' commitment to Christianity and integration (considered the two major symbols of whiteness by the Nation of Islam) also came under fire in the Black Power movement of the late 1960s. In fulfilling their roles as critics and defenders of the faith in the new context of Black Power, younger Negro pastors and theologians converted to blackness while their older counterparts maintained their integrationist approach to the gospel. Profoundly challenged by Black Power's indictment of Christianity and the black church, prophetic African-American pastors publicly issued an honest, internal critique of their religious leadership—a practice seldom seen among contemporary black ministers and theologians. Quite significantly, this prophetic self-criticism was also a means by which black preachers defended biblical Christianity as a truly liberating faith which neither white nor black churches had faithfully practiced.

Finally, we saw how African-American female religious scholars criticized the sexism of black male preachers and theologians and articulated a womanist Christian perspective that sought to build upon the strengths of black liberation theology and eliminate its weaknesses. As the most recent expression of African-American critique examined in this study, womanist theology put white and black Christianity on trial for failure to address the relationship between race, class, and sex as interlocking factors in black women's oppression. Indeed, one awaits the critique of womanist theology that will lead to yet another prophetic expression in the continuous stream of African-American religious thought.

The Right Theology for the Right Time

No theological position speaks for all people for all time. A static theology that does not respond to new socio-cultural events in the community cannot help the Christian church interpret its faith for succeeding generations. Indeed, the rapid developments in African-American Christian thought illustrate the important point that all theology must be carefully scrutinized in light of the gospel. Since no one perspective can capture the breadth of the gospel, there will always be the need for ongoing dialogue on the liberative and oppressive elements of historical manifestations of Christianity.

Given the realization that all theology is conditioned by the social and political forces that produced it, one is in a better position to appreciate the distinctive contribution of each theology examined in this work. For example, there is no need to take the extreme position of celebrating the black theology of James Cone while disparaging the perspective of Benjamin Mays; to do this would be to ignore the fundamental similarities that exist between pre– and post–Black Power religious thought. Both Mays and Cone interpreted the liberating gospel of Jesus in the context of white racism and emphasized the church's radical mission in America and the world. In fact, Benjamin Mays, writing his autobiography at the height of the Black Power movement, hoped to "bridge the wide gap in thinking and experience between my generation and the present generation." Certainly, Mays's comment about the integral relationship between pre– and post–Black Power social activism is directly applicable to the area of theology as well:

> Young black Americans have made great contributions to improve human relations through sit-ins, boycotts, and demonstrations which those of us who are older could hardly have made in our time; *and yet the present generation of young people have built on*

the foundations laid by their elders through "blood, sweat and tears," and through the innocent deaths of millions of Negroes who lived a long time ago.[3]

Moreover, as we have seen, Mays was proud of his racial heritage. Yet, while he appreciated "the current emphasis on blackness," he reminded his young readers that he was "mighty glad I didn't have to wait seventy years for someone in the late 1960s to teach me to appreciate what I am—black!" Hence, any interpretation of African-American religion that ignores the fundamental *continuity* that links pre– and post–Black Power theology is inadequate.

Christianity on Trial argues that the basic *discontinuity* between pre– and post–Black Power male theologians is largely the result of different historical realities which called for different interpretations of Christianity. The universalism of Benjamin Mays, Howard Thurman, and Martin Luther King, Jr., was a necessary response to the racist theology of southern segregationists who preached white supremacy and Negro inferiority. However, the emergence of Black Power brought a new set of concerns raised by disillusioned youth in the ghettos of the urban North. Hence, two different historical and geographical situations created two different theologies. Negro male theologians developed a liberal theology of race relations that was adequate for the South during the 1940s, 1950s, and early 1960s; their perspective served as an important corrective to the theologies of white segregationists as well as southern black conservatives who divorced the gospel from social action. Similarly, black theologians developed a theology of blackness and liberation that was better suited to meet the spiritual, social, and political needs of young northern blacks in the late 1960s and 1970s; their views served as a corrective to the universalism of pre–Black Power theology in a new era of black consciousness. However, both theologies were inadequate for the concern of African-American women, whose unique experience of oppression was overlooked by both Negro and black male theologians. Accordingly, black female religious scholars developed a womanist theology in the mid 1980s as a corrective to the sexism of pre– and post–Black Power male theologians.

It is my contention that this point-counterpoint type of theological activity is a healthy development in African-American religious thought. The value of this ongoing theological debate is that it fosters honest dialogue among segments in the community with different perspectives and helps to deepen theological reflection. As noted earlier, it was because of black preachers' dialogue with non-Christian nationalists that black theology came into being. The Nation of Islam served an invaluable function for the black church by exposing the limitations of Negro Christian theology and forcing black preachers and theologians to take an "outside" view of the black church; this enabled them to tailor their reinterpretation of the gospel for black youth who were on the verge of rejecting Christianity and the black church altogether. Likewise, black women's critique and dialogue with black male theologians and preachers helped to create the emergence of womanist theology. Therefore, I contend that the tradition of African-American prophetic critique of Christianity examined in this work demonstrates the truth of Paul Tillich's insightful interpretation of what he called the Protestant principle:

> For Christianity is final only in so far as it has the power of criticizing and transforming each of its historical manifestations; and just this is the power of the Protestant principle.[4]

Separating Truth from Falsehood in the Black Churches

As a teenager I learned the importance of testing faith statements in light of Jesus' teachings as recorded in the New Testament. I remember vividly my angry reaction to the unethical fundraising tactics of a local radio ministry, which promised spiritual and financial blessings on all who donated ten dollars for a "free" miracle-producing prayer cloth. I wrote a letter to this false prophet expressing my outrage that a so-called Christian ministry would intentionally exploit the desperate plight of suffering people. Even now, years later, I am still outraged at the schemes, tricks, and gimmicks of unchristian preachers and televangelists (in charismatic and denominational churches), convincing me of the vital importance of prophetic theology in black churches.

I believe that as African-American churches prepare for ministry in the twenty-first century, there is an urgent need for critical evaluation of church teaching and preaching in light of the gospel of Jesus. Just as first century Christians were admonished to carefully discern false prophets from true ones (1 Jn 4:1-6; 2 Tm 4:1-5; 2 Pt 2:1-3), twenty-first-century African-American Christians will also need to weigh critically the teachings of their preachers and theologians. Indeed, *Christianity on Trial* seeks to join the prophetic stream of African-American religious thought, which has consistently argued that black churches must encourage honest self-criticism and meaningful dialogue on the important issues of life and faith if they are to be viable instruments of black spiritual and political liberation.

There can be no *true* prophetic theology without the critical self-testing of faith. Unfortunately, in many African-American churches the leadership does not work hard enough to create an atmosphere where constructive criticism and challenging questions about sermons, budgets, and programs are welcomed and encouraged. All too often there seems to be an exclusive emphasis placed on worshiping God with the heart, soul, and strength, but not with the mind. But when the meaningful exchange of ideas and the work of constructive dialogue are not seen as worship, there is little wonder why prophetic theology is not welcome in many churches. Instead of seeking to evade criticism, however, African-American church leaders would do well to embrace the Apostle Paul's admonition to examine themselves by encouraging honest dialogue and demonstrating a willingness to engage in radical self-critique.

I am a firm believer that self-criticism is a prerequisite for growth. People and institutions who are not willing to examine their weaknesses send a clear message (whether consciously or unconsciously) that they do not want to grow and improve. While most African-American Christian leaders would certainly not identify themselves as people who are opposed to personal growth and development, there is often a stubborn reluctance to acknowledge limitations, thus hindering renewal and honest dialogue in the churches. I believe that the path to a more liberated and liberating black church entails a vigorous commitment to truth—truth that begins with radical self-critique.

In what ways do pastors and theologians stifle the voices of those we claim to represent? How can black church leadership create an atmosphere in the context of Christian education classes *and* the Sunday morning worship event that fosters more participation and dialogue? How can we break down the barriers of class, color, gender and sexual orientation that divide clergy, theologians, and members of the very same congregation—not to mention the entire African-American community? These are challenging questions that many pastors and churches do not want to confront with honesty and courage. Yet only a radical commitment to "speak the truth in love" (Eph 4:15) can enable the African-American denominational churches to create a more vibrant, holistic community.

Like the NCBC leaders who responded to Black Power's indictment against the black church by openly confessing their limitations, contemporary black clergy must acknowledge their weaknesses if Christianity and the black church are to have credibility in the African-American community. In fact, it is precisely the churches which do not subject their ministries to continual self-testing that are in the most danger of becoming ineffective, self-righteous, and despotic. As Carlyle Fielding Stewart, III, pastor-scholar of the Hope United Methodist Church in Southfield, Michigan, has argued in *African-American Church Growth: Twelve Principles for Prophetic Ministry*, prophetic ministry involves not only confronting injustice in society, "but equally witnessing to those forces, powers, and principalities which stifle the church from within, thus thwarting the full emergence of the redemptive community."[5] But Stewart is right to also insist that the zeal that inspires prophetic ministers to confront "the tyrannies of church life" should also "*compel pastors to place themselves on trial for the wrongs and injustices they may have committed in the execution of the office of ministry.*"[6] Indeed, I have heard many eloquent sermons and addresses by prophetic black ministers and theologians on the sins of the black church, but only a few that address their own participation in the sins they condemn.

The theological task of separating truth from falsehood in the black church is especially important when we consider the rise in popularity of white conservative evangelicals, who often copy the language and style of black preachers but not their historic commitment to social and political justice for the oppressed. A growing number of African-American young adult Christians have been leaving mainline Protestant churches in favor of the "prosperity gospel" preached by white and black conservative ministers and televangelists. Aside from the consumer culture of the Reagan-Bush years, might not some African-American Christians seek out such congregations because the historic black church has failed to teach its members that the *true* gospel of Jesus has nothing to do with promises of material prosperity, and everything to do with sacrifice and struggle. As pastor-scholar James H. Harris stated in *Pastoral Theology: A Black-Church Perspective*, "Empty religion is spirituality without social consciousness." Regrettably, Harris is right in his observation that the contemporary black denominational churches are often as empty and socially irrelevant as the conservative prosperity churches:

> Few black ministers on radio and television are preaching liberation messages, urging the church to be an active agent of social change . . . If every black preacher in America decided to confront seriously the status quo through sermons and programs that advocated protest against our cavalier treatment of the poor, we could begin the process of transforming the condition of life for the oppressed in society. This radical approach to ministry would enable the church to reclaim its heritage as an institution that has been on the cutting edge of social change.[7]

If the black church does not preserve the legacy of struggle that called it into existence, more and more of its members will abandon it in favor of black imitations of white apolitical and socially irrelevant evangelicalism.

I believe the black church and its theologians must teach Christians that there are essentially two basic types of Christianity manifest in society: liberating Christianity and oppressive Christianity. Liberating Christianity highlights Jesus as the one who frees individuals from sin, guilt, shame, self-hatred, and all other internal demons that keep people from living joyful, productive lives. Liberating Christianity emphasizes an experience with Jesus, who is the spirit of truth itself making broken, fragmented individuals whole and free (Jn 8:31-36). But liberating Christianity also understands Jesus as the One who inspires a community of disciples to pray and fight against external manifestations of

the demonic in the form of social, political, economic, and gender oppression, which threaten to destroy God's people (Lk 10:1-3, 25-37). In
addition to the private devotional reading of scripture, liberating Christianity also entails a critical reading of the Bible that highlights its contemporary relevance for the community's fight against the social and
political dynamics of black oppression.

The emphasis on Jesus the Liberator, who empowers Christians in
their struggle against injustice, is consistent with Delores Williams's
use of the survival/quality-of-life paradigm. The Jesus who enables the
oppressed to survive and attain a productive quality of life is the same
Jesus who inspires them in their political struggle to transform the systems of injustice and achieve full liberation. Indeed, the spirit of Jesus,
which enabled countless black slaves to survive the spiritual and political forces of dehumanization with their dignity intact, also motivated
their descendants to struggle and protest in the civil rights movement's
quest for social and political freedom.

Oppressive Christianity, on the other hand, suffocates believers with
rules and regulations that hinder personal growth and freedom. It neglects the "weightier matters" of justice and mercy for the poor and
places heavy burdens on the people in order to increase the pastor's
prestige. Oppressive Christianity preserves tradition for tradition's sake,
is inflexible and dictatorial, and teaches believers to serve out of fear
instead of love (Mt 23:4, 13-15, 23-27).

Unlike Jesus the Liberator, oppressive Christianity's Jesus reinforces
low self-esteem by convincing the poor that their social plight is irrelevant as long as their souls are saved. Oppressive Christianity is unable to inspire the church to confront social evil because it places *sole*
emphasis on Jesus as a source of emotional comfort and fails to show
the relationship between spirituality and the struggle for justice. All
too often, it sees prayer as the only resource available to Christians;
this leads to a superficial understanding of spirituality as a panacea for
everything that is wrong in the world. In short, oppressive Christianity
cannot lead believers to a positive, productive quality of life; instead it
produces a negative, unhealthy survival/nontransforming mentality that
actually perpetuates oppression. Indeed, this is the type of Christianity
that has drawn the scorn of Elijah Muhammad, Malcolm X, Albert
Cleage, secular Black Power advocates, James Cone, and Delores Williams.

More recently, Grammy Award winning rap group Arrested Development addressed the stifling character of oppressive Christianity in
the song "Fishin' 4 Religion." These young rappers rightly understand
that the tendency to ask God to solve problems that human beings can
resolve is oppressive because it hinders Christians from understanding
their responsibility as followers of Jesus who are called to be engaged
actively in making the world a better place in which to live.

Arrested Development criticizes black church leadership for lulling its members to sleep with an otherworldly theology that discourages collective action against social injustice. As they see it, suffering Christians who bring their "legitimate woes" to the black church are sedated by pastors who recommend "shoutin'" and "prayin'" as coping devices. Dissatisfied with this oppressive approach to the gospel, the rapper in the song decides to leave the church and go "fishin'" for a liberating religion that empowers people to struggle for social change.

If the black church does not do a more effective job of separating truth from falsehood by teaching its members the difference between liberating and oppressive Christianity, more and more young black Christians may also go "fishin' 4 a new religion."[8] What can African-American Christians (pastors, laity, and theologians) do to eliminate the oppressive manifestations of Christianity in their churches and communities, and thereby make them more reflective of the liberating power of the gospel? I believe a good place to begin is by addressing the plight of African-American youth, many of whom already regard Christianity and the black church as relics of an ancient, irrelevant past.

Christianity and the Crisis Facing Black Youth

Any close observer of African-American urban youth culture knows that in the minds of an increasing number of young blacks, especially males, Christianity is white religion that offers no solutions to the harsh realities that shape their everyday lives. In barber shops and on basketball courts and street corners across urban America, many young black men espouse a 1990's version of the black nationalist critique of Christianity examined in this study. Armed with the writings and audiotapes of Malcolm X, Louis Farrakhan, Dr. Yosef ben-Jochannan, and others, many young African-Americans with legal jobs, intellectual discipline, and hopes for a better future have sought to channel their spirituality into non-Christian religions such as Louis Farrakhan's Nation of Islam; orthodox Sunni Islam under the astute leadership of Elijah Muhammad's son, Warith Deen Mohammed; and varieties of traditional African religions and mystery systems.[9]

On the other hand, black youth in the underclass with little formal education, job skills, and family support seem to have abandoned the spiritual quest altogether. Social alienation and endemic joblessness have intensified the pressure to conform to "the code of the streets"[10] and have created an "outlaw culture" among some African-American youth in the underclass. Mark Naison, in "Outlaw Culture and Black Neighborhoods," discusses the spiral of violence in many urban African-American communities that often makes people feel like prisoners in their own homes. Arguing that "the spectacle of neighborhoods being dominated by gun-toting youngsters is a new development in urban African-American history," Naison writes:

An "outlaw culture" has emerged among low-income Black youth that has rejected African-American communal norms in favor of the predatory individualism of the capitalist marketplace . . . Although this worldview is forcefully contested—by teachers, parents, ministers, and now politically conscious rappers—it exerts a powerful hold on the imagination of inner-city youngsters.[11]

J. Deotis Roberts, in *The Prophethood of Black Believers,* writes that "the cult of violence that reigns in our major cities" influences the lives of far too many black youth and makes "our streets like a battlefield where some believe they only have the options of killing and be killed. Many black males have concluded that they will not live to be thirty."[12] Sadly, some black families have even prepaid the funerals of their children because of the senseless violence that pervades their lives. Tragically, the increase of youth gangs and of drug-related violence makes homicide the leading cause of deaths among black youths. Can the black church reach these young people with the liberating power of the gospel, or will its voice be drowned out by the gangster lyrics and seductive images of rap music videos? Can African-American ministers and churches effectively persuade black youth not to sell drugs without helping to provide or locate alternative sources of legal income? Can black churches preach a nonviolent, turn the other cheek Christian ethic when guns and violence are part of many young people's everyday lives? Or is it too late in the day to talk about redeeming the image of Christianity in the minds of young African-Americans, especially when one considers Kelly Brown Douglas's observation that "black youth have found the churches' message virtually irrelevant as they have confronted the challenges of a drug culture, sex, and an uncertain future?"[13] These are hard questions and they require the African-American churches to do some serious soul-searching about their understanding of the gospel and its demands on their ministries.

As the black church and its theologians prepare to meet the challenges of ministry in the twenty-first century, much more serious attention must be paid to the psycho-social issues that shape the lives of African-American youth. Pastors, theologians, and church leaders must make youth ministry their *primary* focus, not merely afterthoughts and postscripts to be handled by seminarians and part-time, untrained volunteers. Viable ongoing youth programs must be an important part of the church budget and demand the best spiritual, intellectual, and financial support churches can muster. Forums and discussion groups on the plight of African-American youth must be regarded as an integral part of the churches' ministry, just like mid-week prayer meetings, Bible study, and revivals. Pastors, Christian educators, religious scholars, and teams of youth workers—especially those who are a generation or two removed from the experience of contemporary African-American youth—should meet regularly to analyze the realities that face many black teenagers and discuss strategies of ministry to address their needs. Here, books like Greg Donaldson's *The Ville: Cops and Kids in Urban America* might help church leaders and theologians to understand the complex factors that shape the lives of far too many black youth. *The Ville* is a dramatic account of youth culture in the Brownsville-East New York section of Brooklyn, one of the most violent areas of the city. Donaldson's account of life in the housing projects and the conflicts between black youth for respect is the raw data that must inform urban youth ministry and contemporary black theology.[14]

In an environment where young people who pursue education and legal jobs are perceived as punks and sellouts, it becomes radically important for churches to wage a determined battle for the minds and souls of black youth, who are susceptible to the nihilism that pervades the African-American community. Philosopher Cornel West has addressed this more effectively than black theologians. West addresses nihilism as a "disease of the soul" that resembles "a kind of collective clinical depression in significant pockets of black America."[15]

While black liberation and womanist theologians have dealt with the *external* social manifestations of black oppression such as institutional racism, sexism, unemployment, and poverty, they have not as yet adequately addressed the *internal* spiritual and psychological factors that compound the oppressive social, political, and economic realities of contemporary black life. Cornel West's philosophical interpretation of the nihilistic threat facing many African-American communities provides helpful clues for the youth ministries of the black denominational churches and informs the work of black and womanist theologians. If more pastors and theologians, along with public school teachers, social workers, youth counselors, and others, continue to commit their energies to resisting the destructive forces that are killing black people, we will be able to redeem our communities and rehabilitate the image of Christianity in the minds of African-American youth.

Bridging the Gap between Black Pastors and Theologians

Thankfully, in recent years there has been a growing concern on the part of prophetic pastors and theologians to develop a closer working relationship in order to make the black church a more effective instrument of human liberation. Although black theologians have always known that their work was not as widely read in the churches as in the seminaries and universities, C. Eric Lincoln's and Lawrence Mamiya's landmark study, *The Black Church in the African-American Experience*, sounded a wake-up call by reminding them that their writings have had little impact on the majority of black pastors and churches. While there are many complex reasons for this, both authors suggest that new methods of teaching black theology are needed if it is to reach the Christians in the pews.[16]

Throughout his ministry, Gayraud Wilmore has also called for a closer relationship between academic black theology and pastoral ministry. His vast experience as a denominational executive in the Presbyterian church during the civil rights movement, and his teaching ministry at seminaries including Pittsburgh Theological Seminary, Colgate-Rochester Divinity School, New York Theological Seminary and the Interdenominational Theological Center in Atlanta, have consistently shaped his pastoral approach to black theology.[17] In addition, J. Deotis Roberts consistently has expressed a similar concern; indeed, his most recent book, *The Prophethood of Black Believers*, is addressed to ministers and theologians in an effort to bridge the gap that has separated black theologians and black pastors. Roberts offers concrete, helpful suggestions for improving the relationship and urges theologians to be more aggressive in reaching out to the churches. Among other things, theologians should welcome opportunities to participate in workshops and seminars in the churches and should write their books "with average churchgoers in mind."[18]

In addition to the important work of the Kelly Miller Smith Institute at Vanderbilt University Divinity School,[19] pastor-scholars such as Dennis Wiley have made significant contributions to healing the relationship between black theologians and black pastors. Wiley, pastor of the Covenant Baptist Church in Washington, D.C., and a Ph.D. from Union Seminary, criticized black theologians for abandoning their prophetic critique of the black church during the 1970s in an effort to improve their strained relationship with the churches. To correct this "unfortunate compromise," Wiley calls for a "prophetic spirituality" that subjects the black church to internal critique, and advocates a grassroots approach to teaching black theology that empowers lay persons to understand themselves as theologians.[20]

An example of Wiley's approach is seen in the April 30–May 6, 1994, Community Institute and Revival sponsored by the Covenant Baptist Church, which addressed the subject "Breaking Down the Barriers that Divide Us." Workshops and panel discussions were held on five barriers that divide the black community: class, gender, age, religious differences, and homosexuality. Featured speakers, panelists, and preachers included James Cone, Eleanor Holmes Norton, Jeremiah Wright, Jawanza Kunjufu, and Kelly Brown Douglas. Moreover, under Wiley's leadership and in partnership with Union and Auburn Theological Seminaries in New York, the Covenant Baptist Church is currently in the process of establishing a grassroots organization called The ChristAfrican Community-Based Theological Institute, which shows great potential for situating black theology in the churches.

The important work of Annie Ruth Powell also provides a helpful paradigm for teaching black and womanist theologies in the churches. Powell, a Ph.D. from Union Seminary and an ordained elder in the

A.M.E. church, organized the Christian Community Learning Center (CCLC) in Brooklyn in 1987. CCLC is a small, nondenominational church that empowers people to do theology from their own experience. Members are encouraged to participate in the nontraditional worship services, which emphasize dialogue and discussion in the context of the worship event. Moreover, through its participation with various social agencies and ministries, CCLC teaches people to relate the gospel to every aspect of their lives. As a member of the Church Based Community Outreach Coalition in New York City, CCLC sponsors health fairs on cancer, AIDS, and other medical problems affecting the masses of black people. In addition, CCLC works in conjunction with groups addressing domestic violence, prison ministry, substance abuse, and homelessness.[21]

A prophetic, emerging womanist voice, Powell expresses a vision for the black church that, if widely embraced, has the potential to make it into a more effective instrument of liberation:

> I dream of a church committed to the total well-being of women, one that is unafraid to address the particular problems of women such as the prevalence of breast cancer, AIDS, sexually transmitted diseases, single parenting, and single and same-sex lifestyles, as well as women's need to appreciate their own beauty, talents, and age . . . I dream of a church that welcomes the poor and combines prayer with social and political action to eliminate poverty . . . I dream of a church where inclusive language about God is not considered too much to ask. I pray that others who share this dream will work together to make it a reality.[22]

I share Powell's vision, and I know there are many others who do as well. I am glad to know that despite the valid criticisms of the black church we have examined in this study, there *are* many committed pastors and lay volunteers who do magnificent work in a quiet, humble, and committed fashion. These pastors and churches are not duped into believing that success in ministry is determined by the size of membership rolls, church budgets, or whether their names appear on *Ebony Magazine*'s list of dynamic preachers. I believe their stories must be told and celebrated, for they—along with the larger, well-known effective ministries throughout the country—demonstrate that Christianity is a liberating faith that is transforming and empowering broken, fragmented lives everyday in African-American communities across this nation.

Notes

Introduction

1. Vincent Harding, "Black Power and the American Christ" in Gayraud S. Wilmore and James H. Cone, eds., *Black Theology: A Documentary History, 1966-1979* (Maryknoll, N.Y.: Orbis Books, 1979), p. 36.

2. Gayraud S. Wilmore, *Black Religion and Black Radicalism* (Maryknoll, N.Y.: Orbis Books, 1983).

3. For more on integration and black nationalism in African-American thought, see James H. Cone, *Martin and Malcolm and America: A Dream or a Nightmare* (Maryknoll, N.Y.: Orbis Books, 1991), pp. 1-17.

4. I am indebted to Dr. Gayraud S. Wilmore for sharing his views on my ideas about pre- and post–Black Power religious thought. In a September 8, 1990, letter to the author, Wilmore writes: "I think you are correct in saying that no one has attempted to deal with the differences between Black religious thinkers before and after the Black Power movement. I would sharpen the question in this way: can we think of the men and women who wrote about religion in the 1930s to 1960s as 'Black theologians,' or must we regard them some other way? 'Negro theologians?' If the latter, what does that mean? . . . No one has dealt with these almost embarrassing questions."

5. See Walter Fluker, *They Looked for a City: A Comparative Analysis of the Ideal of Community in the Thought of Howard Thurman and Martin Luther King, Jr.* (New York: University Press of America, 1989); Carlyle Fielding Stewart, III, *God, Being, and Liberation: A Comparative Analysis of the Theologies and Ethics of James H. Cone and Howard Thurman* (New York: University Press of America, 1989); Lewis V. Baldwin, *To Make the Wounded Whole: The Cultural Legacy of Martin Luther King, Jr.* (Minneapolis: Fortress Press, 1992), especially chapter two; and James H. Cone, "'The Contradictions of Life Are Not Final': Howard Thurman and the Quest for Freedom," in Mozella G. Mitchell, ed., *The Human Search: Howard Thurman and the Quest for Freedom* (New York: Peter Lang, 1992).

6. Significantly, Luther Smith's lecture was entitled "The Discontent of 1949: Howard Thurman as a Source for Black Theology." See also Luther Smith, *Howard Thurman: The Mystic as Prophet* (New York: University Press of America, 1981). Other important Thurman studies from the perspective of black theology include Dennis Wiley, *The Concept of the Church in the Works of Howard Thurman*, Ph.D. dissertation (Union Theological Seminary, N.Y., 1988); and Alonzo Johnson, *Good New for the Disinherited: The Meaning of Jesus Christ in the Writings of Howard Thurman*, Ph.D. dissertation (Union Theological Seminary, N.Y., 1990).

7. See Orville Vernon Burton's Foreword to the 1987 edition of Benjamin Mays's autobiography *Born to Rebel* (Athens: University of Georgia Press, 1987), p. xli.

8. Gilbert H. Caldwell, "Black Folk in White Churches," in *The Christian Century* (February 12, 1969), p. 209.

9. Ibid.

1 *"The Christian Way in Race Relations"*

1. See Benjamin Mays, *Born to Rebel* (Athens: University of Georgia Press, 1987), p. 155; and Howard Thurman, *With Head and Heart* (New York: Harcourt Brace Jovanovich, 1979), p. 124. Thurman was reluctant to go to India in 1936 for fear that he would be looked upon as an apologist for Western Christianity. He was right. "Everywhere we went, we were asked, 'Why are you here, if you are not tools of the Europeans, the white people?' . . . I felt the heat in the question 'If Christianity is not powerless, why is it not changing life in your country and the rest of the world? If it is powerless, why are you here representing it to us?'" (p. 125).

2. Thurman, *With Head and Heart*, p. 114.

3. Negro Christian intellectuals met at the Institute of Religion at the Howard University School of Religion from 1944 to 1948 to discuss "what role should the Christian life play in the solution of the race problem in America." Several important essays presented at the Institute (including ones written by Benjamin Mays and George Kelsey) were published under the title, *The Christian Way in Race Relations*, ed. William Stuart Nelson (New York: Harper and Brothers, 1948).

4. For a thorough resume and complete listing of publications, degrees, and honors received by Mays, see "Biographical Sketch," in *Journal of Religious Thought* 32 (Spring-Summer 1975), pp. 132-37.

5. For an excellent interpretation of Mays's role as an educator whose philosophy molded Martin King, Julian Bond, and other civil rights leaders, see Lerone Bennett, "Benjamin Elijah Mays: The Last of the Great Schoolmasters," in *Ebony* 32 (December 1977), pp. 72-80.

6. Keith D. Miller, *Voice of Deliverance: The Language of Martin Luther King, Jr., and Its Sources* (New York: The Free Press, 1992), p. 44.

7. Mays, *Born to Rebel*, p. 49. For a further description of the incident, see p. 1.

8. Ibid., p. 20.

9. Ibid., p. 17. See also, *Lord, the People Have Driven Me On* (New York: Vantage Press, 1981), p. 2.

10. Basically, Hezekiah Mays wanted his sons to be farmers like himself, and therefore saw education as unnecessary (see Mays, *Born to Rebel*, pp. 35-36, 38).

11. Mays, *Born to Rebel*, p. 36.

12. Because of his responsibilities on the farm, Mays never spent more than four months of the academic year in school until he was nineteen years old—when he finally mustered the courage to disobey his father's command to return home at the end of February (see Mays, *Born to Rebel*, p. 38).

13. Ibid., p. 50.

14. Ibid., p. 55.

15. Concerning his Bates experience, Mays wrote, "Bates College did not 'emancipate' me; it did the far greater service of making it possible for me to

emancipate myself, to accept with dignity my own worth as a free man. Small wonder that I love Bates College!" (ibid., p. 60).

16. Ibid., p. 61.

17. Concerning Mays's impact on Thurman, who was just six years younger, Thurman writes, "The great contribution made to my generation by men like 'Bennie' Mays . . . was this: They heightened our morale. Morale by simple definition is belief in one's own cause" (Howard Thurman, "The New Heaven and the New Earth," in *Journal of Negro Education* 27 (Spring 1958), p. 118.

18. For a discussion of Mays's experience with his University of Chicago mentors—including Henry Nelson Wieman, Shirley Jackson Case, Shailer Matthews, J. Edgar Goodspeed, and J. DeWitt Burton, see *Lord, the People*, pp. 42-48.

19. See Benjamin E. Mays and Joseph W. Nicholson, *The Negro's Church* (New York: Russell and Russell, 1969); and Benjamin E. Mays, *The Negro's God as Reflected in His Literature* (New York: Russell and Russell, 1968). See also his articles, "The Education of Negro Ministers," in *Journal of Negro Education* 2 (July 1933); and "The Religious Life and Needs of Negro Students," in *Journal of Negro Education* 9 (July 1940).

20. It was on this trip to India that Mays first met and talked with Gandhi. For a detailed account of Mays's first trip overseas, see his article, "The Color Line around the World," in *Journal of Negro Education* 6 (January 1937), pp. 134-43.

21. Mays, *Born to Rebel*, p. 167.

22. See Mays's report of his accomplishments as Dean of the School of Religion in *Born to Rebel*, pp. 145-48.

23. Ibid., p. 256.

24. Ibid., p. 254.

25. Ibid., p. 255.

26. See Mays, *Lord, the People*, p. 65.

27. Benjamin E. Mays, "World Aspects of Race and Culture," in *Missions* 40 (February 1949), p. 83.

28. Benjamin E. Mays, "The Eyes of the World Are upon America," in *Missions* 35 (February 1944), p. 75.

29. Benjamin E. Mays, "The Colored Races in the Postwar World," in *Missions* 37 (February 1946), p. 77.

30. W.E.B. Du Bois, *The Souls of Black Folks* (Chicago: A.C. McClurg and Co., 1903), p. 27.

31. Mays, "The Colored Races in the Postwar World," p. 76.

32. Ibid.

33. Ibid.

34. Ibid., p. 77.

35. Ibid., pp. 79-80.

36. Ibid., p. 80.

37. See George D. Kesley, *Racism and the Christian Understanding of Man* (New York: Charles Scribner's Sons, 1965), pp. 24, 27, and 33.

38. Benjamin Mays, "Christian Light on Human Relationships," in *The Eighth Congress of the Baptist World Alliance* (Philadelphia: Judson Press, 1950), p. 149.

39. Ibid.

40. Benjamin Mays, "Of One Blood: Scripture and Science Make No Race Distinctions," in *Presbyterian Life* (February 5, 1955), p. 29.

41. Benjamin E. Mays, *Seeking to Be Christian in Race Relations* (New York: Friendship Press, 1957), pp. 20-21.

42. Mays, "Christian Light on Human Relationships," p. 152. See also *Seeking to Be Christian in Race Relations*, p. 21.

43. Martin Luther King, Jr., "Facing the Challenge of a New Age," in James M. Washington, ed., *A Testament of Hope* (San Francisco: Harper Collins, 1986), p. 138. See also "The American Dream," in Washington, *A Testament of Hope*, p. 210.

44. Howard Thurman, "God and the Race Question," in *Together*, ed. Glenn Clark (Nashville: Abingdon-Cokesbury Press, 1946), p. 120.

45. Benjamin E. Mays, "Democratizing and Christianizing America in This Generation," in *The Journal of Negro Education* 14 (Fall 1945), p. 533.

46. For a discussion of King's understanding of the American dream, see James H. Cone, *Martin and Malcolm and America: A Dream or a Nightmare* (Maryknoll, N.Y.: Orbis Books, 1991), especially chapter 3.

47. Thurman was in his first year as Dean of Marsh Chapel at Boston University when King was completing his doctoral studies. For more on their relationship, see Howard Thurman, *With Head and Heart*, pp. 254-55.

48. Thurman, *The Luminous Darkness* (New York: Harper and Row, 1965), p. 94.

49. Ibid., pp. 98-99.

50. Thurman, *With Head and Heart*, p. 144.

51. Howard Thurman, *Footprints of a Dream* (New York: Harper and Row, 1959), p. 13.

52. Ibid., p. 65. For an interpretation of Thurman's ecclesiology, see Dennis Wiley, *The Concept of the Church in the Theology of Howard Thurman*, Ph.D. dissertation (Union Theological Seminary, N.Y., 1988).

53. Ibid., p. 107.

54. Upon the recommendation of Dr. Charles S. Johnson of Fisk University, Alfred Fisk and Howard Thurman selected Albert Cleage to serve as co-minister until July 1, 1944, when Thurman arrived with his family. See *Footprints of a Dream*, p. 33. I discuss Cleage's reflections of his experience at Fellowship Church in chapter 3.

55. William S. Nelson, "Religion and Racial Tension in America Today," in *Journal of Religious Thought* 2 (Spring-Summer 1945), p. 164.

56. William S. Nelson, "The Influence of Institutional Christianity upon Secular Power," in *The Journal of Religious Thought* 4 (Winter 1946-47), p. 49.

57. See Benjamin E. Mays, "The American Religion and the Christian Religion," p. 533.

58. Nelson, "Religion and Racial Tension in America Today," p. 169.

59. Benjamin E. Mays, *Born to Rebel*, p. 167.

60. Benjamin E. Mays, "The Christian in Race Relations." Delivered as the Second Address in the Henry B. Wright Lecture Series, Yale University Divinity School, April 16, 1952. In this lecture Mays also wrote, "Segregation based on race, therefore, is without Christian foundation and is the greatest scandal within the church" (p. 2).

61. Mays, *Born to Rebel*, p. 243.

62. Ibid., p. 241.

63. Benjamin E. Mays, "The Church amidst Ethnic and Racial Tension," Appendix B in *Born to Rebel*, p. 355.

64. Mays, "The Christian in Race Relations," p. 4.

65. Benjamin E. Mays, "Improving the Morale of Negro Children and Youth," in *The Journal of Negro Education* 19 (Summer 1950), p. 423.

66. Ibid., p. 421.

67. Ibid., p. 424. See also, "Democratizing and Christianizing America in This Generation," pp. 533-34.

68. Benjamin E. Mays, "Obligations of Negro Christians in Relation to an Interracial Program," in *The Journal of Religious Thought* 2 (Autumn-Winter 1945), p. 44.

69. Ibid., p. 45.

70. Ibid., p. 46.

71. Mays, "Obligations of Negro Christians in Relation to an Interracial Program," p. 44. Howard Thurman emphasized the same point in the third chapter of *Jesus and the Disinherited* (Nashville: Abingdon Press, 1949).

72. Benjamin E. Mays wrote a weekly column for the *Pittsburgh Courier* beginning in 1946. This quotation is taken from the January 14, 1950, column entitled, "'Uncle Thomas' May Hold a College Degree from Morehouse or May Be from Columbia U."

73. Mays, "Obligations of Negro Christians in Relation to an Interracial Program," p. 47.

74. Mays, "Democratizing and Christianizing America in This Generation," p. 528.

75. Benjamin E. Mays. *Seeking to Be Christian in Race Relations,* p. 9.

76. Mays, "Democratizing and Christianizing America in This Generation," p. 528.

77. Ibid., p. 530.

78. Ibid., p. 531.

79. Ibid., p. 532.

80. Ibid., p. 533.

81. Mays, "Of One Blood: Scripture and Science Make No Race Distinctions," p. 7.

82. Ibid.

83. Ibid., p. 8. See also, *Seeking to Be Christian in Race Relations,* pp. 56-60.

84. Mays, *Seeking to Be Christian in Race Relations,* p. 26.

85. Ibid., p. 34.

86. Ibid., p. 38.

87. Doris L. Gavins, *The Ceremonial Speaking of Benjamin Elijah Mays: Spokesman for Social Change, 1954-1975,* Ph.D. dissertation (Louisiana State University, 1978), p. 203.

88. Cited in Gavins, *The Ceremonial Speaking of Benjamin Elijah Mays,* p. 104.

89. Mays, *Seeking to Be Christian in Race Relations,* p. 44.

90. Ibid., p. 109.

91. Ibid., pp. 38, 85.

92. Ibid., p. 81.

93. Mays, *Born to Rebel,* p. 156.

94. Sudarshan Kapur, *Raising Up a Prophet: The African-American Encounter with Gandhi* (Boston: Beacon Press, 1992). See especially pp. 81-100. For a discussion of Thurman's encounter with Gandhi, see *With Head and Heart,* pp. 130-35.

95. Mays, *Born to Rebel*, pp. 261-63.

96. See Benjamin Mays's Introduction to *Race: Challenge to Religion*, ed. Matthew Ahmann (Chicago: Henry Regnery Co., 1963), p. 5.

2   *"Christianity Is the White Man's Religion"*

1. C. Eric Lincoln, *The Black Muslims in America* (Westport: Greenwood Press, 1973), p. 198. Originally published in 1961 by Beacon Press.

2. Masco Young, "Elijah Muhammad: Man Chosen for Leadership." Part III of a series entitled, "The Truth about the Muslims," in *The Pittsburgh Courier*, November 3, 1959, sec. 2, p. 1.

3. Louis Lomax, *When the Word Is Given: A Report on Elijah Muhammad, Malcolm X, and the Black Muslim World* (Cleveland: The World Publishing Company, 1963), p. 52.

4. Concerning Fard's disappearance, which state and federal authorities have been unable to solve, see Lomax, *When the Word Is Given*, p. 53; Lincoln, *The Black Muslims in America*, p. 199.

5. Elijah Muhammad, "Atlanta Speech," in Lomax, *When the Word Is Given*, p. 118.

6. Although orthodox Muslims in America (i.e., The Federation of Islamic Associations of Chicago) denounced Elijah Muhammad, his trip to Mecca validated his religious credentials before the world Islamic community. See Lomax, *When the Word Is Given*, pp. 69-73.

7. *Philadelphia Tribune*, January 23, 1962, p. 3.

8. Elijah Muhammad, *Message to the Blackman* (Philadelphia: Hakim's Publications, 1965), p. 297.

9. Muhammad, "Atlanta Speech," p. 129.

10. Muhammad, *Message to the Blackman*, pp. 281-82. Also found in *New Crusader*, January 25, 1964.

11. Elijah Muhammad, *The Supreme Wisdom: Solution to the So-Called Negroes' Problem* (Chicago: University of Islam, 1957), p. 29.

12. Muhammad, *Message to the Blackman*, p. 281.

13. Lincoln, *The Black Muslims in America*, p. 206. See also Lomax, *When the Word Is Given*, pp. 54-55. Muhammad claimed that he was arrested for draft evasion, which he considered to be a false charge. He did not register because he was forty-five years old and a Muslim minister. See *Message to the Blackman*, p. 179.

14. Muhammad, *Message to the Blackman*, p. 285.

15. Lincoln, *The Black Muslims in America*, p. 78.

16. George D. Kelsey used the term *counter-racism* to describe the teachings of Elijah Muhammad, which he considered a black racist answer to white imperialistic racism. See *Racism and the Christian Understanding of Man* (New York: Scribner's Sons, 1965), pp. 10, 39, 42, and 68.

17. Muhammad, *The Supreme Wisdom*, p. 33. According to the myth, the earth and the moon (formerly one planet) were separated by a great explosion six trillion years ago.

18. Muhammad, "Atlanta Speech," p. 125.

19. Muhammad, *Message to the Blackman*, p. 112. Emphasis mine.

20. Ibid., p. 114.

21. This plan included a prohibition against marriages of two black-skinned people and the killing of babies who were too black (ibid., pp. 114-16).

22. Ibid., p. 116.

23. Muhammad, *The Supreme Wisdom*, p. 39.

24. Quoted in Lomax, *When the Word Is Given*, p. 64. See also Cone, *Martin and Malcolm and America*, pp. 97, 103.

25. Muhammad, *Message to the Blackman*, p. 122.

26. Muhammad, *The Supreme Wisdom*, vol. 2, p. 61.

27. Ibid., p. 26.

28. Muhammad, *The Supreme Wisdom*, p. 36.

29. Ibid., pp. 13-14.

30. See Gayraud S. Wilmore, *Black Religion and Black Radicalism* (Maryknoll, N.Y.: Orbis Books, 1983), and Dwight Hopkins and George Cummings, eds., *Cut Loose Your Stammering Tongue: Black Theology in the Slave Narratives* (Maryknoll, N.Y.: Orbis Books, 1992).

31. In Muhammad's theological reading of history, the year 1555 marked the end of the one thousand years of Satan's imprisonment referred to in Revelation 20:6. During that period of time, from 570 to 1555, the white race and Christianity "were bottled up in Europe by the spread of Islam" by the prophet Mohammad and his successors. According to Muhammad, Satan was "loosed from his prison" in 1555 and allowed to deceive the nations of the earth until 1955 (Revelation 20:7-8). See Muhammad, *Message to the Blackman*, p. 3; and *The Supreme Wisdom*, vol. 2, p. 73.

32. Muhammad, *The Supreme Wisdom*, p. 17.

33. However, it should be noted that some historians and theologians have challenged the notion that slave religion was entirely otherworldly. See Wilmore, *Black Religion and Black Radicalism*; and James H. Cone, *The Spirituals and the Blues* (New York: Seabury Press, 1972).

34. Muhammad, "Atlanta Speech," p. 126.

35. Malcolm X, *The Autobiography of Malcolm X* (New York: Random House, 1965), p. 220.

36. Muhammad, *The Supreme Wisdom*, p. 15.

37. Muhammad, "Atlanta Speech," p. 119.

38. Muhammad, *The Supreme Wisdom*, p. 13

39. Ibid., p. 14.

40. Ibid., p. 39.

41. Muhammad, *Message to the Blackman*, p. 226.

42. Ibid., p. 32.

43. Muhammad, *The Supreme Wisdom*, vol. 2, p. 24.

44. Ibid., p. 19

45. Muhammad, *Message to the Blackman*, p. 37.

46. Ibid., p. 231. Muhammad singled out those with college degrees as the target of his scorn: "The college university graduates are poisoned 100% more in mind into the love of the enemy than the uneducated" (p. 232).

47. Muhammad, "Make America to Know Her Sins," in *New Crusader*, January 25, 1964.

48. Martin Luther King, Jr., "The American Dream," in James M. Washington, ed., *The Testament of Hope: The Essential Writings of Martin L. King, Jr.* (San Francisco: Harper & Row, 1986), p. 215.

49. Ibid., pp. 296-97. King used similar language to characterize the Nation of Islam in his 1965 *Playboy* interview. See ibid., p. 363.

50. Muhammad, *Message to the Blackman*, p. 241.

51. Ibid.

52. Ibid., p. 242.

53. Lomax, *When the Word Is Given*, p. 29.

54. Muhammad, *The Supreme Wisdom*, p. 37.

55. Ibid., p. 29.

56. On the Christian background of members of the Nation of Islam, see Lincoln, *The Black Muslims in America*, p. 28.

57. Lomax, *When the Word Is Given*, p. 40.

58. See James H. Cone, *Martin and Malcolm and America: A Dream or a Nightmare* (Maryknoll, N.Y.: Orbis Books, 1991), p. 161.

59. Muhammad, *The Supreme Wisdom*, p. 49.

60. Lincoln, *The Black Muslims in America*, pp. 83-84, 119.

61. Malcolm X, "We Are Rising from the Dead Since We Heard Messenger Muhammad Speak," in *The Pittsburgh Courier*, December 15, 1956.

62. Malcolm X, in the Preface to *The Supreme Wisdom*, p. 8. See also Lincoln, *The Black Muslims in America*, p. 85.

63. Cited in Lomax, *When the Word Is Given*, p. 58.

64. See Dan Burley's column "The Truth about Muhammad," in *The New Crusader*, June 16, 1962.

65. C. Eric Lincoln, "Black Nationalism and Christian Conscience," in *Sounds of the Struggle*, ed. C. Eric Lincoln (New York: William Morrow and Co., 1967), pp. 97-98.

66. See Dan Burley, "The Truth about the Muslims: Muhammad Charges Whites Plot to Destroy Negro with Depravity Program," in *The Negro Crusader*, February 24, 1962.

67. Muhammad, *The Supreme Wisdom*, vol. 2, p. 21.

68. Muhammad, *The Supreme Wisdom*, p. 35.

69. Malcolm X, Preface to *The Supreme Wisdom*, p. 8.

70. Muhammad, *The Supreme Wisdom*, p. 28.

71. Muhammad, *The Supreme Wisdom*, vol. 2, p. 31. Muhammad writes, "My people (the so-called Negroes) know or read no Scripture other than that (Bible). Besides, they don't even understand the Bible—though they read and believe in it—and it is my duty to awaken them from it, because it is surely the graveyard of my people."

72. Muhammad, *Message to the Blackman*, p. 87.

73. Ibid., p. 95.

74. Ibid., pp. 15-16.

75. Muhammad, *The Supreme Wisdom*, vol. 2, p. 39.

76. Ibid., p. 33.

77. Muhammad, *Message to the Blackman*, p. 88.

78. Muhammad, *The Supreme Wisdom*, pp. 19-20.

79. Ibid., p. 17.

80. Muhammad, *Message to the Blackman*, pp. 169-70, 25.

81. Muhammad, *The Supreme Wisdom*, p. 33.

82. Muhammad, *Message to the Blackman*, p. 234.

83. Muhammad, *The Supreme Wisdom*, pp. 16, 34.

84. Muhammad, *Message to the Blackman,* p. 27. See also *The Supreme Wisdom,* vol. 2, p. 80.

85. Muhammad, "Atlanta Speech," p. 123.

86. Ibid.

87. Muhammad, *The Supreme Wisdom,* p. 36.

88. Ibid., p. 27; Muhammad, *Message to the Blackman,* p. 217.

89. Muhammad, *Message to the Blackman,* p. 214.

3   Black Power and Christianity

1. Gayraud S. Wilmore, "Introduction," in Gayraud S. Wilmore and James H. Cone, eds., *Black Theology: A Documentary History, 1966-1979* (Maryknoll, N.Y.: Orbis Books, 1979), p. 69.

2. See Gayraud S. Wilmore's NCBC Theological Commission Report (Fall 1968).

3. Manning Marable, *Race, Reform, and Rebellion* (Jackson: University Press of Mississippi, 1984), p. 106.

4. This subject will be discussed in detail in chapter 5.

5. At the funeral for the slain girls, King said, "History has proven over and over again that unmerited suffering is redemptive. The innocent blood of these little girls may well serve as the redemptive force that will bring new light to this dark city" (Martin Luther King, Jr., "Eulogy for the Martyred Children," in James M. Washington, ed., *A Testament of Hope* (San Francisco: Harper Collins, 1986), pp. 221-23.

6. Since blacks were locked out of the white Jim-Crow Democratic Party of Mississippi, recognition of the MFDP at the national convention would have given blacks the right to participate in the political process for the first time since the Reconstruction era.

7. See Stokely Carmichael and Charles V. Hamilton, *Black Power: The Politics of Liberation in America* (New York: Random House, 1967), pp. 86-97.

8. Ibid., p. 103. Malcolm X was also in Alabama during the 1965 Selma campaign. He was invited to speak by SNCC in early February and was assassinated several weeks later on February 21, 1965, in New York City.

9. See *Eyes on the Prize II:* "The Time Has Come 1964-66" (Alexandria, VA: PBS Adult Learning Service, 1990).

10. Carmichael and Hamilton, *Black Power,* p. 100.

11. Ibid., p. 120.

12. Carmichael ousted John Lewis as national chairman of SNCC in May 1966. This event contributed to the shift away from nonviolence to the philosophy of Black Power.

13. Vincent Harding, *The Other American Revolution* (Atlanta: Institute of the Black World, 1980), p. 186.

14. Ibid., pp. 186-87.

15. Martin L. King, Jr., *Where Do We Go from Here: Chaos or Community* (Boston: Beacon Press, 1967), p. 26.

16. Ibid., pp. 30-31.

17. Robert Brisbane, *Black Activism* (New York: Vantage Press, 1972), p. 146.

18. Carmichael and Hamilton, *Black Power,* p. 44.

19. Julius Lester, *Look Out Whitey! Black Power's Gon Get Your Mama* (New York: Dial Press, 1968), pp. 10-11.

20. Ibid., p. 107. Lester also writes: "We've had our love affair with white America and our virginity is gone . . . Now it's over. The days of singing Freedom songs and the days of combating bullets and billy clubs with Love . . . And as for Love? That's always been better done in the bed than on the picket line and marches."

21. Ibid., p. 137.

22. Nathan Hare, "Black Power Symposium," in *Negro Digest* (November 1966), p. 93.

23. Leon Watts, "The National Conference of Black Churchmen," in *Christianity and Crisis* (November 2 and 6, 1970), p. 238. See also Wilmore, *Black Religion and Black Radicalism*, p. 196.

24. NCBC Statement on "Black Power," in Wilmore and Cone, *Black Theology: A Documentary History, 1966-1979*, p. 26.

25. Ibid., p. 27.

26. See Vincent Harding's analysis of NCBC documents in his "No Turning Back," in *Renewal* 10 (Oct.-Nov. 1970).

27. See William S. Nelson, "Religion and Racial Tension in America," pp. 163-66.

28. Leon Watts, "The National Conference of Black Churchmen," in *Christianity and Crisis* (November 2 and 6, 1970), p. 239.

29. NCBC Statement on "Black Power," in Wilmore and Cone, *Black Theology: A Documentary History, 1966-1979*, pp. 23-24.

30. Ibid., p. 24. Martin Luther King, Jr., used similar language to describe the urban rebellions of the late 1960s. See James H. Cone, *Martin and Malcolm and America: A Dream or a Nightmare* (Maryknoll, N.Y.: Orbis Books, 1991), p. 232.

31. James H. Cone, *For My People* (Maryknoll, N.Y.: Orbis Books, 1984), p. 106.

32. NCBC Statement on "Black Power," in Wilmore and Cone, *Black Theology: A Documentary History, 1966-1979*, p. 27.

33. According to Gayraud S. Wilmore, "This was the first time such a format had been proposed in the history of the ecumenical movement in the United States (see Wilmore, *Black Religion and Black Radicalism*, p. 198).

34. Wilmore, "Introduction," in Wilmore and Cone, *Black Theology: A Documentary History, 1966-1979*, p. 19.

35. "The Church and the Urban Crisis," in Wilmore and Cone, *Black Theology: A Documentary History, 1966-1979*, p. 46.

36. Ibid.

37. Ibid.

38. These include the United Methodist, Unitarian-Universalist, the Disciples of Christ, Protestant Episcopal, American Baptist, Lutheran (American, United, and Missouri Synod), Presbyterian (U.S.A. and U.S.), United Church of Christ, and the Roman Catholic churches (NCBC *Newsletter* [June 1968], p. 6; see also Leon Watts, "The National Committee of Black Churchmen," p. 240).

39. Wilmore, *Black Religion and Black Radicalism*, p. 199. See also Alex Poinsett, "The Black Revolt in White Churches," in *Ebony* (September 1968), pp. 63-68.

40. Leon Watts, "The National Committee of Black Churchmen," p. 239.

41. Needless to say, many concerns were raised about the universality of such a theological position. These issues will be addressed at length in chapter 4.

42. For an important discussion of the 1968 St. Louis convocation, see Grant Shockley, "Ultimatum and Hope," in *Christian Century* (February 12, 1969). Describing the conference, Shockley wrote: "Obvious to even a casual observer at St. Louis was the evidence of a revolution among black church bodies and black constituencies in white church groups. A totally new stance by Negroes toward the concept and existence of blackness as it pertains to self, history, theology and church life and society was evident" (p. 218). See also *Time* (November 15, 1968), p. 78.

43. NCBC Statement on "Black Theology," in Wilmore and Cone, *Black Theology: A Documentary History, 1966-1979,* p. 101. James H. Cone assisted in the writing of the 1969 statement. His first book, *Black Theology and Black Power* (Minneapolis: Seabury Press, 1969), was published several months before the Atlanta meeting.

44. Vincent Harding cites its failure to develop a regional structure and its use of rhetoric rather than sound economic and political analysis leading to a program of black liberation (see "No Turning Back," in *Renewal* [Oct.-Nov. 1970], p. 8; see also Wilmore, *Black Religion and Black Radicalism,* p. 201). For an excellent account of the strengths and weaknesses of the NCBC, see Mary R. Sawyer, *Black Ecumenism: Implementing the Demands of Justice* (Valley Forge, Penn.: Trinity Press International, 1994), pp. 66-89.

45. Metz Rollins, NCBC *Newsletter* (June 1968), p. 5.

46. Ibid.

47. Leon Watts, "The National Committee of Black Churchmen," p. 243.

48. "Black Religion—Past, Present, and Future," in Warner Traynham, *Christian Faith in Black and White: A Primer in Theology from the Black Perspective* (Wakefield, Mass.: Parameter Press, 1973), p. 105.

49. Ibid., p. 109.

50. Calvin Marshall, "The Black Church—Its Mission Is Liberation," in C. Eric Lincoln, *The Black Experience in Religion* (Garden City, N.Y.: Anchor Press, 1974), p. 160.

51. Ibid.

52. "The Black Paper," in Traynham, *Christian Faith in Black and White,* p. 97.

53. Nathan Wright, *Black Power and Urban Unrest* (New York: Hawthorn Books, 1967), p. 136.

54. Nathan Wright, "Power and Reconciliation," in *Concern* (October 1, 1967), p. 15.

55. Ibid., pp. 14, 22.

56. Wright, *Black Power and Urban Unrest,* p. 106.

57. Ibid.

58. Thomas Kilgore, Jr., "The Black Church—A Liberating Force for All," in *Ebony* (1970), pp. 106-7.

59. Ibid., p. 108.

60. Ibid., p. 108. Kilgore writes, "As the future American church works to remain the church, the emotional response of reality so highly developed by black people must be joined with the rational response that white churchmen have so well developed" (p. 110). The implication that white Christians had a more "highly developed" intellectual response to the faith than black Christians was radically challenged by James H. Cone and other black theologians discussed in the next chapter.

61. Ibid., p. 110.

62. Henry Mitchell, "Black Power and the Christian Church," in *Foundations* (April-July 1968), p. 105.

63. Ibid., p. 101.

64. Ibid., p. 100.

65. Gayraud S. Wilmore, "The Case for a New Black Church Style," in H. M. Nelsen and R. Yokley, *The Black Church in America* (New York: Basic Books, 1971), p. 325.

66. Ibid., p. 328.

67. Vincent Harding, "The Religion of Black Power," in Donald R. Cutler, ed., *The Religious Situation: 1968* (Boston: Beacon Press, 1968), p. 10.

68. Ibid., p. 10.

69. Ibid., p. 11.

70. Ibid., p. 12.

71. Ibid., p. 11.

72. Ibid., p. 13.

73. Vincent Harding, "Black Power and the American Christ," in Wilmore and Cone, *Black Theology: A Documentary History, 1966-1979*, p. 37.

74. Ibid., p. 41.

75. John H. Adams, "Black Power: Situation-Judgement-Summons," in *The A.M.E. Church Review* 93 (April-June 1968), p. 69.

76. Cone, *For My People*, p. 59.

77. Cleage attended the October 1968 NCBC convocation in St. Louis, which discussed the viability of a black theology at great length. For an account of Cleage's participation at the St. Louis meeting, see Hiley H. Ward, *Prophet of the Black Nation* (Philadelphia: Pilgrim Press, 1969), pp. 168-70.

78. Albert B. Cleage, *Black Christian Nationalism: New Directions for the Black Church* (New York: William Morrow and Co., 1972), pp. 183-87.

79. Albert B. Cleage, *The Black Messiah* (Kansas City: Sheed and Ward, 1968), p. 87; see also the BCN Covenant in *Black Christian Nationalism*, pp. 259-60.

80. Ward, *Prophet of the Black Nation*, p. 55.

81. Ibid.

82. Cleage, *Black Christian Nationalism*, p. 106.

83. Ward, *Prophet of the Black Nation*, p. 103.

84. For Cleage's critique of Dr. King, see *Black Christian Nationalism*, pp. 105-6; and *The Black Messiah*, chap. 15, "Dr. King and Black Power."

85. See "Cleage-Franklin Split Brewing for Long Time," in *Michigan Chronicle*, November 2, 1963, p. 1.

86. Cleage, *Black Christian Nationalism*, p. 107.

87. Ibid., p. 88.

88. Ibid., p. 108.

89. See *Michigan Chronicle*, June 13, 1964, p. 1. The front page headline reads, "Committee Votes No Censure of Rev. Cleage on 'Hate' Charge."

90. Cited in Ward, *Prophet of the Black Nation*, p. 152.

91. Cleage, *Black Christian Nationalism*, p. 98.

92. Ibid., p. 102.

93. Ibid., p. 101.

94. Ibid., pp. 30-32.

95. Albert Cleage, "Interview: Al Cleage on Black Power," in *United Church Herald* 2 (February 1968), p. 30.

96. Cleage, *The Black Messiah,* p. 46.

97. Ibid., p. 42.

98. Quoted in Alex Poinsett, "The Quest for a Black Christ," *Ebony* (March 1969), p. 176.

99. Cleage, *The Black Messiah,* p. 39.

100. Ibid., p. 186. Cleage goes on to argue that Malcolm had a more difficult task than Jesus, because "the people Jesus preached to wanted to hear the message of the Nation," whereas the people Malcolm encountered wanted to integrate with their enemies and "prayed every night that God would make them cease to be a people" (ibid., p. 188).

101. Ibid., pp. 67, 73.

102. Ibid., pp. 91-93.

103. Ibid., p. 192.

104. Ibid., p. 43.

105. Cleage, *Black Christian Nationalism,* p. 20.

106. See Wilmore, "Introduction," in Wilmore and Cone, *Black Theology: A Documentary History, 1966-1979,* p. 67.

4   Christianity and Black Power

1. Frank T. Wilson, "Critical Evaluation of the Theme—'The Black Revolution: Is There a Black Theology?'" in *The Journal of Religious Thought* 26 (Summer Supplement 1969), p. 6.

2. Ibid., p. 9.

3. Ibid., p. 5.

4. Ibid., p. 7. Leon E. Wright echoed this sentiment in his paper, "Black Theology or Black Experience?" Wright argued that the black experience of suffering is representative of universal human suffering and is thus a viable point of departure for Christian theology in general. However, like Wilson, he argued that this does not constitute "black theology," but rather Christian theological reflection on the black experience (*Journal of Religious Thought* 26 [Summer Supplement 1969], pp. 46-56).

5. Ibid., p. 9.

6. Richard I. McKinney, "Reflections on the Concept of 'Black Theology,'" in *Journal of Religious Thought* 26 (Summer Supplement 1968), pp. 11-12.

7. Ibid., p. 11.

8. Ibid., pp. 12-13.

9. Ibid., p. 12.

10. Ibid., p. 13.

11. Ibid.

12. Ibid., pp. 13-14. The misgivings about black theology expressed at the May 1969 meeting of the Institute of Religion were also voiced at an Interdenominational Theological Center (Atlanta, Georgia) faculty retreat held one month earlier (see Charles Shelby Rooks's analysis of both meetings in *Revolution in Zion* [New York: Pilgrim Press, 1990], pp. 98-99).

13. James H. Cone, *Black Theology and Black Power* (Minneapolis: Seabury Press, 1969), p. 6.

14. Ibid., p. 117.

15. Ibid., pp. 32-33.

16. James H. Cone, *My Soul Looks Back* (Nashville: Abingdon Press, 1982; Maryknoll, N.Y.: Orbis Books, 1986), p. 22.

17. Ibid., pp. 19-21.

18. Ibid., p. 22. Cone writes of his father: "Sometimes I think that everything I feel deeply about and the passion with which I think and write are derived exclusively from him . . . The tenacity with which he defended his rights and spoke the truth, regardless of the risks, earned him much respect among some blacks and the label 'crazy' among others" (see p. 19).

19. Ibid., pp. 18, 27; see also "The Gospel and the Liberation of the Poor," in *Christian Century* 98 (February 1981), p. 162; and "Theological Reflections on Reconciliation," in *Christianity and Crisis* (January 22, 1973), p. 304.

20. James H. Cone, *Martin and Malcolm and America: A Dream or a Nightmare* (Maryknoll, N.Y.: Orbis Books, 1991), pp. 144-45.

21. Cone, *My Soul Looks Back*, pp. 36-37; see also, "The Gospel and the Liberation of the Poor," p. 163.

22. James H. Cone, "'The Contradictions of Life Are Not Final': Howard Thurman and the Quest for Freedom," in Mozella G. Mitchell, ed., *The Human Search: Howard Thurman and the Quest for Freedom* (New York: Peter Lang, 1992), p. 22.

23. Cone, *My Soul Looks Back*, pp. 38-39; see also, "The Gospel and the Liberation of the Poor," p. 163.

24. Ibid., pp. 42-43.

25. Cone, *Black Theology and Black Power*, p. 116. For a discussion of the differences between Cone and Cleage, see James H. Cone, *For My People* (Maryknoll, N.Y.: Orbis Books, 1984), p. 36 and pp. 225-26, note 6.

26. Ibid.

27. Ibid., pp. 33, 131.

28. Rooks, *Revolution in Zion*, p. 93.

29. From my July 1991 interview with Dr. Rooks.

30. Rooks, *Revolution in Zion*, p. 94.

31. Cone, *My Soul Looks Back*, p. 45.

32. James H. Cone, "Christianity and Black Power," in *Is Anybody Listening to Black America*, ed. C. Eric Lincoln (New York: Seabury Press, 1968), p. 4.

33. Ibid., p. 9.

34. Cone, *Black Theology and Black Power*, p. 73.

35. Cone, "Christianity and Black Power," p. 9.

36. Ibid., p. 3.

37. Ibid., p. 8.

38. Ibid.

39. Ibid.,

40. Cone, *Black Theology and Black Power*, p. 48.

41. Cone, *My Soul Looks Back*, p. 46. See Cone's early analysis of the BMCR in *Black Theology and Black Power*, pp. 109-11.

42. Cone, *My Soul Looks Back*, pp. 45, 48.

43. Cone, *Black Theology and Black Power*, p. 2.

44. Ibid., p. 134.

45. Ibid., p. 53. Cone writes: "Black, therefore, is beautiful; oppressors have made it ugly. We glorify it because they despise it; we love it because

they hate it. It is the black way of saying, 'To hell with your stinking white society'" (*A Black Theology of Liberation* [Maryknoll, N.Y.: Orbis Books, 1990], p. 15).

46. James H. Cone, "Black Consciousness and the Black Church," in *Christianity and Crisis* (November 2 & 16, 1970), p. 244.

47. Cone, *Black Theology and Black Power*, pp. 17-18.

48. James H. Cone, "Black Theology and Black Liberation," in *Christian Century* (September 16, 1970), p. 1085.

49. James H. Cone, *A Black Theology of Liberation* (Maryknoll, N.Y.: Orbis Books, 1990), p. 63.

50. Ibid.

51. Cone, *Black Theology and Black Power*, p. 68; see also *A Black Theology of Liberation*, pp. 119-24, and *God of the Oppressed* (New York: Seabury Press, 1975), pp. 133-37. For an excellent analysis of Cone's concept of the Black Christ, see Kelly D. Brown Douglas, *The Black Christ* (Maryknoll, N.Y.: Orbis Books, 1994).

52. Cone, *Black Theology and Black Power*, pp. 68-69. In *God of the Oppressed* Cone writes: "Christ is black, therefore, not because of some cultural or psychological need of black people, but because and only because Christ really enters into our world where the poor, the despised, and the black are, disclosing that he is with them, enduring their humiliation and pain . . . . Indeed, if Christ is not truly black, then the historical Jesus lied" (p. 136).

53. Cone, *My Soul Looks Back*, p. 52.

54. See Dwight N. Hopkins, *Black Theology USA and South Africa: Politics, Culture, and Liberation* (Maryknoll, N.Y.: Orbis Books, 1989), p. 46.

55. J. Deotis Roberts, *Liberation and Reconciliation: A Black Theology* (Philadelphia: Westminster Press, 1971; rev. ed. Maryknoll, N.Y.: Orbis Books, 1994), p. 13.

56. Ibid., pp. 183-84.

57. Ibid., p. 21.

58. J. Deotis Roberts, "A Critique of James H. Cone's *God of the Oppressed*," in *Journal of the Interdenominational Theological Center* 3 (Fall 1975), p. 58.

59. Hopkins, *Black Theology USA and South Africa*, p. 190.

60. Major J. Jones, *Christian Ethics for Black Theology* (Nashville: Abingdon Press, 1974), pp. 59, 40.

61. Ibid., pp. 73-74.

62. Ibid., p. 72.

63. Cone, *A Black Theology of Liberation*, p. 63.

64. Ibid., p. 69. For Cone's response to these criticisms, see *God of the Oppressed*, pp. 270-71, note 14. See also, "An Interpretation of the Debate among Black Theologians," in Gayraud S. Wilmore and James H. Cone, eds., *Black Theology: A Documentary History, 1966-1979* (Maryknoll, N.Y.: Orbis Books, 1979), pp. 612-14.

65. Major J. Jones, "Black Awareness: Theological Implications of the Concept," in *Religion and Life* 38 (Autumn 1969), p. 393.

66. For a complete discussion of this perspective see Dwight Hopkins, "No Black Culture, No Black Theology," in *Black Theology USA and South Africa*, pp. 63-90. For Cone's response to these critics, see *God of the Oppressed*, pp. 252-53, note 38; "An Interpretation of the Debate among Black Theologians," pp. 615-20; and *My Soul Looks Back*, pp. 59-61.

67. Gayraud S. Wilmore, *Black Religion and Black Radicalism* (Garden City, N.Y.: Doubleday and Co., 1972), p. 296.

68. Charles Long, *Significations: Signs, Symbols, and Images in the Interpretation of Religion* (Philadelphia: Fortress Press, 1986), p. 7.

69. Ibid., pp. 193-94. See also Hopkins, *Black Theology USA and South Africa,* pp. 71, 75.

70. Long, *Significations,* p. 7.

71. Ibid., p. 8.

72. Josiah Young rightly observed that, given Long's own commitment to a European-originated discipline, "it is not Cone's Eurocentrism that Long finds to be problematic, but Cone's commitment to Christianity" (p. 273). Young also writes that the Long/Cone debate is essentially "blacks' assimilation of epistemological battles fought in Europe over the meaning of religion. What is at stake, however, is not the valorization of history of religion over theology, but the liberation of the black oppressed" (p. 112). See Josiah Young, *A Pan-African Theology: Providence and the Legacies of the Ancestors* (Trenton, N.J.: Africa World Press, 1992).

73. William R. Jones, "Theology and Methodology in Black Theology: A Critique of Washington, Cone and Cleage," in *Harvard Theological Review* 64 (1971), pp. 541-57. This essay was the foundation for Jones's book *Is God a White Racist? A Preamble to Black Theology* (Garden City, N.Y.: Anchor Books/ Doubleday, 1973).

74. Ibid., p. 544.

75. William R. Jones, "Religious Humanism: Its Problems and Prospects in Black Religion and Culture," in *Journal of the Interdenominational Theological Center* 7 (Spring 1980), p. 183.

76. Mays, "Of One Blood," p. 8.

77. Cone, *God of the Oppressed,* p. 198.

78. Ibid., pp. 198-99.

79. Cone, *A Black Theology of Liberation,* p. 34.

80. Cone, *Black Theology and Black Power,* p. 83.

81. Cone, *God of the Oppressed,* p. 199.

82. James H. Cone, "Black Power, Black Theology, and the Study of Theology and Ethics," in *Theological Education* 6 (Spring 1970), p. 206.

83. For example, see Robinson B. James, "A Tillichian Analysis of James Cone's Black Theology," in *Perspective in Religious Studies* 1 (Spring 1974), pp. 15-28; and Carlyle F. Stewart, III, "The Method of Correlation in the Theology of James H. Cone," in *Journal of Religious Thought* 40 (Fall-Winter, 1983), pp. 27-38.

84. Cone, *Black Theology and Black Power,* p. 32.

85. Rooks, *Revolution in Zion,* pp. 222-26. Notable exceptions include Benjamin Mays, John Eubanks, John Jenkins, and Harry Richardson.

86. James H. Evans, Jr., *We Have Been Believers: An African-American Systematic Theology* (Minneapolis: Fortress Press, 1992), p. 104.

87. See ibid., pp. 104-12.

88. Cone, *Black Theology and Black Power,* p. 155 n.1.

89. George D. Kelsey, "The Christian Way in Race Relations," in *The Christian Way in Race Relations* (New York: Harper and Brothers, 1948), p. 29.

90. Cone, *Black Theology and Black Power,* p. 39

91. Ibid., p. 41.

92. Ibid., p. 42.

93. Kelsey, *Racism and the Christian Understanding of Man*, p. 9.

94. Cone, *Black Theology and Black Power*, p. 73.

95. Kelsey, *Racism and the Christian Understanding of Man*, p. 96.

96. Ibid., pp. 97-116.

97. Cone, *Black Theology and Black Power*, p. 75 (emphasis mine).

98. Cone, *My Soul Looks Back*, p. 49.

99. Cone, *A Black Theology of Liberation* (Maryknoll: N.Y.: Orbis Books, 1986), pp. xvi-xvii.

100. James H. Cone, "Christian Theology and the Afro-American Revolution," in *Christianity and Crisis* (June 8, 1970), p. 124.

101. Cone, "Black Power, Black Theology, and the Study of Theology and Ethics," p. 206. In *My Soul Looks Back* Cone cites William Hordern, Fred Herzog, and Paul Lehmann as notable exceptions (see pp. 57-59).

102. Ibid.

103. See Wilmore and Cone, *Black Theology: A Documentary History, 1966-1979*, pp. 138, 144-219.

104. James H. Cone, "A Theological Challenge to the American Catholic Church," in *Speaking the Truth* (Grand Rapids: Wm. B. Eerdman's Press, 1987), p. 55.

105. Ibid., p. 51.

106. James H. Cone, "Black Theology and the Black College Student," in *Journal of Afro-American Issues* 4 (Summer-Fall 1976), p. 423.

107. See Cone's account of the conference in *My Soul Looks Back*, pp. 54-56.

108. See James H. Cone, "What Time Is It for the A.M.E. Church?," in *The A.M.E. Church Review* 140 (January-March, 1987), p. 34.

109. Cone, "Black Theology and the Black College Student," pp. 424, 428.

110. Cone, "Black Consciousness and the Black Church," p. 249.

111. Rufus Burrow, Jr., *James H. Cone and Black Liberation Theology* (Jefferson, N.C: McFarland & Company, 1994), pp. 169-72.

112. Cone, "What Time Is It for the A.M.E. Church?," p. 35

113. Cone, *Black Theology and Black Power*, p. 103.

114. In his recent book, James H. Harris calls attention to the absence of the black church in Cone's list of sources for black theology in *A Black Theology of Liberation* (1990, pp. 23-35). Consequently, Harris argues that Cone "inadvertently relegates the church to a secondary status when discussing the development of theology." See James H. Harris, *Pastoral Theology: A Black-Church Perspective* (Minneapolis: Fortress Press, 1991), p. 58.

115. Cone, *A Black Theology of Liberation* (1990), p. 26.

116. Cone, *Black Theology and Black Power*, p. 108.

117. Ibid., p. 104.

118. For an important critique of James H. Cone's interpretation of black church history, see Cecil Cone, *The Identity Crisis in Black Theology* (Nashville: The African Methodist Episcopal Church, 1975).

119. Burrow, *James H. Cone and Black Liberation Theology*, p. 159.

120. Cone, "Black Consciousness and the Black Church," p. 249 (emphasis mine).

121. Cone, "What Time Is It for the A.M.E. Church?," p. 37.

122. Ibid., p. 36.

123. James H. Cone, "God Our Father, Christ Our Redeemer, Man Our Brother": A Theological Interpretation of the A.M.E. Church," in *Journal of the Interdenominational Theological Center* 4 (Fall 1976), p. 29. Elsewhere, Cone writes, "How long will we continue to appeal to black heroes of the past as evidence for the contemporary relevance of the black church?" (see "Black Ecumenism and the Liberation Struggle," in *Journal of the Interdenominational Theological Center* 7 [Fall 1979], p. 5).

124. Cone, "What Time Is It for the A.M.E. Church?," p. 39.

125. Ibid., pp. 36, 33.

126. Cone, *My Soul Looks Back*, pp. 89-90.

127. Ibid., pp. 69-79.

5   Christianity and Sexism

1. See Jacquelyn Grant, "Black Theology and the Black Woman," in Gayraud S. Wilmore and James H. Cone, eds., *Black Theology: A Documentary History, 1966-1979* (Maryknoll, N.Y.: Orbis Books, 1979), pp. 418-33.

2. According to Shelby Rooks, the dramatic increase in the number of black women in seminary enrollment constitutes "a revolutionary turn around" in African-American theological education. In the 1987-88 academic year, 29.4 percent of African-American seminarians were women. See Shelby Rooks, *Revolution in Zion*.

3. Delores S. Williams, *Sisters in the Wilderness: The Challenge of Womanist God-Talk* (Maryknoll, N.Y.: Orbis Books, 1993), pp. 1-6.

4. Jo Ann Robinson, *The Montgomery Bus Boycott and the Women Who Started It* (Knoxville: The University of Tennessee Press, 1987), pp. 25-26.

5. See Jualynne Dodson, "Nineteenth-Century A.M.E. Preaching Women," in H. F. Thomas and R. S. Keller, eds., *Women in New Worlds* (Nashville: Abingdon Press, 1981); and Grant, "Black Theology and the Black Woman," p. 433.

6. See "The Life and Religious Experience of Jarena Lee," in *Sisters of the Spirit* (Bloomington: Indiana University Press, 1986), p. 36.

7. Theressa Hoover, "Black Women and the Churches: Triple Jeopardy," in Wilmore and Cone, *Black Theology: A Documentary History, 1966-1979*, pp. 377-78. Hoover also called for more scholarly research on black Christian women: "Any thinking person cannot help wondering why so little has been written, since women are by far the largest supporting groups in our religious institutions, and, in the black church, are the very backbone."

8. Grant, "Black Theology and the Black Woman," p. 423.

9. Cheryl T. Gilkes, "The Role of Women in the Sanctified Church," in *Journal of Religious Thought* 43 (Spring/Summer 1986), p. 29; idem, "Together and in Harness: Women's Traditions in the Sanctified Church," in *Signs* 10 (Summer 1985), p. 683.

10. Anna Arnold Hedgeman, *The Trumpet Sounds: A Memoir of Negro Leadership* (New York: Holt, Rinehart and Winston, 1964), p. 38.

11. Ibid., p. 39. For Hedgeman's positive assessment of Harlem Negro ministers in the 1930s, including Adam C. Powell, Sr. (Abyssinian Baptist), Shelton H. Bishop (St. Phillips Episcopal), John H. Robinson (St. Mark's Methodist), and William Lloyd Imes (St. James Presbyterian), see ibid., pp. 49-50.

12. Ibid., p. 153.

13. Ibid., p. 39.

14. Ibid., p. 27. See also Anna A. Hedgeman, *The Gift of Chaos: Decades of American Discontent* (New York: Oxford University Press, 1977), p. 8, where Hedgeman writes: "I had nothing but contempt for the southern white . . . I actually hated those white people because of their inhumanity."

15. Hedgeman, *The Trumpet Sounds,* p. 176.

16. Pauli Murray, *Song in a Weary Throat: An American Pilgrimage* (New York: Harper and Row, 1987), pp. 370-71. For feminist reflections on the impact of Murray, see Suzanne Hiatt, "Pauli Murray: May Her Song Be Heard at Last"; and Elly Haney, "Pauli Murray: Acting and Remembering," in *Journal of the Feminist Study of Religion* 4 (Fall 1988), pp. 69-79.

17. See Paula Giddings, *When and Where I Enter: The Impact of Black Women on Race and Sex in America* (New York: Bantam Books, 1984); Vicki Crawford (ed.), *Women in the Civil Rights Movement* (New York: Carlson Publishing Co., 1990); Robinson, *The Montgomery Bus Boycott and the Women Who Started It.*

18. Ella Baker, "Developing Community Leadership," in *Black Women in White America,* ed. Gerda Lerner (New York: Vintage Books, 1973), p. 351.

19. Ella Baker, quoted in Giddings, *When and Where I Enter,* p. 312.

20. For a discussion of Hedgeman's work on behalf of black women domestic workers, see Hedgeman, *The Trumpet Sounds,* pp. 68-69.

21. Ibid., pp. 85-86.

22. See Hedgeman, *The Gift of Chaos,* pp. 20-23 and 57-62.

23. Ibid., pp. 172-73.

24. Ibid., p. 179. Note Hedgeman's usage of Malcolm X's term for the six major civil rights leaders involved in the March.

25. Ibid., p. 86.

26. See Sara Evans, *Personal Politics: The Roots of Women's Liberation in the Civil Rights Movement and the New Left* (New York: Vintage Books, 1980), p. 234.

27. For more on SNCC leaders Diane Nash and Ruby Doris Smith Robinson, see Giddings, *When and Where I Enter,* pp. 278-79, 314-15.

28. Despite the prevailing ethos of sexism in SNCC in the mid 1960s, Sara Evans argues that "black women occupied positions of growing strength and power which challenged sexual discrimination" (Evans, *Personal Politics,* p. 88). Likewise, Paula Giddings claims that "the influence of Black women was actually increasing at the time; it was White women who were being relegated to minor responsibilities, in part because of indiscriminate sexual behavior" (Giddings, *When and Where I Enter,* p. 302).

29. Evans, *Personal Politics,* pp. 78-81; and Giddings, *When and Where I Enter,* p. 302.

30. Giddings, *When and Where I Enter,* pp. 314-15.

31. Michele Wallace, *Black Macho and the Myth of the Superwoman* (London: Verso, 1990; originally published New York: Dial Press, 1979), pp. 31-32. See also bell hooks, *Ain't I a Woman: Black Women and Feminism* (Boston: South End Press, 1981). hooks writes: "While the 60s black power movement was a reaction against racism, it was also a movement that allowed black men to overtly announce their support of patriarchy" (p. 98).

32. James H. Cone, *For My People* (Maryknoll, N.Y.: Orbis Books, 1984), p. 133.

33. NCBC Statement on "Black Theology," in Wilmore and Cone, *Black Theology: A Documentary History, 1966-1979*, p. 102.

34. See the NCBC Statement "A Message to the Churches from Oakland, California," in Wilmore and Cone, *Black Theology: A Documentary History, 1966-1979*, p. 105; and "The Black Declaration of Independence," in ibid., p. 111.

35. See Cone, *For My People*, pp. 133, 249-50.

36. See the BMCR Statement "The Black Paper," in Wilmore and Cone, *Black Theology: A Documentary History, 1966-1979*, p. 269.

37. J. Deotis Roberts, "Black Theology and the Theological Revolution," in *Journal of Religious Thought* 28 (Spring/Summer 1971), pp. 10-11.

38. James H. Cone, *My Soul Looks Back* (Nashville: Abingdon Press, 1982; Maryknoll, N.Y.: Orbis Books, 1986), pp. 115-16.

39. See Cone, "Introduction to Part V," in Wilmore and Cone, *Black Theology: A Documentary History, 1966-1979*, p. 364. For more on black theology and sexism, see James H. Evans, "Black Theology and Black Feminism," in *Journal of Religious Thought* (Spring/Summer 1981), pp. 43-53.

40. See Delores S. Williams, "The Color Purple: What Was Missed," in *Christianity and Crisis* (July 14, 1986), pp. 230-32, and "Womanist Theology: Black Women's Voices," in *Christianity and Crisis* (March 2, 1987), p. 66.

41. Delores Williams, *Sisters in the Wilderness*, pp. xiii-xiv.

42. Kelly Brown Douglas, *The Black Christ* (Maryknoll, N.Y.: Orbis Books, 1994), pp. 115-16.

43. Jacquelyn Grant, "Womanist Theology: Black Women's Experience as a Source for Doing Theology, with Special Reference to Christology," in *Journal of the Interdenominational Theological Center* 13 (Spring 1986), p. 202.

44. Ibid., pp. 208, 210. For more on Grant's theology see Jacquelyn Grant, *White Women's Christ and Black Women's Jesus: Feminist Christology and Womanist Response* (Atlanta: Scholars Press, 1989). Note that Kelly Brown Douglas has reservations about calling Christ a black woman because it "is theologically misleading." Brown writes, "Although Christ can certainly be embodied by a black woman, it is more in keeping with black women's testimonies to Jesus and Jesus' own self-understanding if womanist theology describes Christ as being embodied wherever there is a movement to sustain and liberate the entire black community, male and female" (Kelly Brown Douglas, "God Is as Christ Does: Toward a Womanist Theology," in *Journal of Religious Thought* 46 [Summer/Fall 1989], p. 16). For more on the difference between the perspectives of Grant and Brown Douglas, see Brown Douglas, *The Black Christ*, pp. 109-10.

45. According to Brown Douglas, "Wholeness first implies an individual's triumph over her or his wounds of oppression, so that the individual is whole even as she or he struggles for the community's wholeness. Second, wholeness for a community indicates that it is not divided against itself and that it is free, liberated from oppression" ("To Reflect the Image of God: A Womanist Perspective on Right Perspective," in *Living the Intersection: Womanism and Afrocentrism in Theology*, ed. Cheryl J. Sanders [Minneapolis: Fortress Press, 1995], p. 68).

46. Brown Douglas, *The Black Christ*, p. 102.

47. Kelly Brown Douglas, "Womanist Theology: What Is Its Relationship to Black Theology," in James H. Cone and Gayraud Wilmore, *Black Theology: A Documentary History, 1980-1992*, vol. 2 (Maryknoll, N.Y.: Orbis Books, 1993), p. 295.

48. Renee L. Hill, "Who Are We for Each Other?: Sexism, Sexuality and Womanist Theology," in James H. Cone and Gayraud S. Wilmore, eds., *Black Theology: A Documentary History, Vol. 2, 1980-1992* (Maryknoll, N.Y.: Orbis Books, 1993), p. 346.

49. Ibid., pp. 349-50.

50. Williams writes: "While *Sisters in the Wilderness* does not explore christological questions, but rather briefly provides a response to questions surrounding redemption and atonement, there is an assumption here that womanist theology must, in theological areas, render an understanding of Jesus Christ" (p. 202). Note, Williams agrees with Kelly Brown Douglas that calling Christ a black woman is not the best approach for womanist christology because it appears to limit Christ's relevance to black women. Yet, Williams seems to agree with both Brown Douglas and Jacquelyn Grant when she writes: "Whether we talk about Jesus in relation to atonement theory or christology, we womanists must be guided more by black Christian women's voices, faith and experience than by anything that was decided centuries ago at Chalcedon" (p. 203).

51. Williams, *Sisters in the Wilderness*, pp. 243-44, note 7.

52. Ibid., p. x.

53. Ibid., pp. x-xi.

54. Ibid., p. xi.

55. Ibid., pp. 204-6.

56. From my July 30, 1991, interview with Delores S. Williams.

57. Williams, *Sisters in the Wilderness*, p. 206.

58. From the July 30, 1991, interview. Here, Williams's understanding of the "black religious ethos" is similar to her description of the "black church invisible" in *Sisters in the Wilderness*: "The black church gave us spiritual songs and blues and gospel and rap and a singing way to justice, fighting. It is invisible, but we know when we see, hear and feel it quickening the heart, measuring the soul and bathing life with the spirit in time" (p. 206).

59. Delores S. Williams, *The Black Woman Portrayed in Selected Black Imaginative Literature and Some Questions for Black Theology*, M.A. Thesis (Columbia University, 1975), p. 4.

60. Williams, *Sisters in the Wilderness*, p. 53.

61. Delores S. Williams, "Black Women's Literature and the Task of Feminist Theology," in C. W. Atkinson, et al., eds. *Immaculate and Powerful* (Boston: Beacon Press, 1985), p. 97.

62. Delores S. Williams, "The Color Purple," in *Christianity and Crisis* (July 14, 1986), pp. 230-31.

63. Williams, *Sisters in the Wilderness*, p. 50.

64. Williams, "Black Women's Literature and the Task of Feminist Theology," p. 92.

65. Williams, *Sisters in the Wilderness*, p. 52.

66. Williams, "Black Woman's Literature and the Task of Feminist Theology," p. 96.

67. Delores S. Williams, "Women's Oppression and Life-Line Politics in Black Women's Religious Narratives," in *Journal of Feminist Studies in Religion* (Fall 1985), p. 62.

68. Delores S. Williams, "The Color of Feminism: Or Speaking the Black Woman's Tongue," in *Journal of Religious Thought* 43 (Spring/Summer 1986), p. 52.

69. Williams, *Sisters in the Wilderness*, pp. 150-51.

70. Ibid., p. 149. Williams is especially critical of the New Testament scholar Cain Hope Felder, who rightly calls for more attention to the role of Africa and Africans in the Bible, but "gives *very little* attention to the African Hagar." Williams further notes that although Felder "cites countless references from the book of Galatians, he never alludes to Hagar's inferior place in that book" (ibid., p. 269, note 10).

71. Williams, *Sisters in the Wilderness*, p. 245, note 2.

72. Ibid., p. 3.

73. July 30, 1991, interview with the author.

74. Olin P. Moyd makes a similar argument. Moyd claims that the theme of redemption is a more inclusive term than liberation for describing the central motif of the Bible and the black religious experience. Moyd understands redemption as liberation from oppression and the formation of a community in covenantal relationship with God. See Olin P. Moyd, *Redemption in Black Theology* (Valley Forge, Penn.: Judson Press, 1979).

75. Williams, *Sisters in the Wilderness*, p. 161.

76. Ibid., pp. 194-95.

77. Ibid., p. 196. It should be noted that Charles Shelby Rooks also examined the relation between the experience of the Jewish exiles and black Americans. Rooks argued that the image of the African diaspora based on the story of the Babylonian Exile offers more immediate parallels to the contemporary situation of African-Americans than does the Exodus/liberation tradition employed by black theologians ("Toward the Promised Land: An Analysis of the Religious Experience of Black Americans" in *The Black Church* [a journal of the Black Ecumenical Commission of Massachusetts] 2 [1972], pp. 1-48).

78. Ibid., p. 151.

79. In *Black Theology and Black Power* (Minneapolis: Seabury Press, 1969), Cone writes: "Black Theology is not prepared to discuss the doctrine of God, man, Christ, Church, Holy Spirit—the whole spectrum of Christian theology—without making each doctrine an analysis of the emancipation of black people. It believes that, in this time, moment, and situation, all Christian doctrines must be interpreted in such a manner that they unreservedly say something to black people who are living under unbearable oppression" (p. 121).

80. Williams writes that the postbellum mammy tradition produced a stereotypical image of black women "as perpetual mother figures, religious, fat, asexual, loving children better than themselves, self-sacrificing, giving up self-concern for group advancement." Likewise, "the antebellum tradition of masculinizing black women through their work has given rise to the image of black women as unfeminine, physically strong, and having the capacity to bear considerably more pain than white women. These kinds of ideas helped create the notion of black women as superwomen" (Delores S. Williams, "Black Women's Surrogacy Experience and the Christian Notion of Redemption," in Paula M. Cooey and Wm. R. Eakin, eds., *After Patriarchy: Feminist Transformations of the World Religions* [Maryknoll, N.Y.: Orbis Books, 1991], p. 8).

81. Williams, *Sisters in the Wilderness*, p. 162.

82. Delores Williams, "Christian Scapegoating," in *The Other Side* (May-June 1993), p. 43. Williams writes: "After the Civil War, the 'high priests' of the North and South (the economically and politically powerful) laid the emerging social and economic problems on the heads of Negroes. When Reconstruction ended and White power, North and South, began trying to achieve atonement (at-one-ment) among White people, the Negro was the scapegoat 'led into the wilderness' of poverty, neglect, abuse, and often murderous sacrifice."

83. Ibid., p. 44.

84. Williams, *Sisters in the Wilderness*, pp. 164-67.

85. Ibid., p. 167.

86. Williams, "Christian Scapegoating," p. 44.

87. Ibid.

88. Catherine Keller, "Inventing the Goddess," in *Christian Century* (April 6, 1994), pp. 340-42. See also David Heim, "Sophia's Choice," and Joseph D. Small and John P. Burgess, "Evaluating 'Re-Imagining'" in the same issue (pp. 339-40, 342-44). See also Peter Steinfels, "Presbyterians Try to Resolve Long Dispute," in the *New York Times*, June 17, 1994, p. 24.

89. Delores Williams, "Re-Imagining Truth," in *The Other Side* (May-June, 1994), p. 53.

90. Ibid., p. 54.

91. Williams, *Sisters in the Wilderness*, p. 209.

92. Ibid., p. 210.

93. Williams argues that genocide "involves inflicting conditions that weaken the viability of the group. Attempting to destroy the cultural identity of black Americans; destroying the language of the African slaves; attacking African-American leaders; preventing the formation of institutions in the community; trying to destroy the national feelings of African-Americans; destroying the economic existence of the group—all of this amounts to weakening the viability of the black American community. This aspect of the definition brings to light the fact that black people have experienced genocide during every phase of their history in America. And this kind of genocide has been directly caused or indirectly condoned by the state" (*Sisters in the Wilderness*, pp. 133-34).

94. Ibid., p. 201.

95. Ibid., pp. xii-xiii.

96. Williams, "The Color of Feminism: Or Speaking the Black Woman's Tongue," p. 57.

97. Williams, *Sisters in the Wilderness*, pp. xiii, 242, note 4.

98. Williams cites the Glide Memorial United Methodist Church in San Francisco; Allen A.M.E. Church in Queens, New York; and the Bridge Street A.M.E. Church in Brooklyn (ibid., p. 209). It is important to note that there are many smaller, less well-known churches throughout the country who are doing similar work.

99. Williams, *Sisters in the Wilderness*, p. 206.

100. Ibid., pp. 208-9.

101. See St. Clair Drake and Horace R. Cayton, *Black Metropolis* (New York: Harcourt, Brace and Co., 1945), p. 419.

102. Charles Shelby Rooks, *Revolution in Zion* (New York: Pilgrim Press, 1990), p. 43.

103. Williams, *Sisters in the Wilderness*, p. 275, note 5. Williams also writes: "Why is it that when honest, charismatic black leaders emerge who are helping black people obtain a securer life and more prosperous future in America, they get harassed, run out of town or assassinated? There has been no forum in the community to deal with this question. But perhaps there is truth in the black-folk observation that the American government's unwritten policy regarding black leadership is that the leaders either get bought or get buried. Martin Luther King, Jr., and Malcolm X could not be bought; they were buried" (p. 135).

104. Ibid., p. 277, note 6.

105. Ibid., pp. 207-8.

106. Ibid., p. 276, note 6.

107. Ibid., p. 242, note 4.

108. Ibid., p. 273, note 36.

109. Ibid., p. 215.

110. Ibid., p. 218.

111. Delores Williams, "Rituals of Resistance in Womanist Worship," in Majorie Procter-Smith and Janet R. Walton, eds., *Women at Worship: Interpretations of North American Diversity* (Louisville: Westminster/John Knox Press, 1993), p. 221.

112. Ibid., p. 223.

Conclusion

1. See Joseph Washington, "Are American Negro Churches Christian?" in James H. Cone and Gayraud S. Wilmore, eds., *Black Theology: A Documentary History, Vol. 1, 1966-1979* (Maryknoll, N.Y.: Orbis Books, 1993), pp. 92-100; and *Black Religion: The Negro and Christianity in the United States* (Boston: Beacon Press, 1964).

2. William Stuart Nelson, "Crucial Issues in America's Race Relations Today," in *The Christian Way in Race Relations*, ed. W. S. Nelson (New York: Harper and Brothers, 1948), p. 20.

3. Benjamin E. Mays, *Born to Rebel* (Athens: University of Georgia Press, 1987), p. lv (emphasis mine).

4. Paul Tillich, *The Protestant Era* (Chicago: The University of Chicago Press, 1957), p. xviii.

5. Carlyle Fielding Stewart, III, *African-American Church Growth: Twelve Principles for Prophetic Ministry* (Nashville: Abingdon Press, 1994), p. 30.

6. Ibid., p. 31.

7. James H. Harris, *Pastoral Theology: A Black-Church Perspective* (Minneapolis: Fortress Press, 1991), p. 16.

8. See "Fishin' 4 Religion," from the album *Arrested Development: 3 Years, 5 months and 2 Days in the Life of . . .* (New York: Chrysalis Records, Inc., 1992).

9. See Yosef ben-Jochannan, *African Origins of the Major "Western Religions"* (Baltimore: Black Classic Press, 1991; reprint of the 1970 edition); see also W. Deen Mohammed, *Al-Islam: Unity and Leadership* (Chicago: The Sense Maker, 1991); and Don Terry, "Black Muslims Enter Islamic Mainstream," in the *New York Times*, May 3, 1993, p. 1.

10. See Elijah Anderson, "The Code of the Streets," in *The Atlantic Monthly* (May 1994), pp. 81-94.

11. Mark Naison, "Outlaw Culture and Black Neighborhoods," in *Reconstruction*, vol. 1, no. 4 (1992), pp. 128-29.

12. J. Deotis Roberts, *The Prophethood of Black Believers: An African-American Political Theology for Ministry* (Louisville: Westminster/John Knox Press, 1994), pp. 69-70.

13. Kelly Brown Douglas, *The Black Christ*, p. 4.

14. Greg Donaldson, *The Ville: Cops and Kids in Urban America* (New York: Ticknor and Fields, 1993).

15. Cornel West, *Race Matters* (Boston: Beacon Press, 1993), pp. 17-18.

16. C. Eric Lincoln and Lawrence H. Mamiya, *The Black Church in the African-American Experience* (Durham, N.C.: Duke University Press, 1990), pp. 178-82.

17. See Gayraud S. Wilmore essay, "Black Theology and Pastoral Ministry: A Challenge to Ecumenical Renewal and Solidarity," in *The Pastor as Theologian*, ed. Earl E. Shelp and Ronald H. Sunderland (New York: Pilgrim Press, 1988), pp. 30-67.

18. Roberts, *The Prophethood of Black Believers*, pp. 16-18.

19. See James H. Cone's comments on the Institute in Cone and Wilmore, *Black Theology: A Documentary History, Vol. 2, 1980-1992* (Maryknoll, N.Y.: Orbis Books, 1993), p. 6; see also pp. 160-74.

20. Dennis W. Wiley, "Black Theology, the Black Church, and the African-American Community," in ibid., pp. 127-38.

21. For more on Annie Powell's emerging womanist perspective, see "Hold on to Your Dream: African-American Protestant Worship," in Majorie Procter-Smith and Janet R. Walton, eds., *Women at Worship: Interpretations of North American Diversity* (Louisville: Westminster/John Knox Press, 1993), pp. 43-53.

22. Ibid., pp. 51-52.

Index

206